WITHDRAWN

Windows® 365

by Rosemarie and Ken Withee

for dummies®
A Wiley Brand

Windows® 365 For Dummies®

Published by: **John Wiley & Sons, Inc.,** 111 River Street, Hoboken, NJ 07030-5774, www.wiley.com

Copyright © 2022 by John Wiley & Sons, Inc., Hoboken, New Jersey

Published simultaneously in Canada

Contents at a Glance

Table of Contents

Introduction

Hold onto your pants because Microsoft is about to change the world with Windows the same way they did with Office. About a decade ago Microsoft moved Office to a cloud-first product and dubbed it Office 365. Now Microsoft is doing the same with Windows and calling it Windows 365.

Windows 365 is a cloud-based PC. This seems like a strange idea. A PC is something you sit in front of, or sit on your lap, and type on. How could a computer move into the cloud? In a nutshell, the computer is virtual and lives in a Microsoft data center somewhere. You use just about any physical computer to connect to it over the Internet. To get your head around it, imagine your regular old work computer. You look at the screen and move the mouse around and type on the keyboard. You can save files to your desktop and double-click other files on your desktop to open them. You open applications by clicking on Start and then choosing from the list of software on the computer.

Now imagine that you separate all of that from the physical device you are using. In other words, your physical device just becomes a dumb terminal and all the things you normally do on your computer happen on your computer in the cloud. The primary benefit is that you don't need to worry as much about spilling coffee on your computer or saving your work when you move from your office to home or anywhere in between. Your cloud computer always stays in the same state you left it, and you can connect to it and use it from just about any device. You can use a regular Windows computer like a desktop or laptop computer, you can use your Mac (which Rosemarie is a fan of), you can use Linux (which Ken loves), and you can even use your iPhone or Android phone or iPad or Android tablet. In short, like we said, you can use just about any device to connect to, and work on, your cloud PC.

TIP

We hate mixing work with our personal life and our computers are no exception. When we heard about Windows 365 we jumped at the chance to have a work computer that is still accessible from anywhere but is separate from our personal computers.

The next big question to ask is what is the difference between regular Windows, like Windows 11, and this new Windows 365? We answer this question and also speculate about how Windows 365 will unfold into the future.

TIP

Office 365 changed the game by moving apps, such as Word, to the cloud so that we could collaborate on the same document in real-time from any device. In fact, that is how we wrote our previous book, *SharePoint For Dummies*, using Word in the cloud. Office 365 is great for the Office apps, but what about all the rest of the programs you use on your computer? Right now, you have to install all of these programs on every computer you use. If you use both Windows and Mac, then you have to hope the same program is available for both operating systems.

This book covers Windows 365 as of the calendar year 2022 and is designed to be your initial guide. Throughout the book, we offer tips on where you can dig deeper as you progress.

About This Book

This book is intended for anyone who uses Windows or is curious about what Microsoft is up to with Windows 365. Windows is a vast operating system with many nooks and crannies, and no single book can cover everything. This book is designed to provide an introduction and an overview of the new operating system. It shows you how to get up and running and get the most out of Windows 365.

Others who may benefit from this book include

>> **Computer users:** If you use a computer for work, then this book is for you. Currently, Windows 365 is designed only for business, but we suspect in the future it will also be available for home users.

>> **IT professionals:** This book doesn't go into the details of information technology. Most aspects of information technology are far beyond the scope of this book. If you are an IT professional, then this book is designed to provide you with an introduction to Windows 365, and how you can use it to make your life, and the lives of the people in your organization, easier.

>> **Managers:** If you manage a department or business unit, you need to understand how to get the most out of your tools. Windows 365 is designed to simplify the mundane tasks of managing the computers your teams use. By moving your team's PC to the cloud you unlock the need for onsite productivity.

Foolish Assumptions

Because operating systems are such a huge topic, we have to make some assumptions about your initial knowledge, such as

» **You use a computer at work.** Windows 365 is essentially Windows in the cloud. If you don't already use a computer at work, then this book is not for you (unless you are curious about it or will need to use a computer for work in the future).

» **You're a Windows user (or want to become one).** Windows 365 is an operating system based on Windows. You can connect to it from just about any physical computer, but it is Windows once you connect.

» **You have good Internet access.** It might seem like a given that everyone has good Internet access these days, but that is not the case. Windows 365 moves your PC to the cloud and you access it and work with it over the Internet. As such, you need a good Internet connection to get the most out of it.

Icons Used in This Book

A handful of icons are used in this book. Here's what they mean:

TIP

Tips point out handy information and help with sticky situations and important topics in Windows 365.

REMEMBER

This icon marks something to remember, such as how to perform a task or get set up with Windows 365.

TECHNICAL STUFF

This icon provides technical details about Windows 365. We use this icon to provide information about the inner workings of the product.

WARNING

We don't use this icon a lot and when you see it you should take note of something to watch out for. We use this to point out common pitfalls and places we have gotten stuck in the past.

Beyond the Book

In addition to what you're reading right now, this product also comes with a free access-anywhere Cheat Sheet that describes some common Windows 365 tips and resources, among other things. To get this Cheat Sheet, simply go to https://www.dummies.com/ and enter **Windows 365 For Dummies Cheat Sheet** in the Search box.

Where to Go from Here

All right, you're all set and ready to jump into the book. You can jump in anywhere you like — the book was written to allow you to do just that. But if you want to get the full story from the beginning, turn to Chapter 1 — that's where all the action starts.

1

Windows 365 Isn't the Windows You Grew Up With

Chapter **1**

Getting Familiar with the Future of Windows

The concept of a cloud-based PC is not an easy one to get your head around. Until recently, a computer was a physical device that sat on your desk, or perhaps on your lap, or in your pocket. How can Microsoft move that physical computer into the cloud? Keep reading to find out!

In this chapter, you get familiar with the future of Windows and the ways Microsoft is moving the PC into the cloud. We explore the concepts behind Windows 365 and walk through new terminology you will need when thinking and talking about the new Windows. Finally, because this is a brand new way of thinking about a PC, we dig into some of the common questions that we had, and that most people have, when learning about Windows 365 for the first time.

Meeting the Cloud PC

We remember when we bought our first computer. It was a long time ago, and it was a beautiful machine. It had a proud place sitting right on our main desk and we used it frequently. That was decades ago, but over the years not much has changed with the ways we bought and used our PCs. Until now!

Microsoft has moved the PC into the cloud with Windows 365. When we first heard about the concept, we had to scratch our heads. How could it be possible? A PC is something you sit down in front of and type and work on. Unless there is a way to plug our brains into the virtual world (did someone say metaverse?) then a PC will always be a physical thing, right? Well, this is where Windows 365 changes the equation.

Windows 365 is a cloud-based PC, and you interact with it using any physical device you choose.

Yes, for the time being, using a computer will still require you to interact with a physical object, such as a keyboard, mouse, and monitor. What Windows 365 does is detach the keyboard, mouse, and monitor you are physically using from your cloud PC computer. Because the cloud PC is running in a Microsoft data center, you can use any other device to connect to it and use it. All you need is an Internet connection and a physical device you can interact with. In other words, the physical device becomes a simple bridge to work on your cloud PC. Most any physical device will do the job, because your physical computer becomes a "dumb" computer. All the really wonderful things you do for work still live on your Windows 365 computer, as illustrated in Figure 1-1. We cover the requirements of the physical device you use and the Internet connection required to access your cloud PC in Chapter 16.

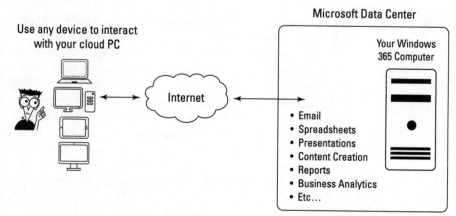

FIGURE 1-1: Windows 365 detaches the physical device (including, for example a keyboard, mouse, and monitor; or touchscreen) from the operating system.

You may find yourself asking, what is a cloud PC good for? What is it not so good for? A cloud PC is great for companies that are remote or hybrid. This is because the cloud PC can be centralized for your organization and remote workers connect to it just like they would come into an office and turn on their desktop computer. As an organization, you can think of all of the cloud PCs as being "inside" your organization. You control them, and remote users connect to them to get work done. The actual cloud PC never "leaves" your organization, though. If someone exits your organization, they simply stop logging in and you retain all information, content, and work that was performed on the cloud PC. Where cloud PCs are not so good is when people in your organization don't have a stable and reliable Internet connection. The cloud PC is streamed over the Internet, and if you don't have a solid Internet connection then a cloud PC will not work.

TIP

Think of your cloud PC as nearly identical to the physical computer you have at home, or in your office, running Windows. Any software you would install on your physical computer running Windows you can also install on your cloud PC running Windows 365. Of course, you still need to keep in mind the requirements for the software such as memory and disk space. Just like your physical computer, your cloud PC has a set amount of memory and disk space. We cover how to select the amount of memory and disk space in Chapter 2.

No, really, what is Windows 365?

To understand what Microsoft is doing with Windows, all you have to do is look back a decade or so ago at what they did with Office. You remember Office, right? Office programs like Word, Excel, and PowerPoint have been around for ages.

It used to be that Microsoft would release a new version of Office every few years. You would buy it and install it on your computer and hope you would remember to make backups frequently and keep your files secure. Then Microsoft moved to a new cloud-based model offered as a subscription called Office 365. With Office 365, you sign up and you always have the latest Office programs. You don't have to wait for the next version of Office to come out in order to get the new features. With Office 365 you get them right away, as they are released. And because these programs are cloud-based, your files are saved to the cloud and automatically backed up and secured for you. We must admit that over the last decade, Office 365 has saved our files from some computer crashes and mishaps on multiple occasions.

Microsoft is starting the same journey with Windows as they did with Office. The success of Office 365 led Microsoft to do the same thing with Windows. In particular, Windows 365 is a subscription based offering that is constantly improved with new features and updated. By adopting the "365" model and moving the PC to the cloud, Microsoft makes Windows a cloud based operating system. This is important because it removes the friction and burden of managing your own physical computer. In a way, when you use a cloud PC you are offloading to Microsoft the burden of running a computer.

You don't have to look further than the 365 in the name to figure it out. And as you can probably guess, using the number 365 is a standard for Microsoft moving forward. You know, because there are 365 days in a year, and you can get new features on any of those days instead of just on a particular day every few years. Figure 1-2 illustrates how Microsoft is doing with Windows what they did with Office.

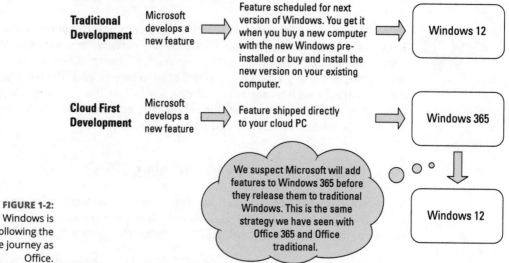

FIGURE 1-2:
Windows is following the same journey as Office.

TIP

Parts of Office 365 have recently been renamed to Microsoft 365. You will still find Office 365 for enterprises but for small business and personal use you will see the branding as Microsoft 365. With Microsoft 365, you still get Office, and Microsoft has bundled a number of other things into the subscription as well. For larger enterprises, you will still see the branding as Office 365.

Looking at a real-world example

To get a better understanding of why Microsoft is on this 365 cloud journey, let's look at a real-world example. As we write this book, we type on many different physical computers. We use our laptops when we are out, in coffee shops, hotels, and elsewhere (hopefully more often as the pandemic fades), and we use a desktop computer both at home and in the office. Office 365 lets us do this because we have the Office programs installed on all of our devices, and our files are saved in the cloud. This works great for the work we do in Office, but what about all the other programs we use at work?

REMEMBER

We cover signing up and getting started with Windows 365 in Chapter 2. We cover using Office 365 with Windows 365 in Chapter 9.

Office 365 moves your apps and files to the cloud so you can work on them from any device as long as you have the Office app installed on that device. Windows 365 moves your entire PC and all of the programs installed on it to the cloud so that you can work on from any device.

On our work computers, we have all sorts of programs. When we need to get work done with those programs, we wait until we are sitting at our work computers. This is where Windows 365 comes into play. Windows 365 takes your entire computer and moves it to the cloud so you can connect to it using any computer or device. We no longer have to wait until we get to the office to work on our computer there. It is always available to us wherever we are in the world and on whatever physical device we happen to be using at the time.

To make the point, though we don't recommend it, you could even chuck your physical computer in the ocean and a minute later pick up another physical computer and continue working on your cloud PC just like nothing ever happened. With Windows 365, your PC becomes detached from the physical world. Have you seen the new *Matrix* movie? Maybe your Windows 365 computer is inside the Matrix — though we aren't sure we want to jack in using a spike in the back of our heads just yet.

Always on, always available, and just how you left it

Your Windows 365 computer stays the same regardless of how you connect to it. For example, you might connect to it from bed in the morning using your Google Chromebook, then move down to your home office using your Mac for breakfast, and then using your Linux laptop on your commute, and finally a Windows desktop computer in your office.

Even though you are moving between physical computers, you are always connecting to the same Windows 365 computer, as shown in Figure 1-3. If you are like us — not good at keeping your computer tidy — and you leave some windows open and some files saved to the desktop of your computer, they will still be in the exact same location when you open your cloud PC from another physical computer.

Your Windows 365 computer has all of your programs installed on it, and when you disconnect it from one physical computer and reconnect it to another, your cloud PC computer is in the exact same state you left it. Did you save a document to your desktop? It will still be there. Did you leave your email program open along with a spreadsheet you were working on? You will find them exactly as you left them.

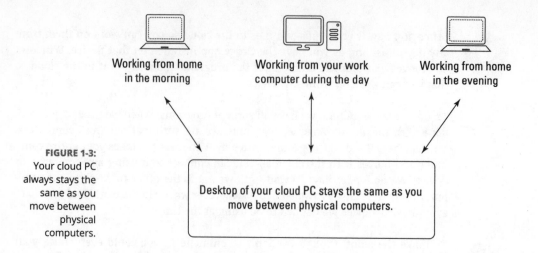

Working from home
in the morning

Working from your work
computer during the day

Working from home
in the evening

Desktop of your cloud PC stays the same as you
move between physical computers.

One of the best things we have found is that you, or your IT team, only have to install your software on a single computer (your cloud PC computer). Your other computers act as a view port into your cloud PC. In other words, your physical computers can come and go but your cloud PC will be there forever.

TIP

Windows 365 provides you a computer in Microsoft's data center that you connect to from any other computer. And the best part is that Microsoft keeps it up to date, secure, and free of viruses for you automatically. The IT team doesn't have to worry about managing your computer for you. Microsoft does it for them. (We cover security with your Windows 365 computer in Chapter 13.)

How Windows 365 Differs from Previous Windows

If you are like us, then you remember your computer running DOS. And then the world changed and a graphical interface in the form of Windows and Macintosh blew our minds. Since the change from text-based to windows-based interactions, there hasn't been a lot more change. Yes, most people moved to using their phones instead of a desktop or laptop computer, but the concepts there are still the same. And for work, most people still use a desktop or laptop computer. Microsoft is changing this paradigm by introducing Windows 365. With Windows 365, you have a single computer that doesn't change and that stays with you, by your side, fighting the good fight. Okay, maybe we got a little bit carried away there. But you get the point.

Jumping off the upgrade merry-go-round

Every few years we all have to buy a new computer that has the latest specifications, the latest operating system, and can run the latest software. We then have to go through the process of installing all of our software again. Looking back on how many times we have been through this cycle, we feel like a hamster on a wheel. The wheel keeps spinning into the future, and the view never changes.

Let's take a look at how Microsoft currently develops features for Windows and how they will do it in the future. In the past, Microsoft would develop features for Windows and then at some point a release would be announced and everyone could go buy that release. For example, right now Windows 11 is out and the next version will likely be Windows 12. Windows 365 changes this model because the operating system is in the cloud and Microsoft can make updates to it automatically. Figure 1-4 illustrates the point.

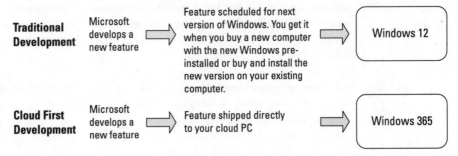

FIGURE 1-4:
Windows 365 is constantly up to date. As Microsoft releases new features, you get them automatically.

As a common practice, hardware is often refreshed every few years. The new hardware will include the latest version of the Windows operating system. Or, your business might buy upgraded hardware and then buy the latest version of Windows separately and install it on your computer. Windows 365 charges a monthly subscription and your cloud PC is always updated to the latest and greatest automatically. Behind the scenes, Microsoft takes care of upgrading any actual hardware such as memory and storage for you. You don't have to keep up with the latest hardware, you just use your cloud PC. You might want to buy a new computer but it won't be a requirement in order to stay up to date with the latest hardware for your cloud PC. Your cloud PC will work fine with hardware you wouldn't have dreamed of using in the past.

Earlier in this chapter we discuss Office 365, and we think this is worth repeating: Microsoft is doing the same thing with Windows that it did with Office. You used to buy a new version of Office every few years. Then Microsoft moved Office to the cloud with Office 365, and you now buy it with a monthly subscription so you always have the latest and greatest Office.

UPDATING YOUR CAR WITH THE CLOUD

Microsoft is not the only company incorporating instant updates to their products. You might think of a car as something you buy and then it stays the same until you buy another car. Tesla changed this model by providing Over-The-Air (OTA) updates.

When you buy a Tesla, you obviously are buying the car. However, you are also buying updates that Tesla provides to your car wirelessly. You might go to sleep at night with one version of the Tesla car and wake up in the morning with the new version.

Other car companies have quickly followed suit, and by doing so, the car industry has shifted customer expectations and experiences dramatically.

With Office 365, you get the latest features as they are released (seemingly daily) instead of waiting a few years in between releases. Windows will follow the same model with new Windows features that are released to Windows 365 first and then eventually released as the "latest" version of Windows at the next major release date.

TIP

Although Microsoft keeps your cloud PC updated to the latest version, you still need to do some things to stay up to date with the rest of your software. We cover keeping things up to date in Chapter 13.

Keeping your knowledge and moving to the cloud

One major concern we often hear about is the cost and pain of learning new things. Learning new software is painful, but learning a new operating system can be unbearable! There is good news on this front, Windows 365 is not much of a change (yet). All it does is take us off the hamster wheel of computer upgrades and reinstalls. Microsoft does all of that for you with your Windows 365 computer. You just use it to get your work done.

TIP

Your Windows 365 computer is always up to date. Microsoft takes care of the security updates for you automatically so you don't have to worry about it. In short, you always have the latest and greatest without having to lift a finger.

Windows 365 is brand new and, as of right now, it is nearly the same Windows that you would get if you went to a store and purchased a physical computer. It runs Windows 11 but in a more streamlined and degunked way, which is built and optimized for the cloud. So when it comes to learning a new operating system, you can take comfort in the fact that you won't have to if you switch to Windows 365. If you are already familiar with Windows, then you are already familiar with Windows 365. We like to think of this as easily packing our long-term Windows knowledge in a suitcase and taking it with us on our journey to the cloud, as shown in Figure 1-5.

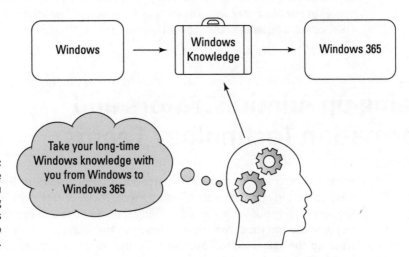

TIP

As of 2022, Windows 365 is available only for business and enterprise. We expect a couple of things to happen in the future:. The first is that Microsoft will extend the offering for home users, too. Technically, anyone can sign up for a Microsoft 365 business license and get Windows 365. At this point, the features are geared toward businesses (and maybe power home users). We expect home versions in the future will focus on features that make sense for home use. The second thing we expect to happen is that Windows 365 will start to have new features that are available only in Windows 365, cloud-enabled features that focus on the benefits only a cloud-based PC can offer.

Building a Mental Model of a Cloud PC

When we started using Windows 365, we liked to think that Microsoft bought us a physical computer and set it up for us and tucked it into their data center. We imagined that computer on a nice pedestal with a great view of Mt. Rainier. This is a great way to envision how Windows 365 works, but it is not accurate. Windows 365 is a virtual computer. In reality, there are a number of major servers all connected together in a data center, and our Windows 365 computer is run on that server hardware.

Our cloud PC computer is not self-contained in the same way we think of a computer on our desk. This has some major advantages, though. For example, imagine we want to upgrade our computer so it has more memory or a bigger hard disk. With a physical computer, we need to buy the upgraded equipment, open our computer, remove the old and install the new. Not complicated, but a pain. With Windows 365, we can upgrade the specifications (think memory and storage space) of our computer with the click of a few buttons on an administration page. (We cover upgrading the specifications for a Windows 365 computer in Chapter 18.)

Freeing up Administrators and Information Technology Teams

Every business needs technical experts and administrators to keep all the computers running and the lights blinking green. Much of this work involves installing new versions of software and keeping it up-to-date and secure. This work can be mundane and time-consuming. Windows 365 shifts this work to Microsoft and frees up the valuable tech experts for other, more important tasks that have a higher business impact (such as optimizing the key business systems). In other words, the experts don't have to run around managing the mundane tasks of administering the operating systems on local computers.

As you may have guessed, we love to build analogies to get across a concept. With Windows 365, we like to think of power plants and power systems. In the old days, power was produced on-site by horses or water or countless other mechanisms. Each of these mechanisms had experts in that area. The experts might be focused on training the horses or optimizing the water wheel. As power evolved and power plants came online, the experts could focus on more import tasks that directly related to whatever the business was trying to achieve. The power necessary to run machines became a given, and no business effort was required to achieve it (except for paying the electric bill). When this happened, the expertise in the company could be shifted. In other words, the value of those experts transformed with the result being a massively greater business impact.

We see the same thing happening with Windows 365. Rather than keeping all the individual computers blinking green, the technical experts in a business can focus on other more important things with the end result being more value (and higher pay).

TIP

The administrative interface for setting up a new Windows 365 computer is very straightforward. You don't need a vast level of technical expertise to do it. Looking back again at Office as an example, it used to require expertise to get Office installed and available to everyone in a business. Now, a technically savvy office administrator can do it. (We cover signing up for Windows 365 in Chapter 2 and administrative tasks in Chapter 18.)

Getting Comfortable with Microsoft Branding

When we say *cloud PC*, we are referring to your Windows 365 computer. However, competitors to Windows 365 also offer similar functionality. For example, you can get a cloud PC from `https://www.parallels.com` too, a direct competitor to Microsoft's Windows 365. Parallels refers to their offering as a hosted virtual desktop. A hosted virtual desktop and a cloud PC are two ways of describing the same thing. A cloud PC is just a computer you access through the Internet (the cloud). In reality that "PC" is running on a computer in a data center somewhere in the world. Because we don't know where that data center is, we just refer to it as "out there" in the "cloud."

One nice thing about a giant company like Microsoft is that they are predictable. Several years ago, Microsoft moved Office to the cloud and called in Office 365. Now Microsoft is moving Windows to the cloud and calling it Windows 365.

TIP

Office 365 and Microsoft 365 can be confusing branding terms. Originally, when Microsoft moved Office to the cloud they called it Office 365. A couple of years ago they added in more software and rebranded some of the subscriptions to Microsoft 365. At the same time, you can still buy Office 365 subscriptions that are geared towards large enterprises. In a general sense, it is safe to use the branding terms Office 365 and Microsoft 365 interchangeably. If you are interested in the differences between Office 365 and Microsoft 365, check out: `https://www.microsoft.com/en-us/microsoft-365/enterprise/compare-microsoft-365-and-office-365`.

If we want to look at the future of Windows 365, all we have to do is look at what Microsoft has already done with Office 365. Office moved from software you install every few years to a continually developed application that is updated constantly and paid for with a subscription. Windows is now taking the same journey, and with Windows, the journey is just getting started.

Questions (and Answers) Likely on Your Mind

What is Windows 365? Windows 365 is a cloud PC. You can think of it as a computer that Microsoft buys, sets up, and manages for you and that you access from any physical device, anywhere in the world.

How is Windows 365 different from Windows 10 or Windows 11? Windows 365 is a computer that is running in a Microsoft data center somewhere. In other words, in the cloud. The computer is running the latest version of Windows. As of this writing, the latest version of Windows is Windows 11. So if you signed up today, you would get Windows 11 on your cloud PC. We expect that in the future Microsoft will develop features that are only available in Windows 365, but for now you can think of Windows 11 and the Windows you use in Windows 365 as nearly identical.

Can I run Windows 365 on my three-year-old PC? Yes! The nice thing with Windows 365 is that it runs in the cloud and you access it using any physical computer you want. We cover requirements in Chapter 15; however, in a nutshell, just about any physical computer can be used to access your Windows 365 cloud PC. Your physical computer becomes a dumb computer and is just used so you have something physical to type on and interact with in the physical world. This concept will become clearer in Chapter 2 where you get up and running with a Windows 365 cloud PC.

How do I pay for Windows 365? You pay monthly on a subscription basis and have a constantly up-to-date computer. In essence, your Windows 365 cloud PC is born and never dies — until you cancel your subscription, that is.

How fast is my Windows 365 computer? Your Windows 365 cloud PC computer is networked at 10 Gigabits per second (Gb/s). That is 10 billion bits per second, which is screaming fast and is as fast as almost any Internet connection available. As for performance for things like memory, CPU, and disk space, you decide what you want, and you can change it any time with a few clicks of your mouse. We cover choosing a Windows 365 computer in Chapter 2 and cover administration and how to upgrade in Chapter 18.

What is Azure Virtual Desktop and how is it different from Windows 365? On the surface, Azure Virtual Desktop and Windows 365 seem nearly identical. The difference is that Azure is a virtual machine you control completely. You have to keep your Azure virtual computer updated yourself. You manage it. Windows 365 is managed by Microsoft and kept up to date by Microsoft.

What is the difference between Windows 365 and Microsoft 365? Windows 365 is the brand name for Microsoft's new cloud PC offering. As we covered previously, Microsoft moved Office to a cloud-based offering and rebranded it as Office 365 and then rebranded that to Microsoft 365. Now Microsoft is moving Windows to the cloud and branding it Windows 365.

Is this concept of using a computer in the cloud something new? No, the concept of a computer that you access remotely has been around for ages. In fact, the first computers used the same concept. The computer was as big as a room and people would access it using a dumb terminal. When personal computers burst onto the scene, the operating system shifted and became local to the personal computer. Now Microsoft is shifting again and moving the operating system to the cloud, and your personal computer becomes a dumb terminal, and your main computer is in the cloud. The same concept is often used in other operating systems, such as Linux. You can connect to a Linux server using just about any device and work on it. However, Windows 365 is the first time Microsoft is offering a cloud PC that is based on their Windows operating system.

TIP

Because Windows 365 is a new concept, Microsoft is constantly adding to a frequently asked questions list. The list of questions and answers is large and continually growing. You can check it out at: `https://www.microsoft.com/en-us/windows-365/faq`.

Now that the first chapter is out of the way and some of the main ideas and concepts of Windows 365 are covered, let's get on with it! In Chapter 2, you get up and running with Windows 365 in just a few minutes. There is no better way to learn something than to just dive in and start doing it. Let's go!

Chapter **2**

Wrangling Requirements for Windows 365

A Windows 365 cloud PC has very few requirements because it runs in a Microsoft data center in the cloud. The main requirements include the physical device you use to connect to your cloud PC and your connection to the Internet.

In this chapter, we take a look at the hardware requirements for the physical device you use and also the network requirements of your Internet connection. We then wrap up by discussing the requirements around subscriptions and accounts. Hint — you need a Microsoft 365 subscription in order to sign up and use Windows 365.

Figuring Out the Requirements Big Picture

After you get some experience using your cloud PC, it will seem like the new normal. We work on our cloud PCs from many different devices and would be surprised if we couldn't just pick up where we left off the last time we stopped working. Gone are the days of having to boot up, get applications started, and get windows situated before we start working. Now we just connect and pick up where we left off. As normal as this feels, for this to work, a lot of complex technical things must happen behind the scenes, and these technical things have requirements.

The two main types of requirements are the physical computer you use to connect to your cloud PC and the network connection you use to make it, as shown in Figure 2-1.

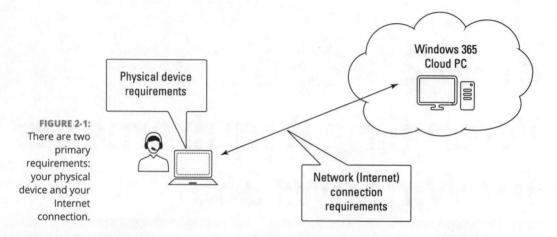

FIGURE 2-1: There are two primary requirements: your physical device and your Internet connection.

Making Sure Your Physical Device Makes the Grade

The first and most important requirement is the physical device you interact with in the physical world. In other words, you need a physical computer that you can interact with in order to work on your cloud PC. As we covered in Chapter 1, the physical device you use can be a desktop computer, a laptop computer, a tablet, or even a phone. Using a small touch-sensitive device like a smartphone works in a pinch, and the functionality has saved us many times when we just needed to do a quick work task on our cloud PC. However, to be the most productive, we find working with a regular keyboard, mouse, and monitor is best.

Maybe in the future you can use AR or wearable devices or a VR headset or things like that. Maybe even a brain implant like in a sci-fi movie! We will stick with the traditional desktop or laptop computer, thank you.

The nice thing with Windows 365 is that just about any computer that has a web browser will work to access your cloud PC. Microsoft officially supports recent operating systems including Windows, macOS, ChromeOS, and Linux. And modern browsers like Edge, Chrome, Safari, and Firefox. With that said, we highly recommend using the Windows 365 Remote Desktop client application to connect to your cloud PC. The client provides a much more seamless interface and has solved problems we have experienced. For example, when conducting a Teams call, the webcam wasn't working on our physical computer. We switched to using the Remote Desktop client to connect to our cloud PC and the webcam worked perfectly. Perhaps there is a way to get the web browser to work with our particular webcam but we didn't spend a lot of time exploring it because we found the client so useful and easy to use.

The Windows 365 Remote Desktop client is available for just about every device. Microsoft has developed the client for Windows and Mac and even for iOS and Android. We cover installing the Remote Desktop client in Chapter 3.

If you are using Windows for your physical computer, then Microsoft recommends some specific minimum hardware requirements. And if you are planning to use Teams for online meetings, then the requirements are increased a bit, as described in Table 2-1.

TABLE 2-1   **Windows 365 Requirements**

Component	Not using Microsoft Teams	Using Microsoft Teams
Windows Operating System Version	Windows 10/11, Windows 8.1, Windows Server 2019, Windows server 2016, Windows Server 2012 R2	Same as not using Teams
CPU	1 GHz or faster processor	4-core processor at 1.6Ghz or faster
RAM	1GB	4GB
Hard Drive	At least 100 MB	At least 3GB
.NET Framework	4.6.1 or later	4.6.1 or later
Video	DirectX 9 or later with WDDM 1.0 driver	Video effects require Windows 10 or 11 or a processor with AVX2 instruction set. Recommended dedicated Graphics Processing Unit (GPU).

If your physical computer is running Windows, you can check the specifications using the System application.

We will use a physical computer running Windows 10 to check the specifications of the computer. Depending on the version of Windows you are running the process might be slightly different. To check your computer specifications, follow these steps:

1. Click the Start button and then type system information.

The Start menu filters to show the System Information application.

2. Click to open the System Information application.

The System Information app opens, and the relevant information appears. The main summary screen shows the Windows version, processor, and memory, as shown in Figure 2-2. You can find the hard drive information by expanding Components and then Storage, as shown in Figure 2-3. Likewise, you will find video information on the Components menu under Display.

TIP

Checking version information for the .NET Framework is not as straightforward. However, if you don't have the latest version installed, you can install it when you install the Windows 365 Remote Desktop application.

FIGURE 2-2:
Viewing computer specifications in the System Information application.

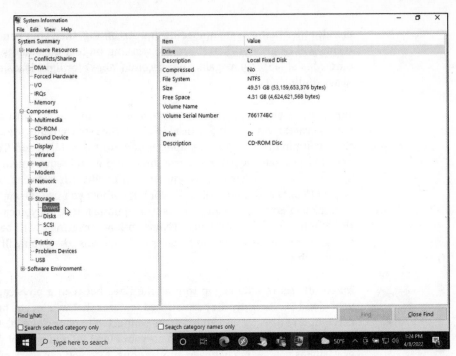

FIGURE 2-3:
Viewing video
information for a
computer in
the System
Information
application.

TIP

Microsoft is rapidly releasing features that allow you to integrate your physical computer with your cloud PC. For example, you can switch between your cloud PC and your physical computer the same way you switch between applications. Or you can boot your physical computer directly into working on your cloud PC. You can even work offline on your cloud PC and have your cloud PC sync the work you did back to the cloud when you have a network connection again. To get these new features you must be using Windows on your physical computer and have the latest updates installed.

We are hoping for a native client for Linux soon, but until then we'll use the web browser from our Linux computers. We haven't used third-party Remote Desktop clients, but Microsoft does provide guidance that clients from Dell, HP, and IGEL will work with the disclaimer that Microsoft Endpoint Manager cannot be used to support these clients on Linux.

Plugging into the Online World

The second most important thing you need is a fast and stable Internet connection. With that said, the amount of bandwidth you require depends on how you use your cloud PC. If you are working with massive computer aided design (CAD) files or video files that you are uploading and streaming, then your bandwidth requirements will be greater than if you are working on text documents. Microsoft recommends at least 1.5 megabits per second (Mbps) for light loads and 15 Mbps for heavy-duty loads.

However, as mentioned, how you use your cloud PC along with the applications you use varies widely and you need to check the requirements for specific applications you plan to use. For example, if you are using Microsoft Teams, then you need to check out the network recommendations and requirements for the Teams app. For Teams, Microsoft recommends a bandwidth between 10 kilobytes per second (KBps) and 4,000 KBps depending on how you use the app. If you are just calling one person and using Teams like a phone line, then you can get away with the minimum. If you are using Teams to have meetings with several people in which everyone uses video and shares their screens, then you will need high-end bandwidth.

TIP

Microsoft has rapidly begun to blur the lines between a physical computer and your cloud PC. Recently they announced features that will let you boot your physical computer directly into an interface connected to your cloud PC. And you will be able to switch back and forth between your cloud PC and your physical computer as easily as you switch between applications. Also you can work on your cloud PC while you are offline and not connected to the Internet. The catch is that you must be using the latest version of Windows on your physical computer to avail these new features.

When most people think of a connection to the Internet, they think of it in terms of whether they can connect. In reality, a network connection can be a fairly complicated topic. This is because network administrators can block some types of network traffic and allow other types. We like to think of it similar to how doors work in buildings. Just because a door is available doesn't mean you are able to access it. You might come to the door, find it locked, and not be able to enter. Of course, life would be simple if every network administrator, and every building, just allowed all types of network traffic and kept all physical doors open and unlocked. Well, life would be simpler and also less secure because unlocking doors provides a convenience for both those who should be entering them and those who should not. All this is to say that even though you can connect your physical device to the Internet and browse to websites you might find that your Windows 365 Remote Desktop application does not connect to your cloud PC. Chances are there is a roadblock along your network route to your cloud PC. If you find this is the case, then the best you can do is contact your network administrator.

TIP

A firewall is a hardware or software networking mechanism for allowing some traffic and blocking other traffic. If a firewall is blocking the network traffic that you need to connect to your cloud PC, then you won't be able to connect. The firewall might be allowing you access to your favorite website and blocking your cloud PC.

Windows 365 Business versus Windows 365 Enterprise Requirements

Microsoft offers two general types of licenses for purchase to allow you to get up and running in Windows 365. The first is called Business and the second is called Enterprise.

A Business license is the simpler version of the two. You can think of a cloud PC you set up with a Business license as similar to buying your own computer for your business and setting it up yourself. It works just fine and for small organizations there aren't any issues.

On the other hand, if your organization has thousands of cloud PCs, then you need an Enterprise license. You can think of a cloud PC setup with an Enterprise license as similar to large organizations that have a massive number of physical computers in their offices. The Information Technology (IT) department manages the computers, and they use tools designed to allow large numbers of devices to be managed remotely and with scale. The Windows 365 Enterprise license is designed for these large organizations, and includes features such as integration with Windows Intune that help the IT team keep everything under control.

Chapter 3 walks you through signing up for Microsoft 365 and then obtaining a Business license for Windows 365. For smaller organizations, this is all you need. For Enterprise licensing, on the other hand, the requirements become a bit more complicated, and we recommend that your organization reach out to its Microsoft account manager. For example, if your organization is going to use Intune, then you must have licensing for it. Enterprises usually already have Windows licensing agreements in place. An account manager can guide you in leveraging those licenses in addition to your Windows 365 licenses. And, of course, at the heart of identity in large organizations is a product called Azure Active Directory. As you can see, licensing for large organizations is best left to a meeting and discussion with a Microsoft account representative. For smaller organizations, we have found that using a Business license works just fine.

TIP

In order to manage Enterprise cloud PCs, you must use a product called Microsoft Endpoint Manager. Microsoft Endpoint Manager is used to manage "endpoints" in large organizations. An endpoint is just another name for an end-user device, and a cloud PC counts as one of those devices (even though it is a virtual device).

Understanding Subscription and Account Requirements

The main subscription requirement for Windows 365 is that you must first have a Microsoft 365 subscription. If your organization already has a Microsoft 365 subscription, then you can add Windows 365 to it. If you are starting from scratch, then you must sign up for Microsoft 365 and then add Windows 365 to your subscription. We cover this process from scratch in Chapter 3.

TIP

In the future, we expect that Microsoft will make Windows 365 available for home use. For now, the cloud PC offering is only available for organizations. Microsoft calls these Microsoft 365 business subscriptions and calls the accounts work and school accounts. In other words, you can't use your Hotmail, Outlook, or Live email address to sign up for Windows 365 yet.

Checking Whether Your Geographic Region Is Supported (Yet)

Microsoft is rolling out Windows 365 globally and in stages. Not every region in the world is supported yet. We see additional regions becoming available regularly. Be sure to check whether your region provides Windows 365.

As of mid-2022, Windows 365 is supported in various Azure regions of the United States, Asia, Australia, Europe, Canada, India, and Japan. Within each geographic area there are Azure regions as well. For example, the United States has an Azure region called US East and another called US West. There is also US Central and each of these can be broken down further such as US West 2 and US West 3. Microsoft maintains a list of supported regions on the docs.microsoft.com website.

TIP

To find the list, open your favorite search engine and type **supported azure regions for cloud pc provisioning**.

Chapter **3**

Getting Up and Running With Windows 365

On the surface, the concept of a cloud-based PC is a bit of a mind-bender. You can read all about it and still struggle to really come to terms with the concepts and how they work and what they mean. With such a tricky concept as Windows 365, we think it is best to jump right in and start clicking around and using it yourself. After you are up and running with your cloud PC, the things you read about cloud PCs will make a lot more sense. You will be able to read something and then do it right in your own environment.

In this chapter, you get up and running with Windows 365. You learn how to get a Microsoft 365 subscription and how to sign up for a cloud PC with Windows 365. When you are up and running, we show you how to sign in and take a peek around at the future of Windows.

Up and Running with Windows 365 in Five Minutes Flat

Getting up and running with Windows 365 is simple and straightforward, but without guidance, it can take some time to get your bearings on how everything works. First, you need to sign up for Microsoft 365, and then sign up to add a Windows 365 subscription. When that is done, you can sign in and start using your new cloud PC desktop.

TIP

When Windows 365 was first released, you could sign up for a free trial. Microsoft quickly paused the free trial due to massive demand. We expect that the free trial will come back at some point, if it is not already back by the time you read this book. Also, there is still a free trial of Microsoft 365 you can sign up for if you don't want to pay for it to get started.

Signing up for Microsoft 365

As we just mentioned, you need a Microsoft 365 business subscription in order to sign up for Windows 365. The easiest way to get up and running is to use your existing Microsoft 365 business subscription. If you don't already have a subscription, you can sign up for a free trial. Here's how:

1. **Open the web browser on your computer and go to** https:// www.office.com/.

   The Office Home page appears, as shown in Figure 3-1.

2. **Click the Get Office button.**

   To get Windows 365, you need to use a business plan subscription. We expect that at some point in the future Microsoft will release a consumer version of Windows 365, but for now it is available only for Microsoft 365 business subscriptions. If you really want to use Windows 365 for home use, however, nothing is stopping you from signing yourself up for a business subscription. We have plenty of friends who run their households better than others run their businesses.

3. **Click the For Business tab to see the available business plans.**

   In the table that appears, you will see the Microsoft 365 business plans. We will choose the Business Standard plan (see Figure 3-2) because it comes with

Office client applications such as Word, Excel, Outlook, and PowerPoint. You can either choose the same plan as we did or you can choose another plan that better fits your circumstances. The Business Standard plan also comes with collaboration tools such as Teams, SharePoint, and OneDrive. We plan to use the Office clients (see Chapter 10) and the collaboration tools (see Chapter 11) on our cloud PC, so we want to be sure they are included in our subscription.

4. **Get a free trial by clicking the Try for Free for 1 Month link just below the Buy Now button.**

   A welcome screen appears that asks for your information.

5. **Walk through the wizard, providing your information as needed, in order to set up your Microsoft 365 business subscription.**

FIGURE 3-1:
The main office.
com landing
page.

After you complete the process, it takes a few minutes to create your Microsoft 365 subscription. When it is done, your free trial will be created, as shown in Figure 3-3. Click the button that says Get Started to sign in to your Microsoft 365 dashboard.

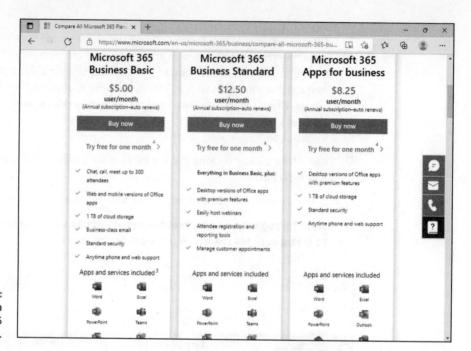

FIGURE 3-2:
Choosing a
Microsoft 365
business plan.

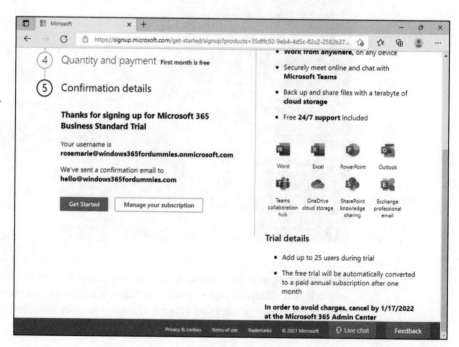

FIGURE 3-3:
Finishing the
sign-up process
for the free trial.

Microsoft 365 walks you through the additional setup items. However, for our purposes, we just want to get to Windows 365, so we click the link to exit setup and get to our Microsoft 365 dashboard, as shown in Figure 3-4.

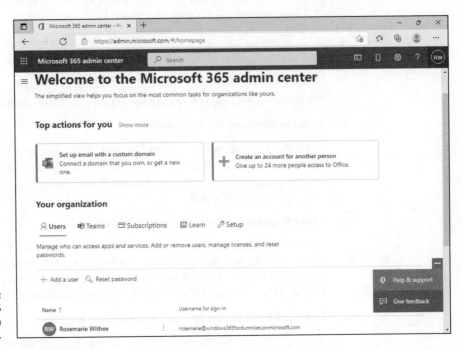

FIGURE 3-4:
The Microsoft 365
administration
dashboard.

TIP

You can always get back to your Microsoft 365 dashboard by navigating your web browser to `https://admin.microsoft.com` and signing in with your admin account. Your admin account is the account that was set up when you first signed up for Microsoft 365. It ends with the domain .onmicrosoft.com. In Figure 3-3, our admin account is `rosemarie@windows365fordummies.onmicrosoft.com`.

Signing up for Windows 365

Now that you have Microsoft 365, you can add Windows 365 to your subscription. When you sign up for Windows 365, you can choose between a Business subscription and an Enterprise subscription. The best way to think of these is to think of two different types of businesses: The first type of business is a small business that buys their computers at their local computer store and then sets everything up themselves. The second type of business is a large enterprise that has a dedicated IT team. The second business gets their computers from some direct supplier and tightly controls and manages the setup using automation and strict governance controls.

The Windows 365 Business subscription is suitable for the first type of business and the Enterprise subscription is suitable for the second type of business. In this chapter, we get set up using the Windows 365 Business subscription because it is straightforward and designed for small business. We cover the Enterprise subscription features later in Chapters 15, 16, and 17.

To sign up for Windows 365:

1. **Navigate to** www.windows365.com **in your web browser.**

   The Windows 365 Cloud PC Home page appears, as shown in Figure 3-5.

2. **Click the Windows 365 Business button.**

   To get Windows 365, you will need to use a Microsoft 365 business plan subscription. If you are following along, you set this up previously in the chapter. If you are using an existing Microsoft 365 subscription then you need to verify it is a business plan.

3. **Click the Compare Plans and Pricing button.**

   In the table that appears, you can view the different specifications for the cloud PC you want to add, as shown in Figure 3-6. We cover the various cloud PC specification options further in Chapter 17. For our purposes, we just want a basic cloud PC for now. It includes 2 virtual CPUs, 4GB of memory, and 128GB of storage.

4. **Select the Basic option and click the Buy Now button.**

   A screen appears that lets you know you can save money if you will be using Windows 10 Pro or Windows 11 Pro on the physical device you will be using to access your cloud PC. They call this the *Windows Hybrid Benefit*. The idea being that if you use Windows locally, and are the primary user of the device and using it regularly, then you are paying a license for that Windows too. On the other hand, if you only use Macs then you don't qualify for the benefit. The benefit is designed to help you reduce the cost of Windows 365 licensing. Select whichever option is relevant for you.

5. **On the next screen, you sign up for Windows 365. In the email address field, be sure to use the email address you set up for your Microsoft 365 business subscription.**

   Earlier in this chapter, when we signed up for Microsoft 365, we used the email address rosemarie@windows365fordummies.onmicrosoft.com, so we enter it here into the form.

6. **Continue filling out the form and then click the Place Order button to complete your order.**

   A screen appears letting you know the order went through and that you have been sent a welcome email. Check your inbox to find details on next steps and getting started, as shown in Figure 3-7.

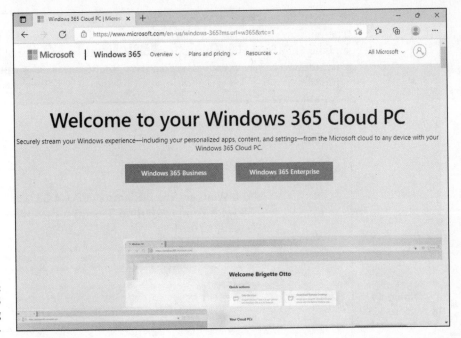

FIGURE 3-5:
The Windows 365 main landing page.

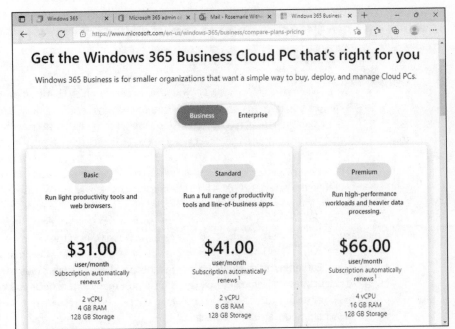

FIGURE 3-6:
The Windows 365 cloud PC options.

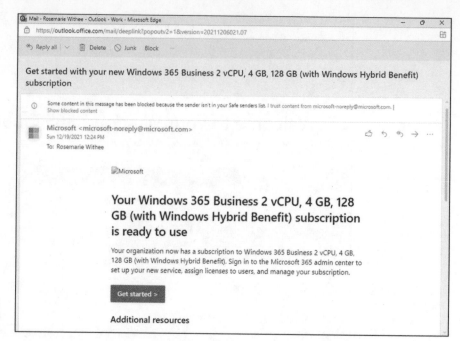

FIGURE 3-7:
The Windows 365 welcome email.

TIP

TAKING A DEEP DIVE INTO COMPUTER COMPONENTS

When you sign up for a cloud PC, you have to decide which specifications you want. For example, you have to decide what processor, the amount of memory, and the amount of storage. Even though your cloud PC is a virtual computer, it still has the components of a physical computer. Let's take a quick look at these components.

The *central processing unit (CPU)*, also called the *processor*, is the main brain of the computer. In the real world, a CPU is a little square chunk of silicon with some metal that you plug into a socket on the motherboard of your computer. It doesn't look very impressive on the surface. It is just a little square and feels a little bit heavy. Inside, however, it is a modern marvel. Two of the main CPU makers in the world are Intel and AMD. With a cloud-based PC the CPU is virtual, and you choose how many of these virtual CPUs you want the PC to have in it. Most physical computers only have a single CPU in them but with a cloud PC you can choose how many virtual CPUs you want to have. Having multiple CPUs allows your work to happen in parallel with the end result being faster and more streamlined computing.

Because the CPU just processes data and doesn't actually store any of that data, a computer needs a way to store information. A computer has two primary ways to store information. The first is short-term memory, often called Random Access Memory (RAM) and the second is long-term storage, often called disk space.

Short-term memory, known as *random access memory (RAM)*, is available only when the computer is turned on. Anything stored in RAM when your computer is powered off will be forgotten.

Long-term memory, on the other hand, persists information whether there is power or not. Long-term memory used to take the form of disks with spinning platters inside. The platters spin similar to how a vinyl record spins but the platters hold 1's and 0's instead of physical gooves. Modern long-term storage is often still called a *disk* even when it uses technology that doesn't have actual disks anymore. For example, a solid-state drive (SSD) stores information even when there is no power just like a disk but inside it is very different. When you choose the memory and disk for your cloud PC you can think of how many programs you need to run and how much memory those programs need.

Short-term memory and long-term memory are both forms of a computer remembering information. In computer speak, *memory* usually refers to only short-term memory that is only available when your computer is powered on and *disk space* or *storage* usually refers to long-term memory that sticks around whether or not you turn the power off on your computer.

Assigning yourself a license to your new cloud PC

When you signed up for Windows 365 in the previous step, you received a welcome email. (Refer to Figure 3-7.) The welcome email includes a Get Started button that automatically directs your web browser to the Windows 365 section of your Microsoft 365 administration center.

In that section, you can assign yourself the new license you just purchased by clicking the Assign License link and then clicking Assign License again to display the user search tool, as shown in Figure 3-8. If you are following along, then you will only have one user so that user shouldn't be hard to find. Select your user and then click the Assign button.

Congratulations! You have successfully signed up for Microsoft 365, Windows 365, and assigned yourself a license. The next step is finding the Windows 365 administration center, signing into your new system, and taking a look around.

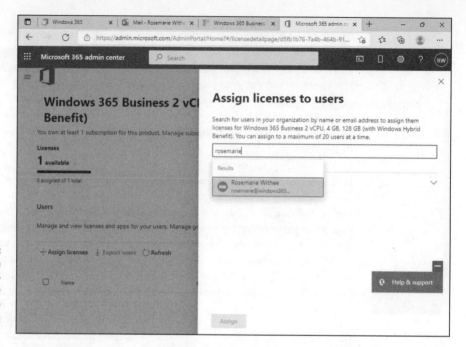

FIGURE 3-8:
Assigning a
Windows 365
license in the
Microsoft 365
administration
center.

TIP

You can always get back to your Microsoft 365 dashboard by opening your web browser and going to `https://www.office.com/` and signing in with the user you created.

Finding the Windows 365 Administration Center

The Windows 365 administration center is where you can see all of the details about your cloud PC. You can see specifications such as the CPU, memory, and storage space and you can also reset and connect to your computer. You access the administration center by navigating your web browser to `https://windows365.microsoft.com`.

The first time you open the administration center you are presented with a message welcoming you to Windows 365. Click the Next button a few times to read about cloud PCs and then you will land on the main administration page, as shown in Figure 3-9. We cover the administration center further in Chapter 18.

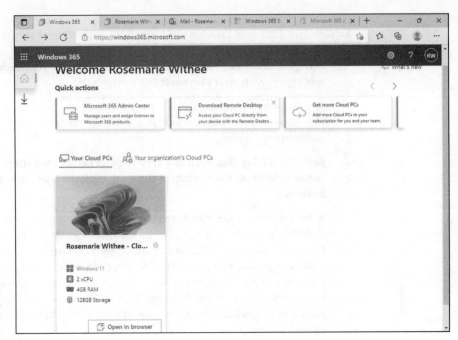

FIGURE 3-9:
The Windows 365
administration
center.

TIP

Your cloud PC takes a little time to get set up. You might see a message above your cloud PC item on the administration page that lets you know it is still being set up.

Signing In to Your New Cloud PC

Now that you have set up your new cloud PC, you are ready to sign in and take a look. Your cloud PC is running out in the cloud and is always on and available and waiting for you. There are two primary ways to interact with it. The first is using the Windows 365 client app you can install on your local computer, and the second is using your web browser.

The Windows 365 client app is a special version of a software application called Remote Desktop, and it provides tight and seamless integration between your physical computer and your cloud computer. To get the most out of your Windows 365 cloud PC, you will want to install the client on whatever computer you plan to use regularly. We cover installing the client and taking a spin around its features in Chapter 4.

Using your web browser, you can also connect to your cloud PC. Your web browser doesn't provide as tight an integration as the Windows 365 client app, but it will get the job done, and it is super easy to use. Let's use the web browser to quickly sign into the cloud PC you just created.

To sign into your new Windows 365 cloud PC, follow these steps:

1. **Navigate to** https://windows365.microsoft.com **in your web browser and sign in with your Microsoft 365 credentials.**

    The Windows 365 Cloud PC Home page appears (refer back to Figure 3-9). Here you can see all of your cloud PCs, including the one you just created earlier in the chapter.

2. **Each cloud PC is displayed as a card with its name, operating system, and specifications. At the bottom of the card, click the Open in Browser button.**

    A new tab on your browser opens that displays a number of features your cloud PC can use from the physical PC with which you are using to connect. Figure 3-10 shows the selections. You can select or deselect these based on how you want to connect the physical computer you are sitting at with the cloud PC you are connecting to. We cover connecting your physical computer to your cloud PC computer in further detail in Chapter 4 and Chapter 5. The Advanced Settings drop-down includes options to select an alternative keyboard layout.

3. **Click the Connect button.**

    A screen appears letting you know your browser window is connecting to your cloud PC, and then you will be asked to sign in.

4. **Enter your Microsoft 365 credentials and then click the Sign In button.**

    Your cloud PC is automatically configured to use your Microsoft 365 credentials. If you are following along with this chapter, these are the credentials you created when you signed up for Microsoft 365. In our example earlier in the book, the credentials are rosemarie@windows365fordummies.onmicrosoft. com. Your cloud PC will take some time to load for the first time, and then you will be presented with a view of your cloud PC, as shown in Figure 3-11.

Congratulations! You are viewing your cloud PC in the web browser on a physical computer. The first time you experience this it can be a bit confusing. Especially if you are also using Windows for your physical computer. You might see a Start menu on your physical computer and a Start menu on your cloud PC, and if you have the web browser maximized, those two Start menus might be really close to each other.

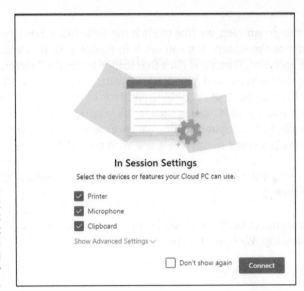

FIGURE 3-10:
Selecting components that your current physical computer will connect to your cloud PC.

Full-screen icon

FIGURE 3-11:
Viewing your cloud PC in the web browser of your physical computer.

To make things simpler, we like to click the little full screen icon in the upper-right corner of the screen. You can see it in Figure 3-11. It is a diagonal line with arrows on each end. When you click that icon, the cloud PC screen takes over your entire physical screen, and you can use your computer just like you normally would. Just remember that everything you do is on your cloud PC. Pressing the Esc key reduces your cloud PC screen back to the smaller window, and you can interact with your physical computer again. We cover working with your cloud PC using the Windows 365 client in Chapter 4 and with your web browser in Chapter 5.

We cover using your web browser to connect to your Windows 365 cloud PC further in Chapter 5.

TIP

You can disconnect from the cloud PC by closing the window that contains your cloud PC desktop. We cover this further in Chapter 4.

TIP

Chapter **4**

Do More with the Windows 365 Client App

You can connect to your Windows 365 cloud PC using just about any device with a web browser, and we cover this more in Chapter 3. To get the most out of your Windows 365 cloud PC, you will want to use the client application. The client app is a special edition of a tried-and-true remote access tool called Remote Desktop.

In this chapter, we walk you through how to get the Windows 365 client installed on your devices and how to use it to connect to your Windows 365 cloud PC. We explain how Remote Desktop has been around for ages and how the Windows 365 client is a specialized version of this remote connectivity tool.

Getting Familiar with the Windows 365 Remote Desktop Client Application

If you have used Windows in the past, then you have likely seen the application called Remote Desktop. It comes free with Windows and has been a popular tool for connecting to PCs remotely. The Windows 365 client application is a specialized version of Remote Desktop. You install the client app on your local device and then use it to remotely connect to your Windows 365 cloud PC. When you're connected, you can work with your cloud PC just like you would a physical computer. For example, you can open your programs, save files to your "desktop," and have meetings with people using Teams.

REMEMBER

It is important to note that the Windows 365 client application is a specialized version of the regular old Remote Desktop that comes with Windows. In other words, you can't use the standard Remote Desktop app that is already installed on your Windows computer to connect to and manage your cloud PC. You need to install the specialized one. We walk you through how to do that later in this chapter.

TIP

In the future, Microsoft will probably add the special Windows 365 pieces into the Remote Desktop app that ships with Windows. For now, however, the version of Remote Desktop that is specifically designed to work with Windows 365 is a separate download and installation.

HOW DOES REMOTE DESKTOP WORK?

Remote Desktop is the name of a software application that Microsoft developed that lets you sign into a Windows computer remotely, such as, for example, when you're in a conference room and need to see something on your computer back in your office. You can open Remote Desktop and connect to the computer in your office and work with it just like if you were sitting in front of it.

Remote Desktop interacts with your remote computer using something called Remote Desktop Protocol or RDP. This is a protocol that essentially streams the user interface from the remote computer to the physical device you are using and relays anything you do on your physical computer to the remote computer. You will often hear people refer to the Remote Desktop software application as *RDP client* or just *RDP*.

We have used Remote Desktop to connect to remote Windows computers for years. By maximizing the Remote Desktop application, the desktop of the remote computer fills the entire screen of the computer you are physically using and typing on. When you do this, it can feel like you are actually sitting in front of the remote computer. More than once we have been working on a far-away computer using Remote Desktop and forgotten we were actually in another room and on another computer.

The concept of using one physical computer to connect to and use another, far-away computer is the same principle behind Windows 365 and cloud PCs. The only difference is that instead of connecting to a physical computer down the hall, you are connecting to a cloud PC somewhere out on the Internet in a Microsoft data center.

Installing the Windows 365 Client on Windows

Windows is still the most popular operating system in business, so it makes sense if your computer is already running Windows. If you are already familiar with Windows, then you will be happy to know that you'll also feel right at home on your Windows 365 cloud PC. That's because your cloud PC is also Windows. In fact, as of this writing, a cloud PC running Windows 11 is nearly identical to a physical PC running Windows 11.

As we talked about in Chapter 2, we expect that Microsoft will do the same thing with Windows as they did with Office. When Microsoft moved Office to the cloud and called it Office 365 it was initially identical. Over time, Microsoft took Office and morphed it into a cloud-first software toolset and the traditional Office slowly faded. Now Office 365, recently rebranded to Microsoft 365, is the primary version of the Office tools people have loved for decades.

This is all to say that over time we expect Windows 365 will become its own cloud-first operating system with features that are only available in Windows 365 versions of Windows. As Microsoft marches towards that goal, you will still find comfort in using all of your existing Windows knowledge when using your Windows 365 cloud PC.

To install the Windows 365 client app on your physical computer running Windows, follow these steps:

1. **Navigate to** `https://windows365.microsoft.com` **in your web browser and sign in with your Microsoft 365 credentials.**

   The Windows 365 Cloud PC Home page appears, as shown in Figure 4-1. Here you can see all of your cloud PCs, including the one you created in Chapter 2.

2. **At the top of the page you will see Quick Actions (see Figure 4-1). Click the Download Remote Desktop option.**

   A new page loads with options to download Remote Desktop.

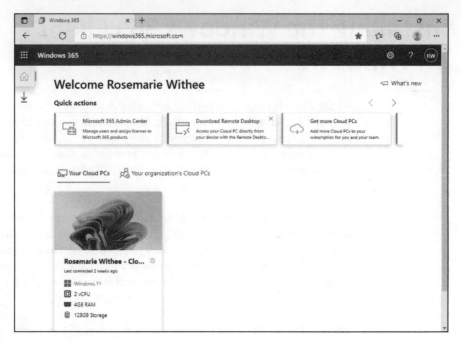

FIGURE 4-1:
The
administration
page for your
Windows 365
cloud PC.

3. **Choose whether to download the client for 64-bit, 32-bit, or ARM 64. The default option is 64-bit. Click Download 64-bit to begin the download, as shown in Figure 4-2.**

   64-bit is the most likely choice, but if you are using an older computer, you might have a 32-bit system. The other option is ARM 64, which is a family of processors built by Arm Ltd.If you aren't sure, you can quickly check:

   - In Windows 11, click Start, type **About** and select About Your PC.

   - In Windows 10, right-click on the Start menu and choose System.

   - In Windows 7, go to the Control Panel and choose System.

4. **When the download completes, you can install it by opening the file, as shown in Figure 4-3.**

   Note that in Figure 4-3 we are using a 32-bit computer, so x86 appears in the filename we downloaded. If you are using 64-bit or ARM 64, your filename will be different.

5. **Walk through the installation wizard to install the Windows 365 client and then click Finish.**

   The wizard guides you through a series of dialogs that require you to accept the terms and conditions and also choose whether access to the program should be limited only to you or whether others on the computer can use it, too.

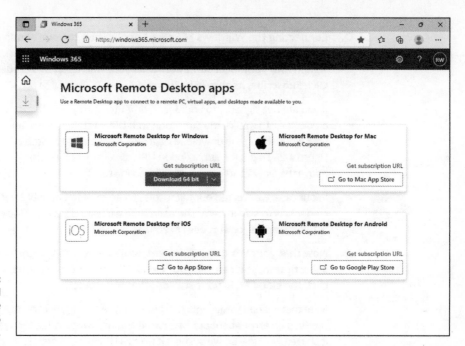

FIGURE 4-2:
The download page for the Windows 365 client application.

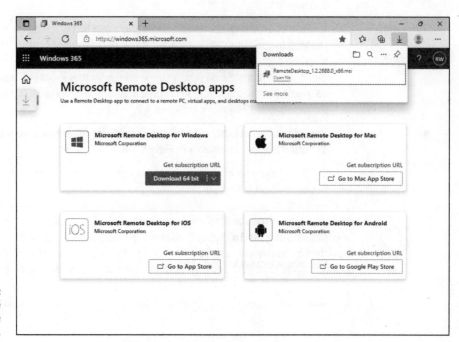

FIGURE 4-3:
Opening the installation file after download.

6. **Connecting the Windows 365 client application to your Windows 365 cloud PC requires you to enter your subscription information. If you are signed into your local computer with your Microsoft 365 credentials, then click Subscribe, as shown in Figure 4-4.**

   If you are not signed into your local computer with your Microsoft 365 credentials, then click the Subscribe with URL button. You will find the URL for your cloud PC on the download page you navigated to in Step 2 (refer to Figure 4-2). To get the subscription URL, click the Get Subscription URL link just above the Download button you clicked in Step 3.

TIP

   In our case, we created our Microsoft 365 account in Chapter 2 and used those credentials to sign in here. The username we used is `rosemarie@windows-365fordummies.onmicrosoft.com`.

7. **Now that your Windows 365 client application is connected to your subscription, you can see your cloud PCs, as shown in Figure 4-5. Double-click the cloud PC in your subscription to connect.**

   Note that we had to sign in a few times before this connection worked. We received an error about our username and password, but after a few minutes it started working. So we suspect it takes a little time to get set up the first time you sign in.

TIP

   You can open the Windows 365 client app again by searching for Remote Desktop in your installed programs. Be careful here! Your computer might also have the default Remote Desktop Connection installed, too. The Windows 365 client has an orange icon with a connection on it that looks like two L's connected at the bottom. You can see the Remote Desktop that was installed as the Windows 365 client in Figure 4-7.

8. **You are automatically signed into your cloud PC and are now able to look at your desktop, as shown in Figure 4-6.**

   Congratulations! You are now using your physical computer to connect to and use your cloud PC.

TIP

By default, the Remote Desktop application might become full screen, which can be confusing at first. In Figure 4-6, notice a small bar at the top of the screen. This bar lets you know you are in your cloud PC. You can minimize the window that contains your cloud PC desktop and get back to your physical computer.

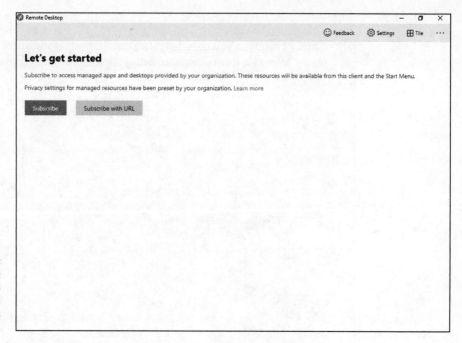

FIGURE 4-4:
Connecting the
Windows 365
client application
to your Windows
365 cloud PC.

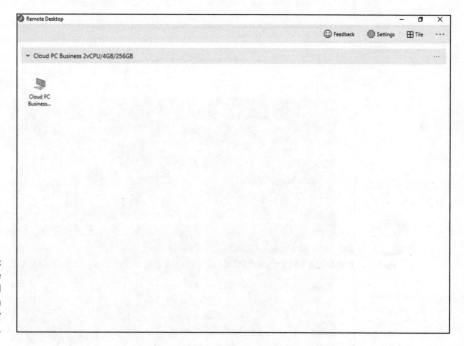

FIGURE 4-5:
Viewing the
available cloud
PCs available in
your
subscription.

Bar indicating you're in your cloud PC

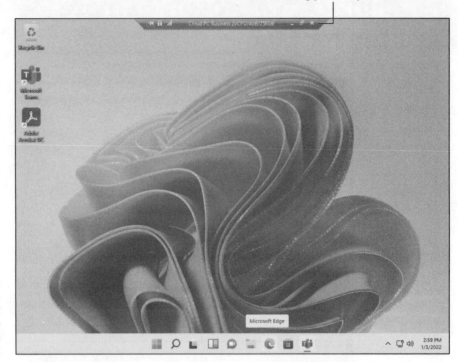

FIGURE 4-6:
Connecting to
your cloud PC
using the
Windows 365
client app.

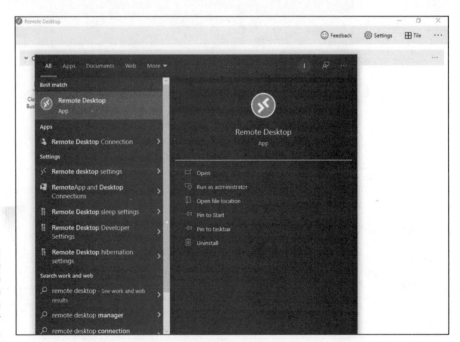

FIGURE 4-7:
Opening the
Windows 365
Remote Desktop
client application
again after
installing it.

Installing the Microsoft Remote Desktop for Mac

Using a cloud-based PC offers a number of major benefits, and one of the bigger ones is that it allows you to use any computer. Your physical computer doesn't need to be Windows. In fact, it can be just about anything that has a web browser. However, as we mentioned, you will get tighter integration between the physical device you are using and your cloud PC when you use the client. Microsoft understands that people also love Mac computers (we are big fans, too!), and they developed a Windows 365 client app specifically for it.

To install the Windows 365 client app on your physical Mac computer:

1. **Open Safari, or another web browser, navigate to** `https://windows365.microsoft.com`, **and sign in with your Microsoft 365 credentials.**

2. **At the top of the page you will see Quick Actions (refer back to Figure 4-1). Click the Download Remote Desktop option.**

   A new page loads with options to download Remote Desktop.

3. **Under the section for Mac, select Go to Mac App Store. (See Figure 4-2.)**

   Your browser takes you to the Windows 365 client version of Remote Desktop, and the App Store app on your Mac also opens with the app, as shown in Figure 4-8.

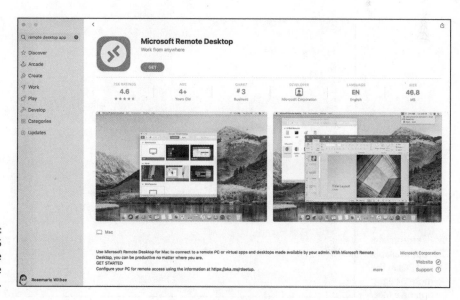

FIGURE 4-8: The Windows 365 client of Remote Desktop in the Mac App Store.

4. Click the Get button to get the app and then click Install App.

5. Walk through the installation wizard to install the Windows 365 Remote Desktop client and then click Finish.

The wizard guides you through a series of dialogs that require you to accept the terms and conditions.

6. Connecting the Windows 365 client application to your Windows 365 cloud PC requires you to enter your subscription information. Click Subscribe to sign in.

You can also click the Subscribe with URL button. You will find the URL for your cloud PC on the download page you navigated to in Step 2 (refer back to Figure 4-2). To get the subscription URL, click the Get Subscription URL link just above the Download button you clicked in Step 3.

TIP

In our case we created our Microsoft 365 account in Chapter 2 and those are the credentials we use to sign in here. The username we used is `rosemarie@ windows365fordummies.onmicrosoft.com`.

7. Now that your Windows 365 client application is connected to your subscription you can see your cloud PCs on the Workspaces tab as shown in Figure 4-9. Double-click the cloud PC in your subscription to connect.

Note that we had to sign in a few times before this connection worked. We received an error about our username and password, but after a few minutes it started working. So we suspect it takes a little time to get setup the first time you sign in.

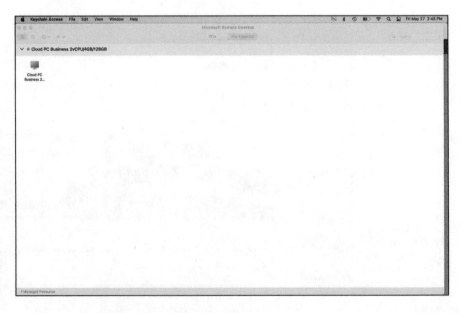

FIGURE 4-9:
Your available cloud PCs in the Remote Desktop app on a Mac.

TIP

You can open the Windows 365 client app again by searching for *Remote Desktop* in your installed programs.

8. **The Windows 365 Remote Desktop application takes over your full screen, and you will be looking at your cloud PC desktop. Because your cloud PC is the same regardless of the device and OS you are using for your physical computer, you will be looking at the same desktop shown back in Figure 4-6. The only difference between the two procedures is the operating system your physical computer is running. Your cloud PC doesn't change as you change devices.**

You are now using your physical computer to connect to and use your cloud PC.

TIP

By default, the Remote Desktop application becomes full screen, which can easily throw you for a loop. To get back to your physical Mac computer, press and hold the Command key and then press the Tab key. You can also move the mouse to the top of the window running your cloud PC and view the Remote Desktop application as shown in Figure 4-10. This bar is what lets you get back to your physical computer. If you minimize the bar, then the Windows 365 Remote Desktop client will minimize and you will be back looking at your physical computer's operating system.

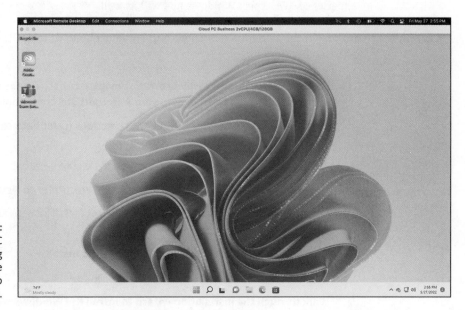

FIGURE 4-10:
Using a cloud PC on a Mac using the Remote Desktop application.

Installing the Windows 365 Client on your iPhone or iPad

You will be hard pressed to find us without our iPhones. On the iPhone, there is an app for just about everything, and we start having anxiety when our phone battery gets low. In other words, we are attached to our phone at the hip, literally! We were excited to find out that Microsoft also has first-class Windows 365 client apps available for phones and tablets. It can feel a bit quirky to be working on your full-fledged work computer using your phone, but it can also be a lifesaver in a pinch.

You can also connect an external monitor and keyboard to your phone or tablet and have the experience of using a traditional computer.

It can feel a bit convoluted getting set up to use your Windows 365 cloud PC from your iPhone or iPad. After you get set up the first time, then accessing your cloud PC is as straightforward as a few taps on your device. Getting to the point where you can just tap to open can test your patience though. We expect Microsoft will streamline the process in the future. The current process reminds us of the first time we used Office 365. Over time Office 365 became a streamlined, cloud-first experience. We expect Windows 365 will as well.

To install the Windows 365 client app on your phone or tablet computer, follow these steps:

1. **Open Safari, or another web browser, navigate to** `https://windows365.microsoft.com`**, and sign in with your Microsoft 365 credentials.**

2. **At the top of the page you will see Quick Actions (refer back to Figure 4-1). Tap the Download Remote Desktop option.**

   A new page loads with the option to download Remote Desktop.

3. **Under the section for iOS, select Go to App Store. (Refer to Figure 4-2.)**

   Your device opens the App Store on the Windows 365 client app called Remote Desktop.

4. **Tap the Get button to get the app and then tap Install.**

   The app downloads and installs, as shown in Figure 4-11.

5. **Walk through the installation wizard to install the Windows 365 Remote Desktop client and then tap Finish.**

   The wizard guides you through a series of dialogs that require you to accept the terms and conditions.

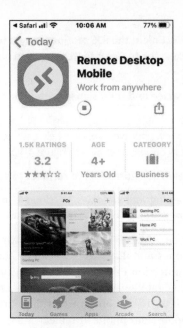

FIGURE 4-11:
The Windows 365
Remote Desktop
client installing
from the iOS App
Store.

6. **Tap Open to open the app on your device.**

   Remote Desktop asks whether other devices on the network should be allowed to discover your device. If you are on a trusted network then you may want other devices to see your device on the network, for example to share files. However, if you are in a public network, such as a coffee shop, then you don't want other devices to see your device for security reasons. You can decide if this is appropriate for your situation. We chose not to allow it in our situation. You are then asked to confirm permissions for Bluetooth, your microphone, and your camera. These are required in order to have meetings from your cloud PC. In essence, when you have a meeting using your cloud PC, you are using the camera and microphone of your local device. Select OK to allow permissions if you plan to use the physical device for meetings from your cloud PC.

7. **When Remote Desktop first opens, it will be empty, and you won't see any PCs or workspaces. You will need to add your Windows 365 PC. Click the plus sign and then select Add Workspace.**

   You are asked for the URL of the workspace. Navigate back to your web browser that shows your Windows 365 dashboard (if you closed the window, it is https://windows365.microsoft.com) and then the Quick Action to Download Remote Desktop — refer back to Figure 4-2).

8. **Tap the Get Subscription URL link in the iOS section, copy it to the clipboard, and then navigate back to Remote Desktop and paste it in the URL textbox.**

9. **Click Next to add the workspace and then sign in with your Microsoft 365 credentials.**

   A dialog appears letting you know your workspace is being set up and then your cloud PC will appear as an option, as shown in Figure 4-12.

10. **Tap your cloud PC icon (shown in Figure 4-12) to connect to your cloud PC.**

    Congratulations! You are accessing your Windows 365 cloud PC from your iPhone or iPad. Figure 4-13 shows our cloud PC desktop on our iPhone.

TIP

As you can see in Figure 4-13, your cloud PC takes over the entire screen on your device. This is standard for iPhones and iPads but this can be alarming and confusing at first. Think of your connection to your cloud PC as just another app on your iPhone or iPad. You can navigate away from it and call someone or send a message and then navigate back to it and continue working. In this way it performs the same as any other app on your phone or tablet.

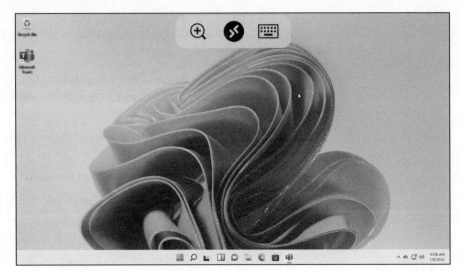

FIGURE 4-13:
Working with
your Windows
365 cloud PC
from an iPhone.

TIP

There are two different ways to interact with the mouse pointer in your cloud PC from your iPhone or iPad. You can drag the mouse pointer around by moving your finger around the screen (the default way) or you can switch the mode so that your finger becomes the mouse and your pointer becomes a hand on your cloud PC. This seems a little crazy to think about but it starts to make sense once you do it a few times.

TIP

To disconnect, click on the Remote Desktop icon (a black icon with two arrows facing each other) and a new screen appears. Click Disconnect All PCs Sessions to disconnect from the cloud PC.

Installing the Windows 365 Client on Your Android Phone or Tablet

Android is the most popular operating system in the world. More devices run Android than anything else. Microsoft was smart to recognize this fact and developed a top-notch Windows 365 Remote Desktop client application.

WARNING

Getting up and running with your cloud PC from your Android phone or tablet can feel like a real challenge. It takes some patience to get things going the first time, but once you are set up, you can connect to your cloud PC from your Android device with just a few taps. In other words, after you are set up, you can think of your cloud PC as just another app running on your device.

To install the Windows 365 client app on your Android phone or tablet computer, follow these steps:

1. **Open Chrome, or another web browser, navigate to** `https://windows365.microsoft.com`, **and sign in with your Microsoft 365 credentials.**

2. **In Quick Actions, at the top of the page (refer to Figure 4-1), tap the Download Remote Desktop option.**

    A new page loads with option to download Remote Desktop.

3. **Under the section for Android, select Go to Google Play Store. You can see the option in Figure 4-2.**

    Your browser takes you to the Windows 365 client version of Remote Desktop, and the Play Store opens on your device with the app as shown in Figure 4-14.

4. **Tap the Install button, tap Open, and then tap Accept for the license terms and the privacy statement.**

5. **When Remote Desktop first opens, it is empty, and you won't see any PCs or workspaces. You will need to add your Windows 365 PC. To do so, tap the plus sign and then select Add Workspace.**

    When you add a workspace, you are asked for the URL of the workspace. Navigate back to your web browser that shows your Windows 365 dashboard (if you closed the window, it is `https://windows365.microsoft.com` and then the Quick Action to Download Remote Desktop — refer to Figure 4-2).

6. **Tap the Get Subscription URL link in the Android section, copy it to the clipboard, and then navigate back to Remote Desktop and paste it in the textbox with the label Email or workspace URL.**

7. **Tap Next to add the workspace and then sign in with your Microsoft 365 credentials.**

    A dialog appears letting you know your workspace is being set up. Then, your cloud PC appears on the Workspaces tab as an option, as shown in Figure 4-15.

8. **Tap the Workspaces tab and then tap your cloud PC icon to connect to your cloud PC. Android asks you to confirm that the remote PC can access resources such as your local storage, microphone, clipboard, and camera. Tap Connect and then allow the microphone and other requests.**

    Congratulations! You are accessing your Windows 365 cloud PC from your Android device. Figure 4-16 shows our cloud PC desktop on our Android phone.

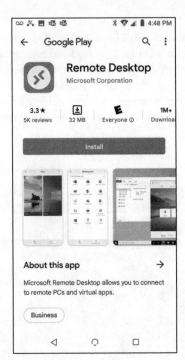

FIGURE 4-14:
The Windows 365 client of Remote Desktop in the Google Play store.

FIGURE 4-15:
The Windows 365 Remote Desktop client running on Android showing a connection to your cloud PC.

Figure 4-16 shows how the Windows 365 Remote Desktop client takes over the entire screen of your device. This is standard for Android phones and tablets but it can be a bit jarring the first time you see it. Think of your connection to your cloud PC as just another app on your Android phone or tablet. You can navigate away from it and call someone or send a message and then navigate back to it and continue working. In this way it performs the same as any other app on your phone or tablet.

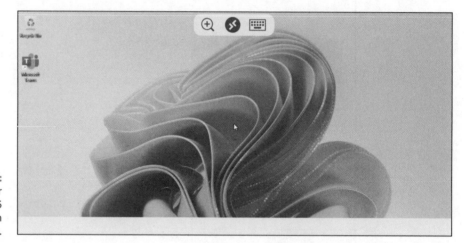

FIGURE 4-16:
Using your
Windows 365
cloud PC from an
Android phone.

To disconnect, click on the Remote Desktop icon (a black icon with two arrows facing each other), and a new screen will appear. Click on the Disconnect All PCs Sessions to disconnect from the cloud PC.

Chapter **5**

One Desktop from Any Device

The *metaverse* is the new name for all things virtual. Facebook went as far as to change their name to *Meta* in order to show how serious they are about the virtual world. The concept of the metaverse is not new. What is new, though, is how connected everything has become and the ubiquity of high-speed and high-quality Internet connections. By moving your PC into the cloud, you don't have to worry about a physical computer anymore. The physical computer you sit in front of, have in your pocket, or rest on your lap is just an interface into your cloud PC. In this way, you can think of your cloud PC as your computer in the metaverse. We expect that in the future you will access your cloud PC from your smart glasses, or maybe even a brain implant that provides an interface between your brain and the metaverse. It sounds outrageous, but Elon Musk is working on it with his company called Neuralink. For now though, you are stuck using regular old computers, laptops, tablets, and smartphones. That is to say, even though your cloud PC is available to nearly any device, you still need a physical device to access it. The good news is that just about any device will do. You literally have one desktop (cloud PC) and you can access it from any device with a web browser.

In this chapter, we walk through the concept of a cloud PC to understand fully what it is and how it works. We talk about how to access your cloud PC from a web browser, and then we discuss some of the differences between using the Windows 365 Remote Desktop client, which we covered installing in Chapter 4, and using your web browser. We take a look at using your smartphone to access your cloud PC, and finally, we take a peek at how you can configure your cloud PC.

Performing a Reality Check on Your New Cloud PC

You interact with your cloud PC from your phone or tablet. Everything you do within the window happens on your cloud PC, not your iPhone or iPad. To test this out, open a Notepad document, type **hello**, and then close the Windows 365 Remote Desktop application. Now go to another computer or device and connect again to your cloud PC. You will see your Notepad document just as you left it. Everything you do on your cloud PC happens in the cloud. This is the primary benefit of Windows 365 in our opinion.

Access the apps you have on your cloud PC from anywhere using just about any device.

Opening Your Cloud PC from a Web Browser

In Chapter 3, you learned how to install the Windows 365 Remote Desktop client on computers, phones, and tablets. You will get the most out of using the client as we explore further later in the chapter. However, with that said, you can connect to, and work with, your cloud PC from just about any device running a web browser. The general process is the same for any device since everything happens using your web browser.

Let's take a look at how to get to our cloud PC using your favorite web browser.

Here's how:

1. **Open your favorite web browser and go to** `https://windows365.microsoft.com`.

   The Windows 365 main page appears.

2. **Sign in using your Microsoft 365 credentials to see your cloud PCs.**

   If you are following along, we created our Microsoft 365 credentials in Chapter 2. Our username is `rosemarie@windows365fordummies.onmicrosoft.com`.

3. **In the PC that you want to work on, click the Open in Browser button at the bottom of the information card, as shown in Figure 5-1.**

   A new tab opens and you are asked if you want to allow your cloud PC to use the printer, microphone, and clipboard of your local computer, as shown in Figure 5-2. The Advanced Settings drop-down includes options to select an alternative keyboard layout.

4. **Click the Connect button and then sign into your cloud PC.**

   Your sign-in to your cloud PC is the same as the sign-in to Microsoft 365. So we use the same credentials that we used in step 2 above. Another advantage of using the Windows 365 Remote Desktop client is that you don't have to sign in all the time. After you get things set up, you can access your cloud PC by just clicking on an icon to connect and get started working with your cloud PC. We cover getting the client installed in Chapter 3.

   TIP

   We experienced errors sometimes when it had been a while since we connected to our cloud PC. We suspect it took a little time for our cloud PC to wake up from its dreams of electric sheep. If you experience an error, then try again after a minute or two. If you keep getting an error, then open a support ticket with Microsoft. You can open a support ticket in your Microsoft 365 administration center at `https://admin.microsoft.com`.

5. **The page loads, and you are presented with the desktop of your cloud PC, as shown in Figure 5-3.**

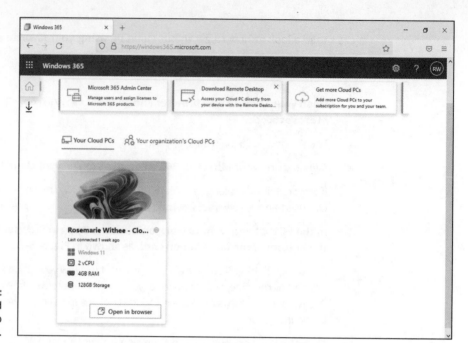

FIGURE 5-1:
Opening a cloud
PC using a web
browser.

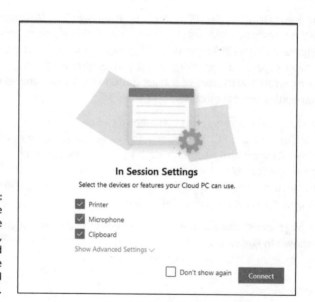

FIGURE 5-2:
Allowing the
cloud PC to use
the printer,
microphone, and
clipboard of the
physical
computer.

Making your cloud PC feel like it is running locally

It can take a while to get used to looking at your PC desktop in your web browser. We find it helpful to maximize the screen so that your cloud PC desktop takes up the full screen of your physical computer. To maximize the screen, click the diagonal line with an arrow at each end. You can see it in the upper-right of Figure 5-3. To get back out of full-screen view, click the icon that shows two lines with arrows pointing towards each other. You can also press the Esc key on your keyboard.

When you make the window full-screen, you can have the feeling you are working on your Windows computer regardless of what operating system your physical computer is running. If, for example, you purchased your physical computer from System76 and it is running the Linux operating system, when you connect to your cloud PC using a web browser and maximize the window then it feels just like you are working on your Windows computer.

TIP

TAKING A LOOK AT MULTIFACTOR AUTHENTICATION AND UNDERSTANDING HOW IT RELATES TO AUTHORIZATION

The language of the day moves quickly and buzzwords come and go. We often find our-selves updating our vocabulary without really understanding what something really means. *Multifactor authentication* is one such buzzword that is worth taking a deep dive on in order to understand what it means and how to make the most of it.

One way most people are familiar with accessing a computer, app, or website is by entering a username and password. Using a username and password has been around since the dawn of the computer age. A username and password has always been the most standard form of authentication.

Authentication is the process of proving that you are the person you say you are. When you sit down at your computer to access it, you have to prove who you are and authen-ticate yourself, and you normally do this by entering your username and password. When you are authenticated, the computer is convinced you are who you say you are. When you need to open a file, the computer checks whether you are authorized. This is the key difference between authentication and authorization. Both you and your co-worker might be able to sign into the same computer (authenticate) but your co-worker may not be able to open the same files you do (authorization).

The problem with a username and password is that anyone who knows the information can sign in as you and pretend to be you. In fact, usernames and passwords are hacked all the time, and bad actors take note of all those hacked username and password files.

You can check to see whether your email address is part of a known hack by going to the website https://haveibeenpwned.com. This is a known website by a known secu-rity expert named Troy Hunt.

A username and password is one way to prove that you are the person you say you are. In other words, it is one form of authenticating yourself. To add a level of security, most systems allow you to add additional methods of authenticating yourself. This is known as *multifactor authentication*. Apple calls this *two-factor authentication*, Google calls it *2-step verification*, and Microsoft calls it *multifactor authentication* (MFA). For example, after you enter your username and password the system might ask you for another code. This may be code sent to your mobile phone by the system or available in a code-generation application you have already pre-installed on your phone. When you enter this code, the system knows that you have received the code in addition to entering your username and password.

Benefits of using your web browser

You can use just about any computer to sign in and use your cloud PC. For example, you might be a globe-trotting nomad working from a remote beach somewhere. As you are working on a deadline, a rogue wave splashes your computer and renders it dead. To make the deadline, you'll have to run down to the local Internet café, sign in using the web browser, and complete your work there. (Okay, maybe our imagination got away from us there, but we would like to think that working from a beach somewhere is definitely within the realm of possibility!) In any case, just remember that most any physical computer will do when you need to get work done on your cloud PC.

TIP

Be careful signing into anything from a public computer. Although you could technically do this through the web browser at an Internet café, you should be aware that security issues are rife around the world these days. The simplest thing a bad actor might do is install a key logger on the computer, which allows them to review the log at a later time to see your username and password. We always recommend multiple factors of authentication, such as using a code sent to your phone. And if you sign in from an untrusted computer, be sure to change your password as soon as possible. You do use a password manager, right?

Another benefit to using your web browser is that you don't need to go through the process of installing the Windows 365 Remote Desktop client application (which we covered in Chapter 3). When using your web browser you just navigate to the Windows 365 dashboard and open up your cloud PC.

TIP

Installing the Windows 365 Remote Desktop client can take some time but it is worth the effort on computers that you use on a regular basis. We cover some of the benefits of using the client, as opposed to your web browser, later in the chapter.

Opening the Windows 365 Remote Desktop Client

After you install it, the Windows 365 Remote Desktop client is just another application on your computer, phone, or tablet. Its name is one area of confusion: *Remote Desktop*. This can be particularly confusing because Microsoft also has an application called Remote Desktop Connection. It is important that you use the correct Remote Desktop app: the Remote Desktop client application from Windows 365 that you learned how to install in Chapter 3. Figure 5-4 shows the two applications in Windows 10 when searching for the word *remote*. The top application was installed from Windows 365, and the second application down was already part of Windows 10.

When you have the Windows 365 Remote Desktop client installed, you can open it just like any other application on your computer. The process is different depending on whether you're running Windows or Mac or whether your phone or tablet is running iOS or Android. In any case, once you have installed the Windows 365 Remote Desktop client you will find it under the name *Remote Desktop*.

Top open the client in Windows 10 or Windows 11, follow these steps:

1. **Click open the Start menu and then type** Remote Desktop **in the search field.**

   Windows filters your applications and shows you everything that contains the word *remote*.

2. **In the list of available applications, click the one that says *Remote Desktop* and that includes an icon that looks like two 'L' letters facing away from each other, as shown in Figure 5-4.**

   The Windows 365 Remote Desktop client opens and you will see all of the available cloud PCs that are available.

3. **Double-click the cloud PC icon that you want to open and then sign in.**

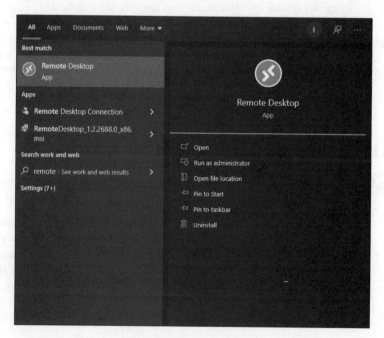

FIGURE 5-4:
The Windows 365
Remote Desktop
client and the
Remote Desktop
Connection app
in Windows 10.

To open the client in MacOS, follow these steps:

1. **Open Spotlight and type** Remote Desktop **in the search field.**

   Spotlight narrows down the list and shows you the Remote Desktop application.

2. **Click the one that says Remote Desktop and that includes an icon that looks like two 'L' letters facing away from each other, as shown in Figure 5-5.**

   The Windows 365 Remote Desktop client opens, and you will see all of the available cloud PCs that are available.

3. **Double-click the cloud PC icon that you want to open and then sign in.**

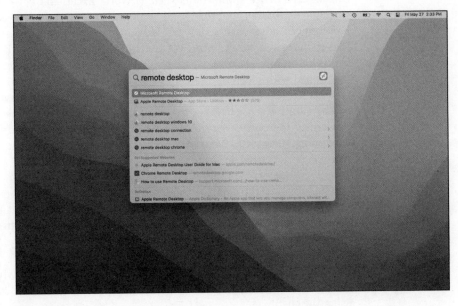

FIGURE 5-5:
The Windows 365 Remote Desktop client and the Microsoft Remote Desktop app in MacOS.

WARNING

Be aware that you should install the Remote Desktop client from the Windows 365 administration center as outlined in Chapter 3. If you have already installed Remote Desktop (separate from the Windows 365 administration download page) then you won't see your cloud PC as an available connection. If you already have Microsoft Remote Desktop installed as an older version you can update the app in the App Store to add the cloud features.

Web Browser vs. the Windows 365 Remote Desktop Client

On the surface, you can use either your web browser or the Windows 365 Remote Desktop client and either should work just fine. In our experience, we have found that the client works better than using the web browser. For example, when we were using Teams on our cloud PC, we were unable to get the video to work in the web browser. When we switched to the Windows 365 Remote Desktop application to connect to our cloud PC, however, the video worked fine.

Other applications, of course, also come in both client and web-browser flavors, and you may find you strongly prefer one of these over the other. For example, consider the Office applications such as Word, Excel, and PowerPoint. These are available both as a client that you install and as a resource accessible from a web browser. When we work with Word, we prefer the actual client and dislike opening files in the web browser. Why? We are hard-pressed to list specifics. It's just how we feel. The same is true with Windows 365. We have some experience, like we mentioned with video in Teams, but on the whole preferring the client is just a feeling. The client seems to have a tighter integration than the web browser. This makes intuitive sense because there are many different web browsers and they all implement the various standards differently. So you might have a perfect experience using Microsoft's Edge web browser with your cloud PC and then have a different experience using Firefox or Safari.

The Remote Desktop client, as opposed to a web browser, is specifically designed from the ground up to be a connection to a remote computer. The Remote Desktop client is specialized, so it makes sense that it would provide a better experience for working remotely with another computer.

TIP

We recommend using the Windows 365 Remote Desktop client whenever possible as opposed to a web browser. We have had a much more consistent experience using the client.

Theoretically, it shouldn't matter which web browser you are using or whether you are using the Remote Desktop client. However, in reality, the Remote Desktop client offers a consistently better experience, and we recommend it whenever possible.

Using Your Phone in a Pinch (pun intended)

In Chapter 3, you learned how to install the Windows 365 Remote Desktop client on iPhone, iPad, and Android devices. Working with a full-fledged version of Windows in the cloud using a device designed for fingering and tapping, however, can be a challenge. We mostly use this method in a pinch when we need to do something critical on our work PC and are away from any regular computer. We always have our phones with us, and this has saved us from a pinch multiple times.

The primary way you work with a Windows computer is using a mouse. It can be tricky to move a pointer around using your finger on a small phone screen or even a larger tablet screen. The Remote Desktop application lets you choose between two different ways of moving the mouse pointer on your cloud computer.

The first method lets you swipe the screen to move the pointer and then tap to click. Microsoft calls this *Mouse Pointer mode*. The mouse pointer on your cloud PC doesn't follow your finger directly. Instead, it moves in more general terms: swipe towards the left anywhere on your phone and the mouse pointer will move over towards the left of wherever it was currently positioned. This mechanism is hard to describe but feels natural after you start working with your desktop on your phone or tablet.

The best comparison we can come up with is the pinch gesture on your phone. You can zoom in and zoom out by pinching your fingers together or expending your fingers apart. It doesn't matter exactly where you pinch the screen, the main thing is the gesture of pinching the screen. The same is true with this method of moving the mouse pointer. Say the mouse pointer on your cloud PC is on the right side of the screen, and touching your finger to the screen and moving it to the left causes the mouse pointer on your cloud PC to move to the left as well. The pointer won't move exactly where you touched the screen, but it moves in the same direction. This can be beneficial for moving the mouse pointer to a particular spot without needing to touch your screen on the exact spot you are targeting.

The second method lets you tie the mouse directly to wherever you touch on the screen. Microsoft calls this method *Direct Touch mode*. So, touching your finger to the screen causes the mouse pointer to move right at that exact spot. If you then move your finger to the left or right, then the mouse pointer will follow exactly where your finger is touching the screen.

Even though it doesn't sound intuitive, we actually prefer the first method, Mouse Pointer mode, where the mouse on your cloud PC can be moved by dragging your finger on your screen instead of appearing exactly wherever you touch the screen.

This lets us move our finger around but still see exactly what the mouse on the cloud PC is doing.

TIP

To left-click on your cloud PC desktop while using your phone or tablet, you tap the screen. To right-click, you tap and hold.

You can switch back and forth between these methods by going back to your Remote Desktop application. To break out of full-screen view, tap the icon that shows two arrows pointing towards each other, as shown in Figure 5-6. Then, tap the icon that looks like a mouse to use Mouse Pointer mode or the icon that looks like a finger to use Direct Touch mode, as shown in Figure 5-7.

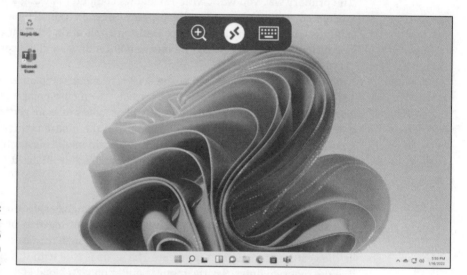

FIGURE 5-6:
Viewing your Windows 365 cloud PC from an iPhone.

FIGURE 5-7:
Switching the mouse pointer mode in Remote Desktop on an iPhone.

Peeking under the Covers of Your Cloud PC

Earlier in this chapter, you used your web browser to sign into your main Windows 365 page at https://windows365.microsoft.com. From this page you can see all of your cloud PCs and perform tasks on them. The main card for each cloud PC provides some basic information such as the Windows version, CPUs, RAM, and file storage.

TIP

Chapter 2 provides information to help understand CPU, RAM, and file storage.

You access the Settings menu on your cloud PC by clicking the gear icon, as shown in Figure 5-8. From this menu you can restart your virtual computer, reset it back to a default setting, or rename it to something that means something to you. You can also start a troubleshooting process if you cannot access your cloud PC for some reason. And finally, you can view the system information about your cloud PC as shown in Figure 5-9.

TIP

We cover administration of Windows 365 cloud PCs in Chapter 18.

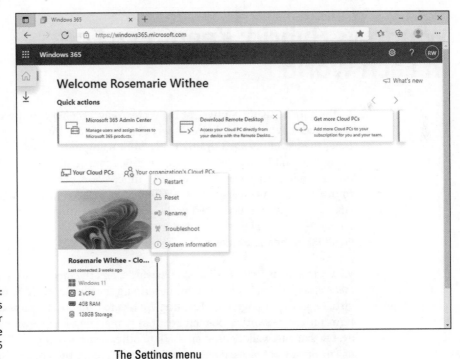

FIGURE 5-8: The Settings menu for your cloud PC on the Windows 365 page.

The Settings menu

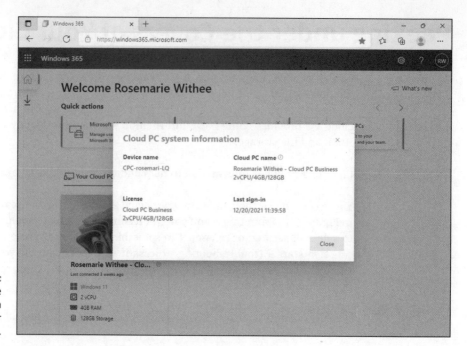

FIGURE 5-9:
Viewing the system information for your cloud PC.

Windows Hybrid: Keeping a Foot in Each World

In the future, using a physical computer may become a thing of the past. We remember how our grandparents were baffled by the Internet. During their lifetime, the world changed dramatically from using horses and traveling slowly to using cars and jet planes. Then the Internet came along, and it was at a level of understanding that was beyond their time. We expect we will be there in the future with the metaverse. People will plug into the metaverse, and the world will change in ways we can't comprehend. Until that time arrives, though, we are happy using our physical computers, phones, and tablets as an interface to our cloud PC in the metaverse.

TIP

We try to keep up with the latest buzzwords, and the metaverse is all the rage. The *metaverse* is just another word for describing the virtual world of online games, or virtual reality, or augmented reality. We like to think of the metaverse as the new term for online worlds. Remember that game The Sims in which you create an avatar that can walk around and talk to other avatars (people)? The virtual world of The Sims was released over two decades ago! And the virtual world is the same thing we call the metaverse. A fantastic new name, *metaverse*, for a very old and well-understood idea. It wouldn't be a great buzzword any other way.

It seems a bit greedy for Microsoft to charge for the Windows operating system on both your physical computer and your virtual computer. We can understand the cost of the virtual computer because behind the scenes there are real computers in a real-world data center somewhere, and someone needs to continually maintain them. The operating system also requires work to build and maintain, so we understand the need to charge money for it. But it would be nice if Microsoft would give a bit of a bonus for people that choose to use the Windows operating system on both their physical computer and their virtual cloud PC. The good news is that Microsoft agrees with us, and they provide a discount on your cloud PC when you use Windows for your physical PC. The discount is called the *hybrid discount,* and you obtain it when you sign up for your cloud PC. We walk through the process and point out the place where you get the discount in Chapter 3.

TIP

Another benefit to using Windows on both your physical and cloud PCs, though this one is arguable, is that getting familiar with a single operating system makes it easier to move between your physical computer and your virtual cloud computer. You get used to how things work, and the same knowledge transfers between both. Personally, we love our operating systems and we use Linux, Mac, and Windows all at the same time on many different computers. If you aren't happy to be techy nerds like us, it can save you a lot of time and effort to just learn one operating system, though.

2

Getting the Most Out of Windows 365

Chapter **6**

Personalizing Your Desktop

E veryone is different, and each person has their own preferred way of setting things up. Maybe you like to have your desk in your office super-neat and tidy or maybe you have a disorderly set of piles around you, organized in a way that makes perfect sense to you. No one way is the best way, and how you organize your work environment is completely up to you. The desktop on your cloud PC is no different.

In this chapter, you learn how to customize and organize your cloud PC desktop to fit your work style and preferences. You start with the Start menu (what a perfect pun) and then move onto the look and feel of other areas of the desktop, such as the taskbar and the desktop. Next, you learn some of the ways to work with your desktop. Finally, you learn how to do some basic security tasks like locking your cloud PC when you are not actively using it and disconnecting when you are done working.

Finding the Best Place to Start

Before you begin, check whether your cloud PC is using Windows 10 or Windows 11. In the future, we expect your cloud PC will always be using the latest version of Windows and will use a rolling update, like Office does with Office 365. For now, in the early days, the version of Windows in your cloud PC can be either Windows 10 or Windows 11. We use Windows 11 in our examples.

To check which version of Windows your cloud PC is running, follow these steps:

1. **Open your web browser and sign in to** `https://windows365.microsoft.com`.

2. **Each cloud PC has an information card associated with it. Find the version of Windows you're running on the information card, as shown in Figure 6-1.**

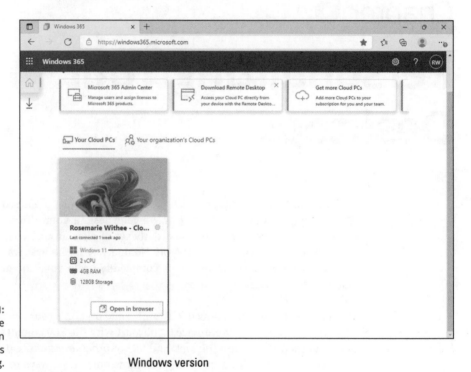

FIGURE 6-1: Viewing the Windows version a cloud PC is running.

Windows version

In Chapter 3, we cover how to install the Windows 365 Remote Desktop client on your physical computer. We recommend using it to connect to your cloud PC. If you can't use the client, you can always use a web browser, and we cover using a web browser to connect to your cloud PC in Chapter 4.

TIP

When you have connected to your cloud PC, we recommend making the window full screen. This provides the illusion that your cloud PC is the actual computer you are typing on. In our experience, the client becomes full screen by default, and you can minimize or resize the window just like you would any other window. Look for the floating display bar. The display bar can also be hidden unless you move the mouse over it. You can pin and unpin using the thumbtack icon at the very left side of the bar.

Taking a trip around your desktop

The main screen of your cloud PC is called the *desktop* (see Figure 6-2). This is a reference to the top of a physical desk, the kind you pull up a chair and sit at to get work done. On the top of your physical desk, you might set out some files and folders that you want to read through. Your virtual desktop is similar. You can save files and folders there, too, so that they are right on top in plain sight. You can also store files in folders that are tucked away in your computer, much like you can store files in a filing cabinet. We cover working with files in Chapter 8.

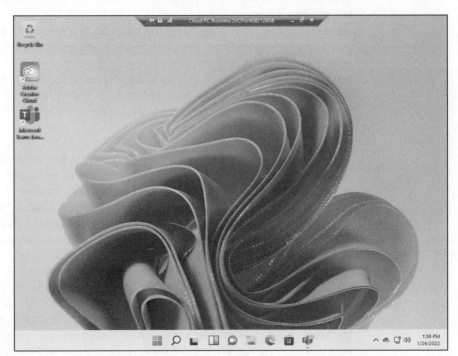

FIGURE 6-2:
The main desktop
of Windows 365.

TIP

In Figure 6-2, you can also see a couple of shortcuts on the desktop. A *shortcut* is a link to a file, folder, or application. We like to think of a shortcut as a sticky note we put on our physical desktop that says to look in the third drawer down or in the second file cabinet from the left to find a physical file. You access the shortcut by double-clicking it on your desktop; when you do so, whatever the shortcut points to will be opened.

Your cloud PC desktop includes a taskbar along the bottom and a small control menu. The location of the control menu depends on the physical device you are using to connect to your cloud PC. In Figure 6-2, we are using the Windows 365 Remote Desktop client running on our Windows 10 physical computer. The control menu is specific to your cloud PC and is your key to your cloud PC connection. The taskbar along the bottom is what you use to control your cloud PC operating system. The taskbar in your cloud PC, along with all other aspects of your cloud PC user interface, stays the same regardless of the physical computer you are using. The easiest way to get your mind around this is to think of your cloud PC running inside of a window on your physical device. The way you work with the window running your cloud PC depends on how your physical device handles the user interface of windows. For example, if you are using a web browser on Linux, then the window running your cloud PC is a tab on your web browser on the Linux operating system. If you are using the Windows 365 Remote Desktop client on a Mac, then the way you open the client and how you maximize and minimize windows on your Mac is different. The same goes for using your iPhone to connect to your cloud PC. The key thing to keep in mind is that regardless of how you connect to your cloud PC, the desktop of your cloud PC is always the same. The control bar that you use to interact with your physical computer might be slightly different, but your cloud PC desktop is a constant.

TIP

Whenever you are signed into your cloud PC, your window displays your Windows 365 cloud PC desktop. You can maximize or minimize the window you use to view your cloud PC desktop. If you are using Windows for your physical computer, then it is easy to get confused about which taskbar belongs to which computer (the physical computer or the virtual computer). To avoid confusion, we like to keep our virtual PC maximized until we are done working on it.

TIP

One major shift between Windows 10 and Windows 11 is that Microsoft moved the Start button. In Windows 11, the taskbar, which includes the Start button, is more centered, whereas in Windows 10 it was always in the lower-left corner of the desktop. If you set up your cloud PC with Windows 11 and find you hate that the Start button is not on the lower-left corner of your desktop, then you can move it back to match the Windows 10 behavior. You do this in the Personalization section of Settings, which we cover later in this chapter.

Getting comfortable with the Start menu and the Taskbar

The Taskbar includes three primary sections, the Start button, taskbar items, and taskbar corner icons. The Start button is how you open the Start menu. When you click the Start button, a menu pops up in which you can search to find applications and files, open applications pinned to the menu, view recommended files, lock your screen, sign out, update your settings, or disconnect or restart your virtual computer. The Start menu is shown in Figure 6-3.

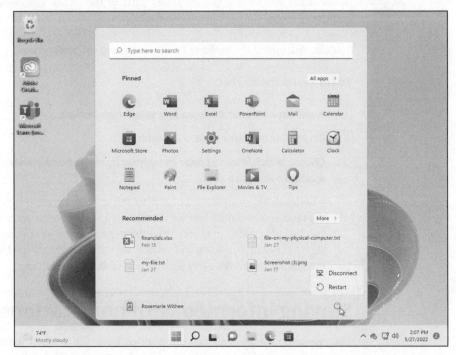

FIGURE 6-3:
The Start menu in Windows 365.

Just to the right of the Start button are *taskbar items*. The taskbar items area is where you have quickly accessible items. You can configure which items are shown here. In addition, you will also find open applications. For example, if you open a Word document then a new icon will appear that represents the Word application. When you close Word, the icon will disappear. You can also "pin" applications so that the icon is stuck to the taskbar regardless of whether or not you have it open. When you do this, you can open the application by just clicking the icon on the taskbar.

Finally, on the right side are the taskbar *corner icons*. The corner icons show various information about the status of applications that are running that are not actively opened windows. For example, if you use OneDrive or Dropbox (we use both), then you will see icons for them in this area. You will also find the date and time and other useful information such as the status of the network connection and sound. As you add software to your system, you might notice new corner icons appear. You can get information about what each icon represents by hovering the mouse pointer over it.

TIP

The corner icons area only shows a limited number of icons. You can see the rest of the icons by clicking the up arrow (just to the left of the corner icons) to see additional icons.

You can customize the taskbar to fit your personal preferences.

To customize the taskbar:

1. **Right-click on your desktop and select Personalize.**

2. **On the list of options, choose Taskbar.**

3. **Choose which items appear as taskbar items and as taskbar corner icons, as shown in Figure 6-4.**

   You can also customize the behavior of the taskbar such as the alignment of the taskbar (remember how we mentioned it is centered in Windows 11?). You can hide the taskbar until you hover the mouse over it, you can show badges such as unread messages, and you can set it so that clicking the far corner of the taskbar minimizes every window and reveals your desktop.

Staying informed with notifications

The operating system can provide notifications. *Notifications* include information such as the result of a recent virus scan by Windows Defender, new email messages, and things like that. New notifications appear on the rightmost side of the taskbar as a light-blue circle with a number inside. That number lets you know how many new notifications you have. To view new notifications, you click the blue circle, and a pop-up appears showing you the notifications.

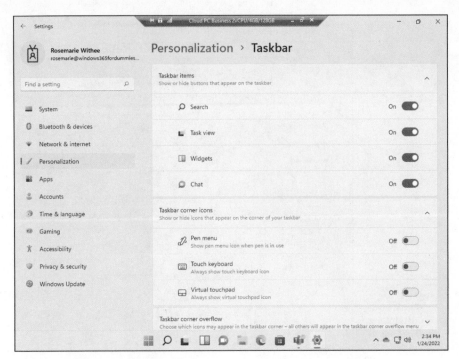

FIGURE 6-4:
Customizing the
taskbar.

You can configure what notifications you receive in System settings.

To customize notifications, follow these steps:

1. **Click the Start button and then click the Settings app. It appears in the Pinned section by default. However, if you don't see it, you can type** *settings* **in the Search box to find it.**

   The Start menu filters results based on what you typed, so you will see the Settings app.

2. **To open the Settings app, click it, or, if it is already highlighted, just press Enter.**

3. **In the list of settings, select Notifications, as shown in Figure 6-5.**

   You can configure which apps are allowed to send you information. You can also configure notifications from the operating system. The operating system notifications include tips and suggestions as well as ways you can improve your device. One of the main features we like is the Focus Assistant. The Focus Assistant lets you configure when the system is allowed to send you notifications and when it should be quiet so you can focus. With so many things vying for our attention these days, we love being able to turn things off and just focus during certain times.

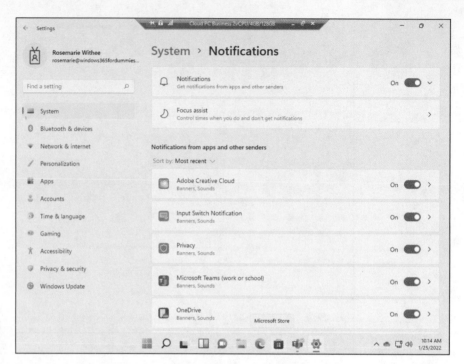

FIGURE 6-5:
Customizing
notifications in
system settings.

Making Your Desktop Your Own

You can customize your desktop and the look and feel of your cloud PC. You can set the background of your desktop (often called *wallpaper*), change colors and themes, change the lock screen, customize the Start menu and taskbar, change fonts, and set notifications based on how you plan to use your computer.

Picking a memorable background

We think that the main background of your desktop is particularly important when using a cloud PC. The reason being is that it is easy to get confused when your physical computer also uses Windows. We set our cloud PC background to an image that we use only on our cloud PC. That way, just looking at the desktop tells us which computer we are working on, our cloud PC or our physical PC.

To change the background, follow these steps:

1. **Right-click anywhere on your desktop and select Personalize, as shown in Figure 6-6.**

    The Settings app opens with the Personalize section automatically selected for you.

You can also get to Settings by clicking the Start button and looking in the Pinned section. If you don't see the Settings app there, you can type the word **settings**, and then pressing Enter. From there, you can select the Personalize section.

2. **On the list of sections, choose Background.**

The Background customization page appears, as shown in Figure 6-7.

3. **Choose an existing picture, upload a new image, or select a color.**

After you have selected an image, you can close the Settings app and view the new image on your desktop. If you choose something that is specific to your cloud PC, then you will always have a visual reminder when working on your cloud PC as opposed to your physical PC.

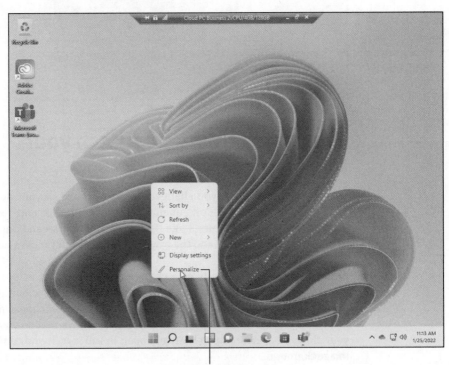

FIGURE 6-6:
Right-clicking anywhere on the desktop and selecting Personalize to customize the desktop.

Personalize button

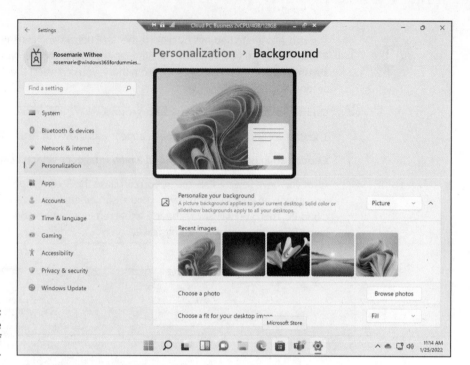

FIGURE 6-7:
Personalizing the
Background of
your cloud PC.

Selecting a theme to match your personality

In the previous section, you changed the background of your desktop. Changing your background is one component of the overall look and feel of your cloud PC. The *theme* includes things like the colors of windows and buttons, the sounds used for different events, and the way the mouse pointer moves around the screen.

TIP

Earlier we mentioned we like to change the background of our desktop on our cloud PC so that we always know we are working on our cloud PC as opposed to our physical PC. Taking this a step further, you can also choose a theme that you use only on your cloud PC. That way, you will always realize you are working on your cloud PC even if you have an app open in full screen and can't see your desktop background.

You change the theme of your cloud PC in much the same way you changed the background of your desktop in the previous section. Right-click anywhere on your desktop and choose Personalize. Then, instead of selecting Background from the list of items you can customize, you choose Theme. You can choose from several existing themes, or you can browse additional themes from the Microsoft store. The Themes customization screen is shown in Figure 6-8.

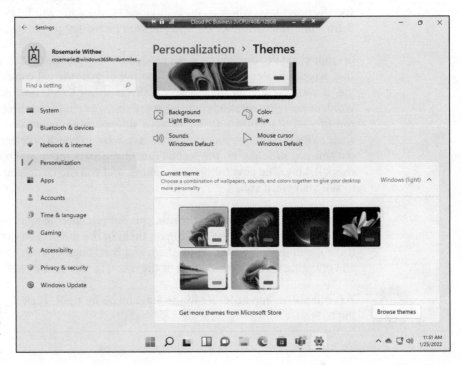

FIGURE 6-8:
Personalizing the Theme of your cloud PC.

TIP

Many people prefer a darker overall look and feel to the way their computer works. For example, most of the settings pages in Windows are a light-colored background with dark-colored font. This is called *light mode*. Windows uses light mode by default. In *dark mode*, the scheme is reversed: The primary background is a dark color, and the fonts are lighter colors. You can switch to dark mode in Personalization settings on the Colors page.

Customizing the Start menu to increase your productivity

When you click the Start button, a menu pops up called the Start menu which includes a section for Pinned apps. The Start menu is where you open new apps either by clicking on them from the Pinned section or by searching for them. The way you set up your Start menu will likely be different for a cloud PC than for a traditional physical PC. This is because the apps in a cloud PC are always exactly how you left them when you last ended the connection. On your physical computer, you might start your day by turning on the computer and then opening specific programs, whereas, on your cloud PC the apps will be exactly as you left them when you disconnected, and you won't need to open them again each day.

On your cloud PC, it might be more productive to organize the Start menu in a way that accommodates the "always on" nature of your virtual computer. For example, if you create a lot of new spreadsheets using Excel, new documents using Word, or new presentations using PowerPoint, you could pin these apps to the top row of your Start menu. Or if you have an application or a folder that you don't want to keep open but you want to be reminded to check occasionally, you could put this app or folder on the second line of the Start menu and build a routine to check it daily. The possibilities are endless, and you can customize the Start menu to suit your work style.

When you customize the Start menu, you can pin specific apps or folders so that you can open them by just clicking on them in the menu. You can also rearrange these menu items by clicking on them and then holding down the mouse button and dragging them to other areas of the menu to suit your needs.

TIP

You can pin an app or folder to the Start menu by right-clicking it and choosing Pin to Start.

To customize the Start menu, follow these steps:

1. **Right-click anywhere on your desktop and select Personalize, as shown back in Figure 6-6.**

   The Settings app opens with the Personalize section automatically selected for you.

2. **On the list of sections, choose Start.**

   The Start menu customization page appears, as shown in Figure 6-9.

3. **Choose the options to suit your work style.**

   If you don't want your recently used apps to appear on the Start menu, toggle the option off. (It is on by default.) You can also toggle on the option to show your most frequently used apps. Other options include showing recently used items and other apps such as File Explorer (which is used to browse folders on your system).

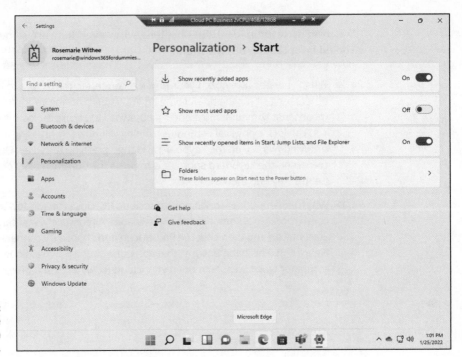

FIGURE 6-9:
Personalizing the
Start menu in
Windows 365.

TIP

You can configure the Start menu to automatically pin apps that you recently used or that you use frequently. This avoids you having to pin them manually.

Security Habits Worth Adopting

The good thing about the Internet is that you can be sitting on a beach somewhere and get just as much work done as if you were sitting in a stuffy office in a downtown hub. The bad part about being so connected is that anyone else on the Internet can attack you and your work from wherever they happen to be, too. As a result, security is more important now than it has ever been in the past.

We cover security in-depth in Chapter 14; however, here are some quick tips that should be at the top of your mind:

>> When you step away from your physical computer, make sure to lock it so others can't sit down and become an imposter. "Locking your computer" means that someone must enter a password to access the computer again. You can lock a physical computer running Windows by pressing and holding the Windows key on the keyboard and then pressing the L key. On a Mac computer, the keyboard shortcut is to press the Command key plus the Control key and then the Q key.

>> When you are done working on your cloud PC, close the window and your connection will automatically be terminated. Alternatively, you can click the Start button and then click the Power icon and choose Disconnect (refer to Figure 6-3). This habit ensures that someone sitting down at your physical computer won't be able to open your cloud PC window and pretend to be you.

Chapter **7**

Expanding the Reach of Your Cloud PC

Your Windows 365 computer lives in a virtual world out on the Internet. The latest word to describe this world is the metaverse. By the way, buzzwords like *metaverse* are a great way to impress your friends and family. You might slip into a conversation that you just wrapped up some work on your cloud PC in the metaverse and that later you might jump back into the metaverse using your virtual reality goggles to have a virtual happy hour with your co-workers and discuss finalizing a report.

With the cloud, and the virtual worlds it enables, reality becomes a bit confusing. How do physical devices that we need to interact with in the real world fit into this picture? I mean, the metaverse and our cloud PC are great, but what if we need to print something, or have a call with someone using a headset, or get a file off a USB stick?

In this chapter, you learn how you extend your cloud PC to the physical world. You walk through how to print and how to interact with files on USB devices, aka *thumb drives*. Next, you discover how to get the most out of your cloud PC using a tablet. Then you learn some tips about traveling and what it means to move around while your cloud PC remains in the cloud. Finally, you learn how to use headphones, speakers, and other peripheral devices that connect your physical world with your virtual computer.

Introducing Your Cloud PC to Your Peripherals

When you are using the Windows 365 Remote Desktop client, you can connect most peripheral devices and use them in your cloud PC. When you are using your web browser to connect to your cloud PC, you can still use some peripherals, such as speakers, but others won't work. For example, we weren't able to use the camera in Teams on our cloud PC when using our web browser. When we switched to using the Windows 365 Remote Desktop client, our camera worked just fine.

DIGGING INTO WEB BROWSERS

A *web browser* is a piece of software designed to run on a specific operating system. Different companies and organizations make web browser software. For example, you can install the Firefox web browser on your Windows computer, your Mac computer, and your Linux computer. The web browser software — Firefox in this example — is different for each operating system. Generally, the software should have very similar functionality; however, each operating system has its own way of doing things and the fact of the matter is that the same web browser on different operating systems is not always the same. To complicate matters further, there are different versions of each web browser. If you're using a Firefox browser, for example, you might be using Firefox version 91, or version 96, or a version the developers are currently working on, such as version 108.

These days quite a few web browsers are available. In the past, however, Microsoft's Internet Explorer web browser was the top of the list. In fact, it was so popular, the U.S. Department of Justice brought an antitrust case against Microsoft in 1998. Today, Microsoft has replaced Internet Explorer with a new web browser called Edge. As of 2022, Edge is nowhere near the most used web browser.

Today's top web browser is made by Google and is called Chrome. The second most popular is made by Apple and is called Safari. Microsoft's Edge and Firefox are the third and fourth place browsers. Firefox is made by an organization called Mozilla and has a long and storied history worth checking out. If you are using a Samsung device, then your web browser is probably called Samsung Internet. Samsung devices also have Chrome preinstalled so you could be using either one. Another well-known web browser, Opera, is made by a company of the same name. In addition to these, you can also find several other less well-known web browsers such as the security-focused browsers Brave and Vivaldi.

We cover installing the Windows 365 Remote Desktop client in Chapter 3 and cover connecting to your cloud PC in Chapter 4.

How your cloud PC views peripheral devices

A *peripheral* is any device that you plug into your computer. In other words, it's a device that is outside of the box of your physical computer, which often you connect to your computer by plugging a wire into a port. The connection to your computer can be of many different styles with the most common these days being USB plugs. Many peripheral devices even connect to your computer wirelessly instead of using a physical wire. The most common type of wireless connection is called Bluetooth. Some common peripheral devices you might have used include printers, USB thumb drives, cameras, speakers, headsets, mouses, and keyboards.

After you plug your peripheral into your physical computer, the computer's operating system recognizes it and makes it available for you to use. Most devices are "plug and play," meaning that when you plug in the device the physical computer automatically recognizes it and makes it available for you to use. If you are using a wireless peripheral connected via Bluetooth, then some minimal setup is also necessary so that your computer trusts the wireless device. For example, you must pair the peripheral and the physical computer to establish a trust relationship between them. Your cloud PC then uses the trust relationship between your physical computer and your peripheral so everything works correctly.

After you have connected a peripheral to your physical computer and your physical computer recognizes it, the next step is to use it with your cloud PC. What happens next depends on whether you connect to your cloud PC via the Windows 365 Remote Desktop client or via a web browser:

>> **Windows 365 Remote Desktop client:** If you are using the Windows 365 Remote Desktop client, then the connection happens automatically. The client allows you to use your peripherals on your cloud PC just like you would on your physical PC.

>> **Web browser:** When you connect to your cloud PC using your web browser, you are presented with a dialog that asks whether you want to allow your web browser to use the available peripheral devices on your physical computer. You must agree to allow your web browser access to your peripherals.

Note that using a web browser does not grant your cloud PC access to all peripherals. Figure 7-1 shows the permissions request dialog when connecting using a web browser. Notice that a webcam is not listed. When we make the same connection using the Windows 365 Remote Desktop client, our cloud PC recognizes our webcam so we can use it just like we would on a physical computer. (Figure 7-2 shows the webcam in the devices list on Teams running on our cloud PC.) We used the same physical computer with both connections. The difference is that using the Remote Desktop client allows us to use our webcam whereas the web browser does not. If we try to use our webcam when connected to our cloud PC using our web browser, we see that None are available, as shown in Figure 7-3.

We cover working with Teams on your cloud PC in Chapter 11.

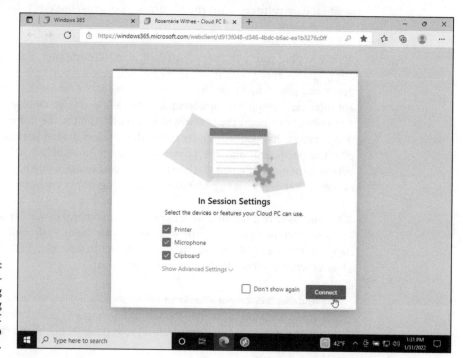

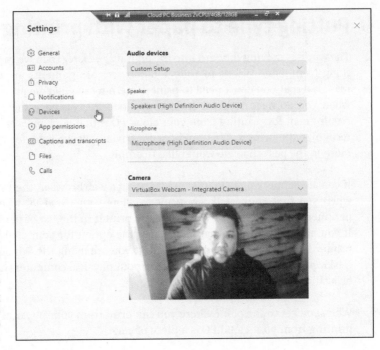

FIGURE 7-2:
Using the webcam of our physical computer when connected to our cloud PC using the Windows 365 Remote Desktop client.

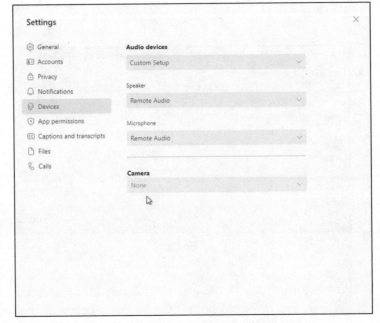

FIGURE 7-3:
The webcam peripheral device is not available in our cloud PC when we are connected to it using a web browser.

Putting type to paper with printing

The world is moving forward into the digital age faster than we can believe. Everything from plane tickets to college homework assignments are now digital. You may find that you don't need to print something to good ole paper very often, but when you do need to print from your cloud PC you have the option. The only requirement for printing from your cloud PC is that your physical computer must recognize the printer. This might seem trivial, but we have fought with printers more in the past than we would like to admit.

If you are connecting to your cloud PC using a web browser, then you will be asked when you first connect if you want to allow your cloud PC to use your printer peripheral. Refer to Figure 7-1 to see the printer in the list of permission options. If you plan on printing, then make sure the option for your cloud PC to use your printer is selected. On the other hand, if you are using the Windows 365 Remote Desktop client, the printer connected to your physical computer will automatically be available for use with your cloud PC.

TIP

When you get to the point where you can print from your physical computer, then printing from your cloud PC is a piece of cake.

Figure 7-4 shows the printer we use on our physical computer being available on our cloud PC.

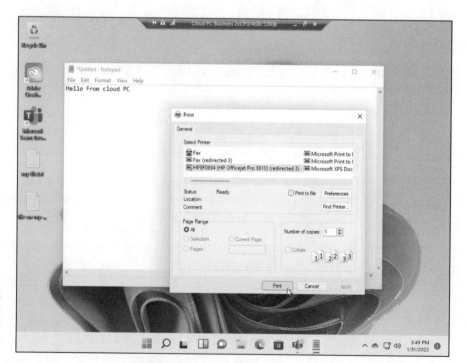

FIGURE 7-4:
Printing from a
Notepad
document from
our cloud PC.

Using a USB drive with your cloud PC, aka sneaker-net

Moving files around is often done over the Internet these days. To do so, you might use File Transfer Protocol (FTP) or email or a shared drive like OneDrive or Dropbox. There comes a time, though, when so-called sneaker-net is required. *Sneaker-net* is a term used to describe moving files by physically walking them between computers. The media often used to store files in this portable manner is a small drive that plugs into the USB port on your computer. These small storage devices with a USB plug are often called *thumb drives*, *flash drives*, or *jump drives*. If you have worked with computers as long as we have, then you might also slip up and refer to them as a Zip drive. *Zip drive* is the brand name for the removable floppy storage system of yesteryear.

To move files from a USB drive to your cloud PC, you first need to make your physical computer aware of the USB device. Usually, all you have to do is plug in the USB drive to a USB port on your computer and the computer will automatically open the folder on it. When your physical computer sees the USB drive, you can then sign in to your cloud PC and move files between your physical computer and your cloud PC. In other words, your physical computer must first recognize the USB device because your physical computer acts as an intermediary between your USB device and your cloud PC.

TIP

We cover moving files from your physical computer to your cloud PC in Chapter 8.

REMEMBER

USB drives are a huge security risk. It is not uncommon for IT administrators to turn off USB functionality completely, or at least disable AutoRun and AutoPlay on office computers due to the danger of introducing viruses onto the devices and the network. You should never plug in a USB device that you are not 100 percent sure is secure. A popular attack involves dropping infected USB drives in parking lots and waiting for unsuspecting office workers to pick them up, take them inside to their desk, and plug them in. When a bad USB drive is plugged in, the attackers have compromised the computer. If you want to learn more about these dangers, use your favorite search engine and type **BadUSB**. The name *BadUSB* refers to the attack mentioned above. You might be surprised to learn how easy it is to create a bad USB device. You can even buy them right on Amazon!

TIP

When your cloud PC is aware of a peripheral device, then you can use it just like you would on a physical computer. You can attend video calls using your webcam and headset or microphone and speakers. We cover using Teams for collaboration in Chapter 11.

Working with Your Cloud PC from Your Tablet or Phone

If you primarily get work done by sitting in front of your computer using a standard keyboard, mouse, and monitor, then your Windows 365 cloud PC will feel very comfortable, and you won't notice much change. However, one of the big changes that comes with your cloud PC is the ability to work on it using other computer devices such as a tablet or phone.

Tablets and phones are touch-based devices designed for interaction using your fingers. For example, when you interact with your tablet or phone, you usually don't break out a keyboard and mouse. Likewise, you might have a Windows laptop known as a 2-in-1. These devices provide two ways of working with them: a keyboard, like a regular laptop, and a touchscreen, which you can interact with like a tablet if you flip the screen around and hide the keyboard. Beginning with Windows 11, the user interface has been designed to accommodate both forms of interaction. Your cloud PC is like a 2-in-1 in that you can interact with it using a traditional physical computer with a keyboard or mouse or with a physical phone or tablet. The physical device doesn't matter.

When you are using the Windows 365 Remote Desktop client, the way you interact with your cloud PC can be adjusted in the client. You can set the mouse to move exactly where you touch the screen, or you can set the mouse to move based on the gesture you make on the screen. For example, you might set the mouse to match exactly where you touch on the screen. So, touching part of the screen causes the mouse to jump to that point. On the other hand, you might want to be able to see the mouse on the screen while you make movements with your finger to drag the mouse around. Working with the mouse in these two ways can be difficult to understand, but once you do it becomes very intuitive. When using a touch device to connect to our cloud PC, we find ourselves switching back and forth between these two behaviors based on the size of the screen we are using. We cover these user interface details further in Chapter 4.

Traveling with Your Cloud PC

Before the pandemic, travel while working was relegated to a few specific roles. The rest of us had to slog into the office every day, sit down at our computer, and work from the same boring location day in and day out. The pandemic forced almost everyone who works on a computer to work from home. Over the last two years of the pandemic, the world has shifted to a primarily remote workforce. Now people are ready to travel again. If there was a silver lining from the pandemic, it is that many people can work from anywhere in the world as long as they have a good Internet connection and a way to access their work computer. Windows 365 achieves part of this equation by moving the work computer into the cloud in the form of a cloud PC.

After you are set up with your cloud PC, you can connect to it from just about any device and get work done. The primary thing to keep in mind is that you will still need a physical computer to act as the gateway to your cloud PC. This could mean that you bring a laptop with you, or it could mean that you buy an inexpensive computer at your destination. We like to keep a computer at each of the places around the world where we spend time. The physical computer only acts as the gateway to our cloud PC, so it doesn't matter so much. If it is damaged, then we just buy a new one. All our work happens on our cloud PC.

Your physical computer as a gateway to your cloud PC

As we just mentioned, your physical computer acts as a gateway to your cloud PC. However, you still need to make sure your physical computer is up to date with patches and to maintain good security practices.

Writing down your passwords on sticky notes or scraps of paper and using the same passwords across multiple accounts are critical security risks. Anyone who stumbles across the paper will be able to access your accounts. For example, if your password for your physical computer is the same as the password for your cloud PC, then anyone with the physical computer's password will be able to access your cloud PC from anywhere in the world.

We recommend using a password manager. We prefer LastPass, but other good choices include 1Password, Bitwarden, Zoho Vault, and Keeper Password Manager & Vault. There are countless others, too. Use the password manager to generate a complicated and unique password for every account. When you need to access your passwords, you login to your password manager. Many password managers have advanced features designed for organizations. We like to think of a password manager as the next evolution in passwords. Some of the features password managers provide include logging you into accounts automatically and offering suggestions on creating and rotating passwords for each account. If your organization doesn't provide a password manager, then you can get brownie points for doing the research and suggesting one that fits your needs.

TIP

Using a password manager is critical in maintaining security. We cover using a password manager to log into your cloud PC and other Microsoft accounts in Chapter 14.

In closing, remember that your physical computer is a gateway to your cloud PC. You want to make sure the gateway is secure so that someone else doesn't pretend to be you. When you travel, your cloud PC is always available in the cloud, and where you are physically located doesn't matter. However, just as you are careful with your physical security and wouldn't open your laptop and start working in a dark alley, you shouldn't hop onto a shared computer in a sketchy Internet café or connect to a suspiciously named Wi-Fi signal to access your cloud PC. You can improve your security when you travel by using a Virtual Private Network (VPN), which we cover how to do in Chapter 14.

Keeping your meetings organized across time zones

When you set up your cloud PC, the time zone is automatically set for you based on your location. You can change the time zone of your cloud PC so that it matches your physical location.

To change the time zone on your cloud PC, follow these steps:

1. **Click the Start button on your cloud PC**

   The Start menu opens.

REMEMBER

   Make sure you click the Start button on your cloud PC. If your physical computer is also running Windows, then it is easy to make a mistake and click the Start button on your physical computer. To avoid confusion, we recommend changing the background to alter the look and feel of your cloud PC so it is clear which computer you are working on. We cover making these changes in Chapter 5.

2. **Click the Settings icon to open the Settings app, as shown in Figure 7-5.**

   The Settings app opens.

3. **In the left navigation area, select Time & Language.**

4. **On the Time and Language screen, select Date & Time.**

5. **On the Date and Time screen, select the drop-down to change your time zone, as shown in Figure 7-6.**

TIP

   When we are only in a time zone for a short time, we prefer not to change our cloud PC. More than once we have changed our time zone and then forgot to change it back when we were in a longer-term location.

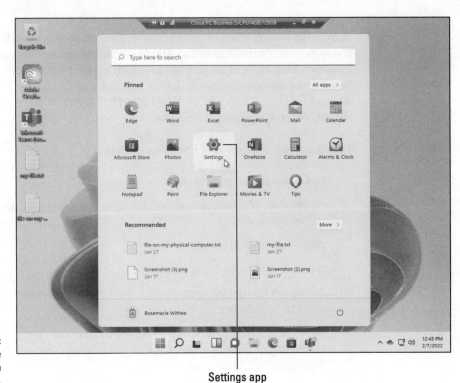

FIGURE 7-5:
Opening the
Settings app on
your cloud PC.

Settings app

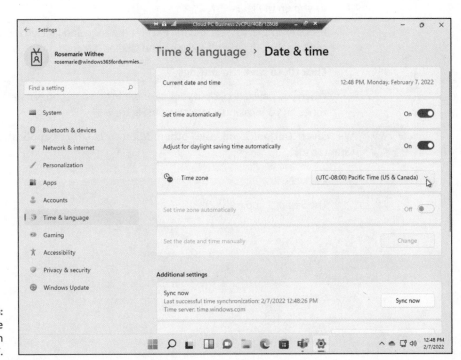

FIGURE 7-6:
Changing the
time zone on
your cloud PC.

To avoid confusion when moving between time zones, you can add additional time zones to your Outlook calendar. Having multiple time zones on your calendar helps you keep track of when a virtual meeting will be at various locations in the world. For example, it might be handy to know that 10:30 a.m. in French Polynesia, and Hawaii, is 3:30 p.m. in New York. That way, you can plan your meetings and out of work activities accordingly.

To add another time on your Outlook calendar:

TIP

1. **Open Outlook on your cloud PC.**

   We cover working with Outlook and the other Microsoft Office applications further in Chapter 10.

2. **Click File and then select Options.**

   The Outlook Options dialog appears.

3. **On the left navigation area, select Calendar and, in the options, scroll down to Time Zones.**

   You can add a label for each time zone you add. For example, you might want to label one time zone Tahiti and the second one San Francisco. Or whatever your locations happen to be.

4. **Select the box to add a second time zone and then select the time zone, as shown in Figure 7-7.**

   In our example, we selected the Pacific time zone and labeled it *Seattle*, and selected the Singapore time zone and labeled it *Manila*.

5. **Click OK to save the settings.**

   When you navigate back to your calendar in Outlook, you will see both time zones on your calendar, as shown in Figure 7-8.

TIP

We cover Outlook and the other Microsoft Office applications further in Chapter 10.

FIGURE 7-7:
Adding a second time zone to Outlook on a cloud PC.

Time zones

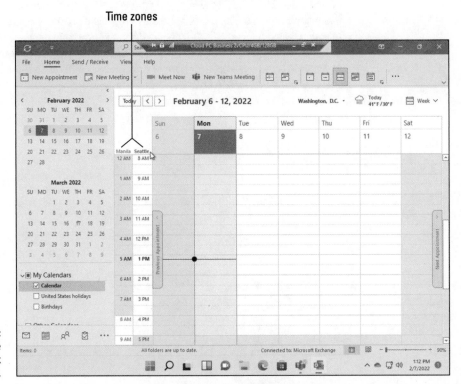

FIGURE 7-8:
Viewing two time zones in Outlook on a cloud PC.

THE FUTURE OF TIME

Time zones are a relatively recent invention that were forced on the world back when trains started traveling so quickly that something had to be done beyond a time for each city. As we move into the metaverse, or whatever you prefer to call online life, we expect there will come a point when there is just a single time zone. This may seem outrageous at first. However, the more we think about it the more we like the idea: One single time zone, and everyone adapts to whatever time it happens to be. For example, in Italy maybe it becomes standard that sunrise is around 18:00 global time and your 9-to-5 working hours are 20:00 to 04:00. If the entire planet followed the same time, then a meeting time would just be whatever time the meeting is and nobody would have to calculate their own time zone. For example, a meeting at 04:00 might be the evening in Europe and the middle of the night in China. The time is the same for the entire world and each location adapts to what the time 'means' to them. Like we said, it seems like an outrageous idea until you start to really think about it. The only thing holding back a global time is the connotation that comes with 9 a.m. being the start of a workday regardless of geographical location. To make the current system work requires a constantly changing time zone so that the sun rises in the "morning" hours and sets in the "evening" hours. If there is one single global time, then the time becomes the constant and the relation between the time of day and the sun rising and setting would become an old-school way of thinking. The benefit is that the entire world becomes in sync and meetings in the metaverse are standardized. In other words, our working hours might become 01:00 to 09:00 and anything outside of those hours are off limits. And your working hours might be 07:00 to 15:00 and everything outside of those global hours are off limits. You might be on the other side of the world from your colleagues and yet 03:00 is the same time for both of you. The only difference being that at 03:00 global time one of you might be asleep and the other working.

Chapter **8**

Digging into Software Applications in Windows 365

Your Windows 365 cloud PC can run any of the software you would normally run on a physical computer. A lot of software comes with your cloud PC by default. You might find some of this software useful and you might enjoy exploring it. On the other hand, some of this software you might want to uninstall right away. A computer is only as useful as its software applications, and your cloud PC is no different.

In this chapter, you look at using your cloud PC to run software. You learn about the software that is already installed by default on your cloud PC. Next, you learn how to install new software both from the Microsoft Store and from other sources. You learn about the importance of security and about installing only legitimate software. Finally, you learn how to uninstall software that you don't want or need on your cloud PC.

Discovering Programs Already Installed on Your Cloud PC

Your Windows 365 cloud PC comes pre-installed with many software applications that Microsoft thinks you might find useful. Of course, among these are the familiar Office applications and collaboration applications such as Teams. In addition, you will also find many other familiar apps: apps for multimedia, such as Media Player and Photos; apps for generating content, such as Voice Recorder, Snipping Tool, and Video Editor; and apps for most basic computing tasks, such as Alarms & Clock, Calculator, and Notepad. There is even an app for checking the weather, aptly named Weather, and an app for checking the news, called Microsoft News. Covering every app on your Windows 365 cloud PC would require a book unto itself, so in this chapter we cover only a few of the most popular types of apps.

TIP

The apps installed on your cloud PC can vary depending on whether your organization uses a Business plan or an Enterprise plan. Some applications, such as Office, depend on other subscriptions, like the Microsoft 365 subscription your organization uses. In addition, for large organizations, your IT team may have already pre-installed software you will use in your job duties. For example, if your organization uses an Enterprise Resource Planning (ERP) system, then that software may already be installed for you and ready to go when you log in for the first time.

You can find all the apps on your cloud PC by clicking on the Start button and then clicking the All Apps button in the upper-right part of the menu, as shown in Figure 8-1. All your apps are listed in alphabetical order, as shown in Figure 8-2. You can drag the slider on the right of the menu to scroll down the list of apps. Alternatively, you can type in the search box to filter down the list of apps based on an app's name. When you find an app, you open it by clicking it in the list.

Finding our dear friends, the Office apps

We absolutely love Microsoft Office and have used it seemingly forever. Office 365 began the transition of moving the familiar Office apps such as Word, Excel, and PowerPoint (and many others) into a cloud-based world. We were happy to see our favorite apps were included as part of the future of Windows and pre-installed in Windows 365. We already pay for these apps through our Microsoft 365 subscription, so we were excited to see that we could continue using them when we logged into our cloud PC for the first time. We cover finding and opening the Office apps in Chapter 8 and go into more detail in Chapter 10.

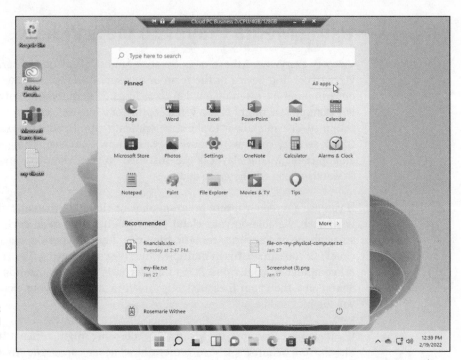

FIGURE 8-1:
Finding the All
Apps option on
the Start menu.

FIGURE 8-2:
Viewing the list of
apps installed on
your cloud PC.

Using Media Player to view videos

Video is everywhere these days because almost all of us are carrying around a video-recording device in the form of our smartphones. Also, when working on our computer we often take video recordings to capture and convey information. For example, we might take a video capture of a bug we found in a software application so we can show it to the development team. In addition, web-based video (think security cameras) is more prevalent now than ever. The good news is that an app called Media Player is pre-installed on your cloud PC, and you can use it to watch videos and listen to audio.

If you use a screen-capture program on your cloud PC, then any video you record is already available on your cloud PC. If you use a physical device, such as your smartphone or a security camera, then you'll need to get the video file onto your cloud PC. You can do this in multiple ways. We cover getting files from your physical computer to your cloud PC in Chapter 8. If your organization uses Teams or SharePoint, then your files are likely already available on your cloud PC as soon as you log in.

TIP

We have heard rumors for years that Microsoft might remove Windows Media Player from Windows. Those rumors have never come true. Instead, Microsoft added a brand new player called Media Player. When you search for *Media Player*, you will see in the results both the older Windows Media Player and the new Media Player. We suspect Microsoft added the new Media Player because many organizations still use video files distributed locally, or via a web URL, instead of using cloud-based services such as YouTube and Vimeo.

TIP

A common task in any organization is taking training in the form of videos. Although many videos can be streamed on a website, others can be found in the form of local files or web URLs. You can use Media Player to watch these videos and listen to audio files.

To open Media Player and watch a video, follow these steps:

1. **Make sure you are logged into your cloud PC and then click the Start button.**

    The Start menu appears.

2. **Click the All Apps button in the top-right corner of the Start menu.**

    A list of all the apps installed on your cloud PC appears (refer back to Figure 8-1 and Figure 8-2).

3. **Scroll down the list of apps until you see Media Player and then click it.**

    The Media Player app opens, as shown in Figure 8-3.

4. **Click the drop-down arrow on the right side of the orange Open Files button shown in Figure 8-3.**

You can open a file, a folder, or even a URL to load videos. When you open more than one video file, you queue up the files in a playlist. You can then watch the videos in the playlist.

TIP

If you can't find the video file you are looking for, it might be on your physical device (such as your phone or tablet). You can move the video file to your cloud PC. We cover how to do that in Chapter 8.

5. **Click the Play button to begin watching the video.**

Your cloud PC uses the speakers attached to your physical computer. We cover working with physical peripherals, like speakers, in Chapter 6.

FIGURE 8-3:
Opening the
Media Player app
in Windows 365.

TIP

You can also listen to radio stations over the Internet using Media Player. The key is that they must broadcast in a format that Media Player understands. This is a nice concept; however, we find we mostly use Spotify or Pandora these days.

Content-generation apps

Creating new content for others to consume is fun and a great way to boost your career. Some of the most popular apps used to create content are part of Office.

However, there are other apps you can use, too. Your Windows 365 cloud PC ships with apps pre-installed that you can use to capture voice recordings, screenshots, and videos.

The Voice Recorder app is installed by default. We cover earlier in this chapter how to find and open apps. When you open the Voice Recorder app for the first time, it asks whether it can use your microphone. This seems like a straightforward request, and it brings us back to thinking about the ways our cloud PC and whatever physical device we happen to be using interact with each other. The microphone you use to record your voice on your cloud PC is located on your physical device. Microsoft does a good job with Windows 365 of making this complicated arrangement invisible. When you open the Voice Recorder app, or any app that requires a component of your physical computer, you are benefiting from a complicated feat of engineering. You are using the Internet to connect your physical device with a computer running in some other location. Such an arrangement is incredibly complex under the covers. However, Microsoft has developed Windows 365 to be as seamless as possible so you shouldn't experience any friction.

The Voice Recorder app is extremely simple. Click one button and you begin recording from your microphone. All your recordings appear along the left side of the app; just select them and then select the Play button to listen to them. The Voice Recorder app is shown in Figure 8-4.

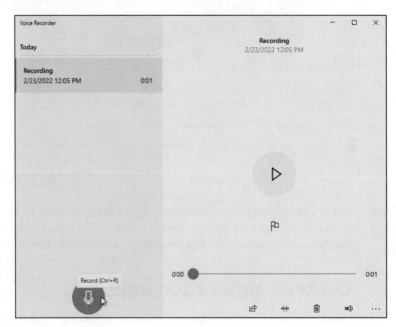

FIGURE 8-4:
The Voice
Recorder app on
a Windows 365
cloud PC.

A picture, they say, is worth a thousand words. We couldn't agree more! To convey meaning about something we are working on, we often take a screenshot.

A *screenshot* is a picture you take of your screen at a specific point in time. You can capture your entire screen or just parts of your screen.

Your cloud PC comes pre-installed with a screenshot-taking app called Snipping Tool. The Snipping Tool app is what we have used to take all the images you see in this book. Open the Snipping Tool app and then click the New button to begin the capture process. By default, the app captures the entire screen of your cloud PC in what is known as Full-Screen mode. After you take a capture, you can edit the image using basic features built into the app. When you are satisfied, save the image to your cloud PC. Figure 8-5 shows a screen capture of our cloud PC screen.

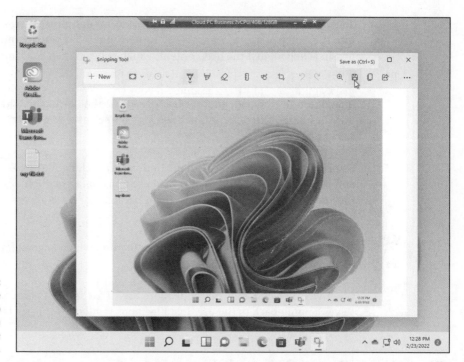

FIGURE 8-5:
Using the Snipping Tool app to capture an image of the cloud PC screen.

A shortcut to taking a screenshot with the Snipping Tool app is to press and hold both the Windows and Shift keys on your keyboard and then press the S key. When you do so, the Snipping Tool app automatically opens in capture mode, and you can use your mouse to click and hold and draw a rectangle of the area of your screen you want to capture.

If a picture represents a thousand words, then a video represents more words than we can count. Professional video-editing software is numerous, but it can be expensive. A basic video-creation-and-editing app, called Video Editor, comes already installed with your cloud PC. The app provides basic functionality that lets you create videos by adding sound and combining video clips. The app provides basic functionality, and we have found it useful for the videos we create.

Oldie but goodie apps

Some of the apps installed on your cloud PC have been around for ages and are still some of our favorites. The Notepad app, for example, is a very simple, bare-bones text editor. We use it all the time to take quick notes and when we just want to type text from our keyboard and capture it in a digital format.

You can copy text from a web browser or document-processing app and paste it into the Notepad app to remove any formatting. What you are left with is simple text in Notepad, just the text content, which you can then copy and paste into any other app.

In addition to Notepad, another favorite app is the Calculator. The Calculator app provides basic functionality, and we find ourselves using it constantly for basic calculations.

Some of the other apps you might find useful include Alarms & Clock, Weather, and Microsoft News. The names of these apps do a good job of describing what they do. We find ourselves using them because they are always available on our cloud PC and easy to use.

The Clock app includes a Focus Sessions feature, which is good for time management systems such as Pomodoro.

Other websites and apps might be more useful for specific tasks, yet we find ourselves coming back to the pre-installed apps regularly for basic tasks.

Getting Comfortable with Apps on Your Physical Computer versus Your Cloud Computer

Your cloud PC is a separate computer that lives in the cloud. This is a concept that can take some time to adjust to. It is separate from any of your physical devices. There are applications that are installed, and that you use, on your physical device, and there are applications that are installed, and that you work with, on your cloud PC. Figure 8-6 illustrates the point.

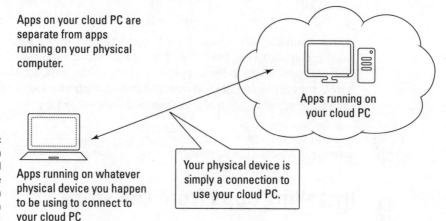

Apps on your cloud PC are separate from apps running on your physical computer.

Apps running on your cloud PC

Your physical device is simply a connection to use your cloud PC.

Apps running on whatever physical device you happen to be using to connect to your cloud PC

FIGURE 8-6:
Apps installed on your physical computer are separate from apps installed on your cloud PC.

REMEMBER

It is important to remember that your cloud PC is separate from any of your physical devices. The software running on your physical device is completely separate from the software running on your cloud PC.

The separation of software between your cloud PC and physical device is straightforward when your physical device is running MacOS or when it is a phone or a tablet. However, it is easy to get confused when both your physical device and cloud PC are running the Windows operating system, especially when you have the same software installed in both locations. We have caught ourselves opening apps such as Notepad on our physical computer when we meant to be working on our cloud PC. This is one of the reasons we decided to change the look and feel of our cloud PC compared to our physical computers. We cover how to do this in Chapter 5.

After some adjustment, however, the difference becomes intuitive. We now use many different physical devices as a gateway into our cloud PC. We use our cloud PC as our primary work environment and don't worry about backing up our physical devices anymore. If one of our physical devices crashes and burns, we just grab another one, or a new one, and continue working on our cloud PC right where we left off. It can take some time to get comfortable with this new way of working, but when you do having your work environment always available and separate from the physical world is a great feeling.

TIP

Be sure you are aware of the location where the software you open is running. It is easy to open a software application on your physical device when you meant to open it on your cloud PC.

Finding and Installing Software on Your Cloud PC

The Microsoft Store is a centralized place where you can find and install apps. Microsoft makes both free and paid apps available in the store. The benefit of installing applications from the store (as opposed to somewhere else) is that Microsoft puts all the store's apps through its vetting process, which ensures the store's apps are legitimate and free of malware. With that said, you can, of course, still install software you buy and download from other locations.

TIP

Think of the Microsoft Store as being similar to app stores on other devices. For example, Apple has the App Store and Google has the Play Store.

Installing apps from the store

The Microsoft Store is available on your Windows 365 cloud PC by default. To find applications, simply open the store and browse for apps that you want to install.

TIP

The Microsoft Store offers more than just software apps. You can also browse for games, movies, and TV shows.

There are many web browsers to choose from. Microsoft Edge, for example, is already installed on your cloud PC. We like to have options, however; another web browser we like is Firefox by Mozilla. Firefox is a free app and is available in the Microsoft Store.

To install the Firefox web browser from the Microsoft Store, follow these steps:

1. **Make sure you are logged into your cloud PC and then click the Start button.**

   The Start menu appears.

2. **Click the All Apps button in the top-right corner of the Start menu.**

   A list of all the apps installed on your cloud PC appears (refer to Figure 8-2). Alternatively, you can type the word **store** in the search box and then jump to step 3 below to open the Microsoft Store app.

3. **Scroll down the list of apps until you see Microsoft Store, and then click it.**

   The Microsoft Store app opens, as shown in Figure 8-7.

4. **In the search field at the top of the store, type** firefox **and press Enter.**

The Firefox app is displayed, as shown in Figure 8-8.

5. **Click the blue Get button to download and install the app.**

The button you clicked provides status updates as the app is downloaded and installed. When it is done, the blue button will change to say *Open.* Click the same button again to open Firefox.

FIGURE 8-7:
The Microsoft Store app on your cloud PC.

Another app that we use regularly is called Adobe Creative Cloud. Adobe Creative Cloud requires a paid subscription and includes a number of Adobe apps such as Acrobat, Photoshop, Illustrator, and InDesign. Rosemarie is an avid photographer and uses these apps on a regular basis.

TIP

The Microsoft Store includes apps you can install and use for free and apps that you must pay for. For example, the Firefox web browser is free, whereas the Adobe Creative Cloud is subscription-based software you must purchase. Be sure to check the subscription requirements for any app you want to try. Many apps offer a free trial. Some apps charge a one-time purchase fee and others charge a monthly or yearly subscription.

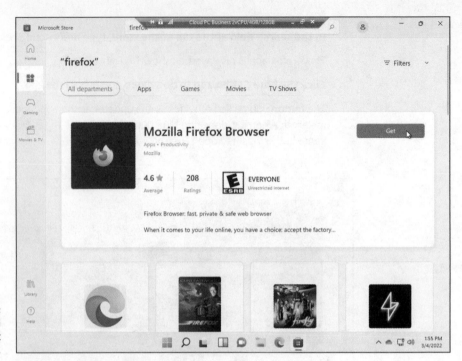

FIGURE 8-8:
The Firefox app in
the Microsoft
Store.

Installing Apps from Other Sources

If you use an iPhone, then you are aware that you can only install software from the Apple App Store. Microsoft has the Microsoft Store, but it's not so restrictive: You can also install software on your cloud PC directly from the Internet. This can be a risky proposition, however, and we recommend taking every precaution should you decide to install software you download.

TIP

The Microsoft Store is a great way to install software that you know is trusted and free of malware.

One of our favorite screen-capture programs is called Snagit, made by a company called TechSmith. When we want to install this software, we must make sure we are buying it and downloading it from the company that makes it. In other words, we need to use our web browser and go to the website, `https://www.techsmith.com`. If you happened to do this from an untrusted Internet connection, such as a coffee shop Wi-Fi, then you should take extra precautions as well. You should make sure the certificate for the website shows the verified name of the company — otherwise, a bad actor could be displaying a fake site to you in the hopes you will enter your personal and payment information. To check the certificate for the site, look to the left of the website's URL in your web browser. In Google Chrome and Microsoft Edge, you will see a padlock icon. Click on the padlock icon to view the details of the certificate, as shown in Figure 8-9. When you verify that the site is legitimate and has a valid certificate, you can then interact with the site to purchase, download, and install software.

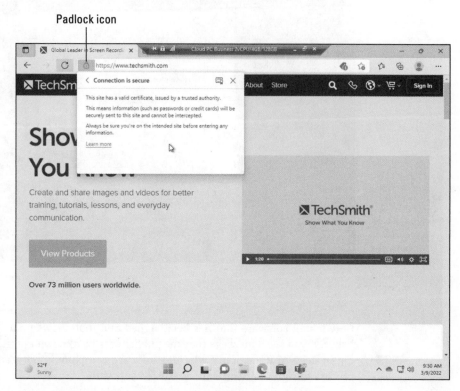

Padlock icon

FIGURE 8-9:
Viewing the certificate for a website to validate it is legitimate.

TIP

When viewing a website in a browser, you should check to make sure the site has a verified certificate. For most web browsers a padlock icon will appear to the right of the website. If you don't see a padlock on a website, then the website has not been verified and you should not trust it.

One of the most important steps in installing software you have downloaded is verifying the publisher of the software. When you install software, a warning pops up asking you to confirm you want to install the software. You should confirm that the software is a verified publisher before installing. If you see a message that the publisher is "Unknown Publisher" then consider it a red flag and avoid installing the software. Only in rare cases does a software company fail to go through the process of obtaining a software signing certificate and still wants people to install their software so we recommend putting your radar on high alert before installing any software that has not been signed with a certificate. Figure 8-10 shows the trusted publisher information when we installed Snagit.

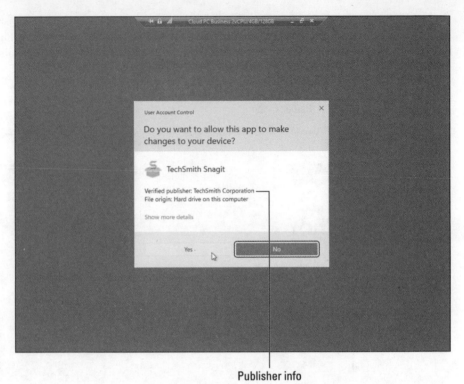

FIGURE 8-10:
The trusted
publisher
notification when
installing
software.

Publisher info

WARNING

Only install software that has been signed and that shows up as a verified publisher. If you see a message that the publisher is "Unknown Publisher," be sure to dig in deep to understand why the software company is not going through the process to sign their software as trusted software.

Cleaning Up and Uninstalling Apps

Everyone has a different level of comfort when it comes to the number of apps installed on their computer. Some people prefer to install and uninstall apps that they use frequently, and others prefer to keep all the apps they might ever want to use installed at all times. We lean towards limiting the number of apps installed to those that you use because it lowers the attack surface for any hackers.

TIP

Uninstalling software that you don't use is important in maintaining security. We cover security further in Chapter 13.

To view the apps installed on your cloud PC and uninstall the ones you don't need, follow these steps:

1. Make sure you are logged into your cloud PC and then click the Start button.

The Start menu appears.

2. **In the search box type** add or remove programs **and then click the app, as shown in Figure 8-11.**

   The Apps & Features settings page appears with a list of apps found on your computer.

3. **Scroll down and find the app you want to uninstall, click the vertical ellipsis to the right of the app, and choose Uninstall, as shown in Figure 8-12.**

   A warning is displayed for you to confirm that you want to uninstall the app and all its associated data.

REMEMBER

If you are using Windows for your physical computer, then it is easy to get confused and uninstall apps from your physical computer instead of your cloud PC. Make sure you are working in your cloud PC if that is where you want to uninstall an app. We found ourselves thinking we were in our cloud PC when we were really on our physical computer many times before we came up with a strategy and habit to avoid the confusion. We changed the look and feel of our cloud PC and physical computer, so we always have a visual clue as to where we are working. We cover this in more detail in Chapter 5.

4. **Select Uninstall to confirm you want to remove the app and all its associated data.**

   The app is uninstalled and removed from the list.

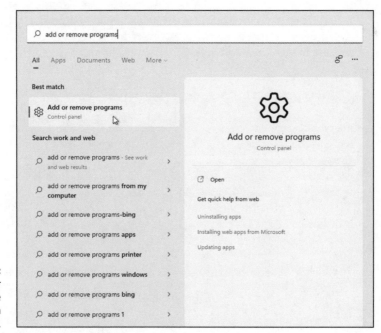

FIGURE 8-11:
Opening Add or Remove Programs from the Start menu.

FIGURE 8-12:
Uninstalling an app from the Apps & Features settings page of your cloud PC.

3
Getting Work Done with Microsoft 365

IN THIS PART . . .

Discover how Windows 365 and Microsoft 365 go hand-in-hand

Making the most of your cloud-based Office apps

Learn how to collaborate with others with Teams, SharePoint, and OneDrive

Get comfortable with using Word, Excel, PowerPoint, and Outlook on your cloud PC

Chapter 9

Working with Documents and Folders

I f you are like us, then you remember the days when the world ran using paper. Big file cabinets contained all sorts of documents in the form of pieces of paper. Each piece of paper represented information of some type, and they were grouped together in folders. Some of those pieces of paper were drawings or photographs, some were typewritten text, and others were a combination of both. And then the digital age swept the world.

If you are an experienced computer user, then you are already familiar with documents and folders in the digital age. Documents became digital, and working with them involved using specific software applications such as the popular Office applications Word, Excel, and PowerPoint. We like to think of the migration from paper to digital documents as the first great wave of transition. We are now well into the second great wave of transition, which involves software developed in a hyperconnected world using the Internet (aka the cloud).

As computing has moved into a cloud-first world, the concept of a document has morphed from a piece of paper into something that is not so easy to understand. Yes, a document still represents a type of information, such as a Word document, an Excel spreadsheet, or a PowerPoint presentation. However, with cloud-first software, the file can be synchronized automatically between cloud locations and physical devices. In other words, a shift has happened so that a document can magically be many places at the same time. This requires a mental shift, the familiar reference of a digital document representing a physical document no longer works. Microsoft undertook this shift nearly a decade ago when they introduced Office 365. With Office 365, your documents are often available on all your devices without you having to think of where you left them. For example, in order to work on a file in the days before Office 365, you would first have to remember whether your file was on your laptop or maybe on your computer at the office. If you wanted to move a file between devices, then you could put it on a disk or email it to yourself or a colleague. Office 365 removed this burden with the result being that your files were always available on every device.

Now Microsoft is doing the same with the Windows operating system in the form of Windows 365. Windows 365 makes your entire operating system available just as Office 365 did with your documents. Which brings us to the current chapter. Microsoft provided a gradual on-ramp to the cloud-first world with the move from Office to Office 365. Microsoft is doing the same in the move from Windows to Windows 365. When thinking about your documents and folders on your cloud PC, you'll have to make mental adjustments to some things, although for now, most of your current knowledge will directly translate.

In this chapter, you learn how to create new files on your cloud PC. You learn how the new Office application is a one-stop shop for creating Office documents. You then learn how to open a particular Office application, such as Word, directly and how to create a document. Next, you explore how to work with files using File Explorer, how backups work in Windows 365, and finally, how to move files between your cloud PC and your physical computer.

Finding Microsoft Office

The traditional Office apps, such as Word, Excel, and PowerPoint, are a major part of Windows in your cloud PC. Microsoft has created a unified Office experience in the form of a single Office app (although you can still launch each Office app individually). From the single Office app, you can find all your Office formats and create and open files.

We expect that in the future, Windows 365 will continue to integrate with Office and other popular Microsoft products such as Teams and SharePoint. At some point, it might be hard to tell where the operating system of your cloud PC ends and the apps it runs begin. Your cloud PC will become your productivity portal in the metaverse and any device with an Internet connection will work. We feel that Microsoft is laying the groundwork for a new era of computing in the metaverse. Perhaps an augmented reality device, such as HoloLens, or a virtual reality device, such as Oculus, will be your primary cloud PC interface at some point in the future. Some people are even working on direct brain-computer implant interfaces, like Elon Musk and his company Neuralink, so perhaps the future of computing will see our brains integrating completely with the cloud! Seems a scary thought — although probably no more radical than the concept of the Internet would have been 100 years ago.

The Office apps are integrated and available in a single app that feels like part of your cloud PC. Microsoft has named this new app simply Office. You can still find the stand-alone apps and open them individually, too. We walk you through both methods of accessing your favorite Office apps next and cover the SharePoint and OneDrive apps (which are part of Office 365) further in Chapter 11.

Creating a new Excel spreadsheet from the Office app

Microsoft has evolved Office into much more than the traditional apps such as Word, Excel, and PowerPoint. As Office transitioned to a cloud-first strategy with Office 365, a significant number of apps were added to the product. To help you wrangle all these new apps, Microsoft created a super-app called simply Office. The Office app has the same name as the Office suite of products from yesteryear, although it is so much more. All these new Office apps might boggle your brain, but if you are just trying to open Excel to create a spreadsheet, you should know that it is as easy as ever.

To open Microsoft Excel from the Office app on your cloud PC, follow these steps:

1. **Make sure you are logged into your cloud PC and then click the Start button.**

2. **Type** office **and then click the Office app, as shown in Figure 9-1.**

   The main Office app opens, and you can see all the individual apps along the left side of the screen, as shown in Figure 9-2.

3. **Click the icon to load the Excel app. Alternatively, you can click the plus sign at the top of the list and then select the type of file you want to create, as shown in Figure 9-3.**

   The Excel app then launches, and you can create a new blank spreadsheet, open an existing spreadsheet, or create a new spreadsheet from a template.

FIGURE 9-1:
Opening the
Office app from
the Start menu.

FIGURE 9-2:
The main screen
of the Office app.

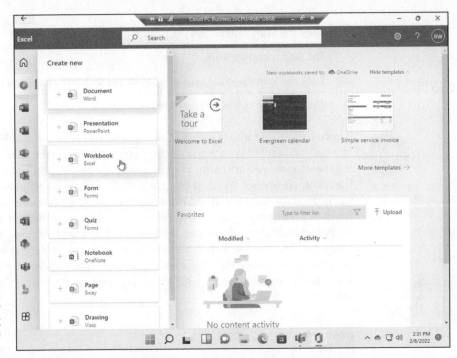

FIGURE 9-3:
Creating a new
file by launching
one of the Office
apps.

Working in full-screen mode when creating a new document

REMEMBER

When you open an app such as Microsoft Word, you must make sure you are open-ing it in your cloud PC, not your physical PC. It can be easy to make a mistake if your cloud PC and your physical computer have the same apps running. If your physical computer is running MacOS, on the other hand, then it is easier to avoid the mistake. If your physical computer is running Windows 11 and your theme and background are identical on both systems, then it is easy to make the mistake. As we mentioned earlier, we like to change the look and feel of our cloud PC so that we never make the mistake of working on physical computer when we thought we were working on our cloud computer.

To open Microsoft Word on your cloud PC, follow these steps:

1. Be sure you are in the window you are using to connect to your cloud PC.

We covered connecting to your cloud PC using the Windows 365 Remote Desktop client or a web browser in Chapter 4.

2. **Click the Start button (on your cloud PC).**

The Start menu appears.

3. **Click the Word app (or type** word **in the search bar and press Enter).**

The Word app opens on your cloud PC.

TIP

A good habit to get into is making the look and feel of your cloud PC different from any look and feel of your physical computers. Another good habit is always making the window you are using to connect to your cloud PC full screen. To illustrate the point, we opened Word on our cloud PC and made the window smaller so that you can see the Start menu and the desktop of our physical computer as well as the cloud PC, as shown in Figure 9-4. When we put the window that shows our cloud PC (which is the Windows 365 Remote Desktop client running on our physical computer) into full-screen mode, then our entire physical display is filled with our cloud PC desktop. This concept can take some time to get used to, but after you are familiar with it, using your cloud PC from any physical device is a piece of cake.

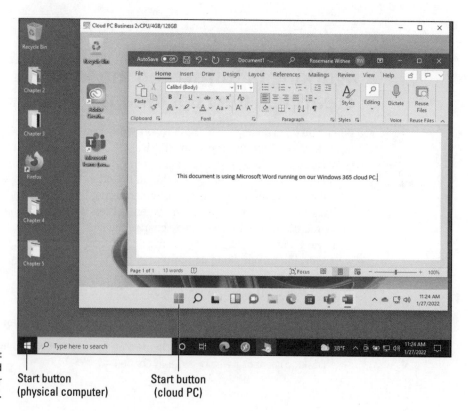

FIGURE 9-4: Microsoft Word running on our cloud PC.

Start button (physical computer)

Start button (cloud PC)

Saving a document

When you sign into your cloud PC, you are using your Microsoft 365 credentials as we outlined in Chapter 1. This means that when you sign into your cloud PC you get all the Office 365 cloud-enabled features by default. A perfect example is saving a document. You won't see the Save menu item if the AutoSave toggle is on. This is because your document is automatically saved for you by default. In other words, when you stop working, move to another computer, or throw your computer in the ocean, and then come back to work on the document again, using whatever physical device you decide you want to use, your cloud PC and the document you were working on will be exactly as you left them.

WARNING

The AutoSave toggle is turned on automatically when you are logged in to your Microsoft 365 account. When you are using your cloud PC, you sign in using your Microsoft 365 account. If you are using a traditional version of Windows on a physical computer, however, then you need to keep in mind the document might not be saved automatically. We experienced this when we got used to working on our cloud PC and then had to work on a document on a traditional version of Windows. We forgot to constantly save the document and lost a significant amount of work. To avoid making the same mistake, you should always remember to save your document when not working in your cloud PC.

WARNING

The AutoSave feature can be tricky when you are used to the traditional method of saving a file as you work. We have run into issues where we were used to saving a file with a new name as we made changes, and this doesn't work with AutoSave. Microsoft is trying to be helpful and automatically save your work; however, it can be a struggle to get used to the feature.

Copying and pasting

When you first begin to use your cloud PC, you will likely have information on your physical computer that you will want to get into your cloud PC. Later in this chapter, we tell you how to move files. However, you might want to move only a paragraph of text, or an image, or some financial data. To move information to your cloud PC, you can copy from a document on your physical computer and then paste into a document on your cloud PC. Copy-and-paste works because of a shared clipboard between your physical device and your cloud PC.

The way you add information to your clipboard on your physical device depends on the operating system the device is using. For example, in Windows you can right-click and select the Copy icon. You can also use the keyboard shortcut by pressing and holding the Ctrl key and then pressing the C key. On a Mac, the keyboard shortcut is to press and hold the Command key and then press the C key to copy. On a tablet or smartphone, you tap and hold and then select Copy. After you've successfully copied the information, you can paste it in your Windows 365 cloud PC by right-clicking and selecting the Paste icon or by using the keyboard shortcut (Ctrl-V).

TIP

Copying and pasting from your physical computer to your cloud PC can also be done when using your web browser. When you connect to your cloud PC using a web browser, make sure that the selection for Clipboard is selected, as shown in Figure 9-5.

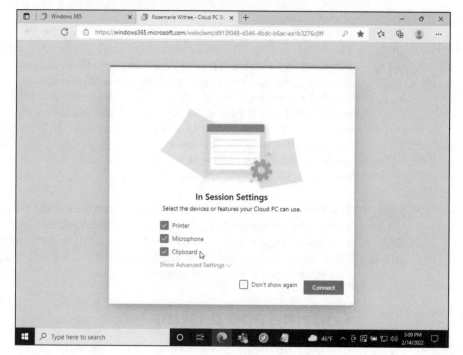

FIGURE 9-5:
Allowing copy and paste from your physical computer to your cloud PC when using a web browser.

Closing a document

Because your cloud PC is always on and always available you don't necessarily need to close a document. When we first started using Windows 365, we were in the habit of closing documents when we shut down our computer. Over time, we adjusted to the fact that our cloud PC is always on and always available and exactly how we left it. Now we keep documents open and when we close them, we think of it as archiving it or moving our thinking about it to a closed state. If you want to close a document, click the X in the upper-right corner of the document. Alternatively, you can click on the File menu in the upper-left of a document and then select Close.

Getting Familiar with Windows in Windows 365

Microsoft tends to use the same words for various meanings. It is especially the case with software like Teams where your team can work together. Teams is relatively new, and we cover it further in Chapter 9. Windows, on the other hand, has been around for ages. An eternity, in Internet time. *Windows* refers to the operating system that runs all the hardware on a computer. A *window* is also a box that is displayed on your computer that represents the user interface for an application. So, it makes some sense that Windows, the operating system, is focused around using windows to get things done. If you are already familiar with Windows, then this concept is all too familiar. What makes Windows 365 different is that the entire Windows operating system is also running within a window on your physical computer. It doesn't matter what physical computer you are using or what operating system that physical computer is running. When you connect to your cloud PC, you are viewing it through a window on your physical computer. This can take some getting used to. As we mentioned previously, we like to make the window we are using work with our cloud PC full screen, so we have the illusion that our cloud PC is running on our physical computer.

TIP

One of the most important concepts to keep in mind when using your cloud PC is that it is separate from whatever physical computer you happen to be using to connect to it. The best way we have found to get our minds around it is to think of your cloud PC as an actual computer that Microsoft has set up for you and that you log into and use remotely over the Internet. Using this way of thinking makes it easier to think about apps and files and where they live and run. The apps either live and run on your cloud PC or they live and run on whatever physical computer you are using to connect to your cloud PC.

Looking at Files and Folders

There is a special app in Windows called File Explorer. When you open this app, you are presented with the files and folders on your computer. Be sure you are in the correct window and looking at the desktop of your cloud PC and then click the Start button, type **file explorer**, and press Enter. The File Explorer app opens, and you can see all your files and folders, as shown in Figure 9-6. By default, it opens and shows you quick access areas that you might want to look at, but you can also click on the left side of the app to explore the files and folders in other places on your computer.

TIP

If the File Explorer application is pinned to the tray, which it is by default, then you can click the icon to open it. In Figure 9-6, you can see the icon, which looks like a file folder, on the tray. In general, there are multiple ways to perform the same task in Windows 365.

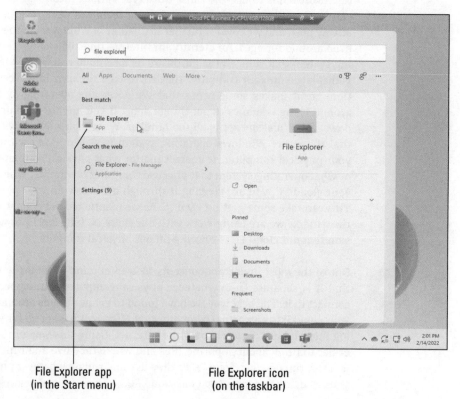

FIGURE 9-6: Opening the File Explorer application.

File Explorer app (in the Start menu)

File Explorer icon (on the taskbar)

Moving and copying files

You can move files between folders by clicking on them, holding the mouse button down, and then dragging them to another folder. You can make copies by right-clicking on a file and choosing the Copy icon, as shown in Figure 9-7. You can then go to another folder, right-click, and choose the Paste icon, which makes an exact copy of the file in the new location.

Copy icon

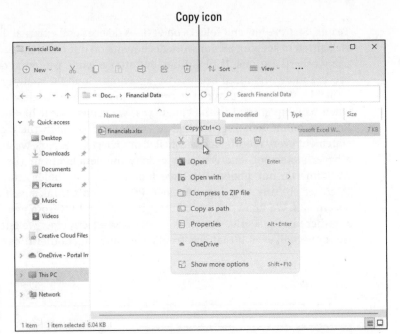

Creating folders

You can create new folders and name them so that you can organize your documents. A folder can be created within another folder. To create a new folder, navigate to the location you want to create the folder, then right-click in File Explorer and select New from the menu and then choose Folder, as shown in Figure 9-8.

TIP

Figure 9-8 shows you how to right-click and create a new folder. Notice that you can also choose to create a new document using the same process. It is often the case in Microsoft products that you can achieve the same result in multiple ways.

After you create a folder, you can move it just like you move files: Click on it and hold down the mouse button and then drag it to the new location and release the mouse button.

Organizing files

Keeping files, as well as our homes, organized can be a challenge for us all. On the surface, it can feel overwhelming to start using a new cloud PC. It seems like it is just one more place you might have to look for your digital files. If you are dreading this aspect of Windows 365, then you are not alone. We felt the same way when we started using our cloud PC. We already used Dropbox, Box, OneDrive,

Teams, SharePoint, and folders on various devices and external drives. Over time, we shifted to keeping all our work documents on our cloud PC and slowly stopped using other locations. It took time, but after a while we found our work lives to become more organized because we know our cloud PC is always on and always available. We like to think of it as being like the mental shift we went through when banking shifted to the cloud (yes, we remember it like it was yesterday). Prior to online banking, we had to correspond through the mail, waited for a statement every month, and reconciled our checkbook. Now we don't even receive a paper statement, and we know exactly the details of our checking account in real-time on our phone. We have found the same holds true with our cloud PC. After shifting to using our cloud PC, we don't think much about our work documents. We know we can connect to our cloud PC from any device and from anywhere in the world. Our work progress is exactly how we left it the last time we connected, even if that was from a computer in another time zone.

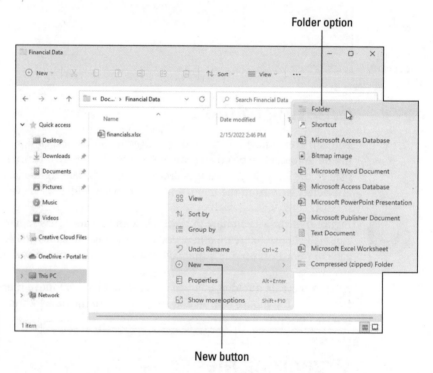

FIGURE 9-8:
Right-clicking and creating a new folder.

When you get your mind around your cloud PC being always on and always available, the next step is organizing your files. If you are already familiar with folders, then you will feel right at home in Windows 365. You can create new folders (described in the previous section) and you can put documents inside those folders. You can also put folders within other folders in a hierarchy of folders. To move a folder into another folder, click on it, hold down the mouse button, drag the folder over the top of another folder, and then release the mouse button. The folder will be moved inside of the other folder. You can continue this process in a way that makes the most sense for you.

Sharing documents with others

Sharing folders with other people in your organization is a concept that has been around for a long time. Windows 365 provides the same functionality through Teams, SharePoint, and OneDrive. The Teams application has a place where you can store and share files with others. When you put documents in Teams, they are shared with others on the team, and you can work on them and collaborate in real time. We cover using Teams in detail in Chapter 10, but if you want to dive even further check out *Teams For Dummies* by Rosemarie Withee (Wiley). You can think of OneDrive and SharePoint as almost the same thing. SharePoint includes a web interface and OneDrive is used to sync files with SharePoint sites and colleagues. In fact, SharePoint uses OneDrive to sync files. We cover OneDrive in more detail in Chapter 11.

TIP

If you are using Teams to store your files, then you are already using SharePoint. Teams uses SharePoint behind the scenes for document storage.

Deleting and recovering documents and folders

You can delete a document or folder by selecting it and pressing the Delete key on your keyboard. Alternatively, you can right-click and select the Delete icon (it looks like a trashcan, which you can see by referring back to Figure 9-7). When you delete a document or folder, you move it to a special folder called the Recycle Bin. The Recycle Bin in your cloud PC is like the recycle bin at the food court in a mall. When you throw something like an empty soda can into the recycle bin, it remains there for a while, but eventually it is removed and recycled and used to make a new can. In the same way, when you delete a file, it is moved to the Recycle Bin, and you are letting your cloud PC know that it can recycle the digital space that it took up and make it available to create new documents.

TIP

By default, the Recycle Bin keeps your deleted files until the space reserved for recycled items runs out. The default size of the Recycle Bin on our cloud PC is 1638 megabytes. When we have deleted more than 1638 megabytes, the Recycle Bin folder will start permanently deleting older Recycle Bin files to make room for files we recently deleted. You can change these settings by right-clicking the Recycle Bin icon on your desktop and selecting Properties.

If you accidentally delete something, you can still retrieve it for some time by looking for it in the Recycle Bin. To restore an item you deleted, double-click the Recycle Bin folder on your desktop to open it, right-click the item, and select Restore.

Getting files from your physical computer to your cloud PC

One of the first tasks most people want to achieve with a cloud PC is to get the files on their physical computer into their cloud PC. The good news is that when you are using the Windows 365 Remote Desktop client, the storage on your physical computer shows up in the File Explorer app on your cloud PC. You can find that storage by selecting "This PC" on the left side of File Explorer. You will see the storage on your cloud PC, and at the bottom you will see the Redirected Drives and Folders section, as shown in Figure 9-9.

TIP Using the Windows 365 Remote Desktop client on MacOS is slightly different than on Windows. On MacOS you will find the Folders options on the Folders tab where you can redirect folders.

TIP Keep in mind that the contents you see in the Redirected Drives and Folders section are specific to whatever physical computer you happen to be using to connect to your cloud PC. If you connect from your laptop in the morning, then you will see the files and folders on your laptop. If you connect from your desktop computer, then you will see the files and folders in your desktop. When using the Windows 365 Remote Desktop client, you can even see the storage on your phone, if that is the device you happen to be connecting from.

To move files from your physical computer to your cloud PC, use File Explorer. The process is similar to moving a file between folders within the same computer. On your cloud PC, open File Explorer twice so you have two windows open. In one window, open the files on your physical computer, found in the Redirected Files and Folders section. In the second window, open the location on your cloud PC to where you want to move the files. Then, click on a file in one window and drag and drop it in the other window, as shown in Figure 9-10.

TIP By default, dragging and dropping files between computers creates a copy. If you want to move the file instead of copying it, then use the right mouse button to drag and drop. When you use the right mouse button and drop a file, you are presented with a menu with options other than copy.

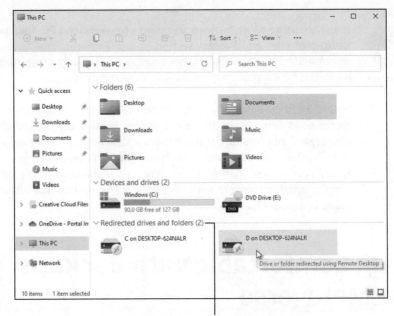

FIGURE 9-9:
Viewing the
storage on your
physical
computer from
your cloud PC.

Redirected Drives and Folders section

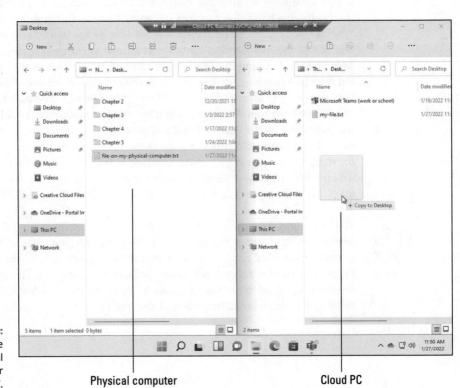

FIGURE 9-10:
Copying a file
from our physical
computer to our
cloud PC.

Physical computer　　　　**Cloud PC**

If you are using a web browser to connect to your cloud PC, then you won't see the Redirected Files and Folders section in File Explorer. This is another reason we recommend using the client whenever possible. Using a web browser is fine in a pinch but for everyday work we always use the client.

With files in so many places it can be easy to get confused. For this reason, we recommend using a content management system like SharePoint to keep your files organized and share and collaborate with others in your organization. If your organization uses Teams and you have files in Teams, then you are using Share-Point. Teams uses SharePoint as a content management system and provides a simpler interface to work with files than going directly into SharePoint. We cover using Teams in Chapter 10 and SharePoint in Chapter 11.

Getting Comfortable with Backups in the Metaverse

If you have used a computer connected to the Internet to interact with others, then you are a bona fide member of the metaverse. Congratulations! We love the "metaverse" buzzword because it sounds like we are in a sci-fi movie such as *The Matrix*. Cue the movie voice, "in a world known as the metaverse, a young heroine fights evil . . .". Using the previous buzzword, the *cloud*, was cool for a long time, but it is time to move into the future. Both terms mean essentially the same thing. You are using resources "out there" that are being hosted and run by someone else. Since "out there" isn't very catchy most people prefer to call it the *cloud* or the *metaverse*. In the case of Windows 365, the group out there hosting the software is Microsoft. And this is a good thing because it means they are on the hook for making sure our digital infrastructure is backed up and secure. Even though we are offloading most things to Microsoft, there are still some backup considerations we need to keep in mind.

The term *cloud* derives from the early days of drawing diagrams of networks. Networks consist of pieces of equipment such as routers, switches, cables, and plugs. Drawing a network can be time consuming so engineers, being inventive, decided to just draw a cloud shape for a complex network diagram. The Internet became the network of all networks and thus became the cloud shape in diagrams. This tidbit is a great conversation piece at cocktail parties.

You can think of backups in two primary ways. The first way is to think of the personal work you are doing on your cloud PC in the form of your documents and files. The second way is to think of your cloud PC and the settings and applications you have installed.

Making sure you don't lose work

Modern computing is very forgiving to the mistakes we humans make. Lately, we are more surprised when we can't recover from a mistake with the few clicks of a button. With that said, you still need to be aware of the content on your cloud PC and take the proper precautions so that you never lose your work. For example, if you accidentally delete data in a spreadsheet and don't realize it, then the data is likely lost unless you have a previous version backed up.

TIP

If you keep your documents in SharePoint and have versioning on, then you can easily go back and see all the different versions from when you saved and worked on a document.

To keep your hard work safe, we recommend keeping your documents in a content management system such as Teams or SharePoint (hint, Teams uses SharePoint behind the scenes). When your files are in a content management system they are automatically backed up. You can turn on automatic versioning and avail of all sorts of great features. We cover Teams in Chapter 10 and SharePoint in Chapter 11. We have even written entire books on Teams and SharePoint. If you want to dive deep in these areas, check out *Teams For Dummies* and *SharePoint For Dummies* (Wiley).

Keeping your cloud PC safe and backed up

The cost of a cloud PC is not insignificant. One of the benefits of having Microsoft take on the ownership of managing the infrastructure is that they are on the hook for backing up your cloud PC. Going into the details of what this entails would require several books. If you are interested in learning more about this, open your favorite search engine and type in "how does a Microsoft data center work." We think understanding all the pieces of a data center is on par with understanding all the pieces of the U.S. Government. In other words, a lot of people have careers focused on various aspects of the process. With all this in mind it is important to know that you or your administrator can cause problems for yourself by performing actions such as resetting a cloud PC from the Microsoft 365 administrative interface.

If you have followed along with the book, then you personalized your cloud PC in Chapter 5. Making your cloud PC your own can consume a lot of time, and you don't want to lose the work. If you are an administrator, then keep in mind that you can reset a cloud PC back to a fresh state. However, when you do this, you are removing all the changes that have happened to the cloud PC since it was first created. If you are not the administrator for your cloud PC, then make sure to tell the administrator not to reset things without checking with you first.

WARNING

An administrator can reset your cloud PC, which removes all apps and local documents you have created on it. We cover administration further in Chapter 18.

Chapter **10**

Using Microsoft Teams to Stay Connected

First, Office went to the cloud with the introduction of Office 365. Then the Office suite of apps grew with the addition of SharePoint, Teams, OneDrive, and so on. Windows 365 completes the seamless cloud experience. As previously mentioned, you need to have a Microsoft 365 account in order to use Windows 365. The good news is that Microsoft Teams is already preinstalled with your cloud PC so you don't have to take the extra steps of installing it.

We admit that when we first heard about Microsoft Teams, we were not very impressed. The market was already filled with chat programs. Microsoft even purchased the most popular one, Skype! So why did Microsoft decide to create redundant software? Well, that was years ago. Since then, our opinion has undergone a radical transformation. Now we understand the vision Microsoft had for Teams, we have seen what it has become, and we know why it has surpassed SharePoint as the fastest-growing product in Microsoft's history.

In this chapter, you see what makes Teams so special. First, you take a quick spin around the Teams interface and learn some of the basic Teams terminology. Then, you get up and running with the Teams app in a quick tutorial. After that, you find out how to sign up and sign in. Let's get Team-ing!

Wrapping Your Head around Microsoft Teams

Microsoft Teams is a relative newcomer to the world of business communication software. It was first announced in 2017, and when we first heard about it, we weren't sure what to make of it. We had been using Skype to chat with friends and family for years, and we had used Lync (later rebranded Skype for Business) for business communications. Since its announcement, Teams has been integrated with just about every product Microsoft offers and has swallowed all the features that used to make Skype for Business so great. You can make phone calls, chat, conduct meetings, share your screen, and have video calls, to name just a few of the features Teams offers.

Microsoft Teams as a communications platform, replacing Skype for Business, is nice, but that is not what has made it the fastest-growing product in Microsoft history. What makes Teams so special is that Microsoft has invested heavily to make it the face and entry point to almost all other Office services. This means you can use Teams to not only collaborate in real time to chat but also work with others using the Office apps such as Word and without having to leave Teams. For example, we are writing this book using Microsoft Word, but we are doing so from within the Teams app, as shown in Figure 10-1. We really like having one main app that acts as a hub and think you will, too.

In addition to integrating with Microsoft Office, Teams also integrates with many third-party applications. The app section, as shown in Figure 10-2, includes Microsoft apps and also many others.

To be fair, the big competitor to Teams called Slack (https://slack.com), is also racing to integrate other software and be the primary business tool you use for communications and productivity. Slack had a head start — hitting the market in 2013 — and became incredibly popular very quickly. However, Microsoft had a big advantage in that so many people already used Office products, so when Microsoft integrated Office with Teams, it was an easy move for users to start using Teams. In fact, in 2020 it was announced that Teams now has more active users than Slack. That is a big milestone!

Don't get us wrong; We still use Slack in Rosemarie's consulting business, because some of her clients only use Slack and don't use Teams. In fact, we use other apps, too, such as Google Workspace (https://workspace.google.com) and Zoom (https://zoom.us). Zoom has become extremely popular for video-calling especially for groups. However, Zoom is focused on video-calling and lacks the integrated capabilities needed to do effective remote work and collaboration.

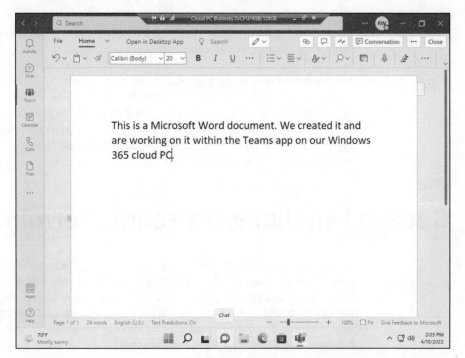

FIGURE 10-1:
Using Microsoft
Word from within
Teams.

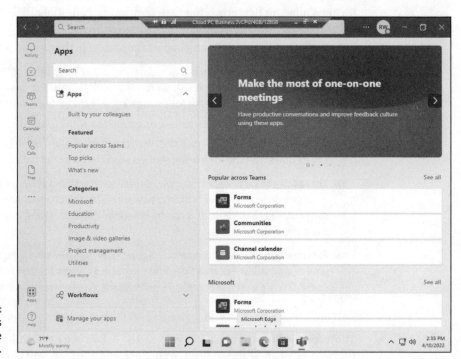

FIGURE 10-2:
Some of the apps
that integrate
with Teams.

It is this software diversity resulting from Rosemarie's consulting that gives us confidence to contrast and compare these tools.

Microsoft Teams is becoming the one app to rule them all in the Microsoft world. It has become the entry point for Office applications as well as other non-Microsoft software. This is the reason it has grown so quickly. If you are using Microsoft 365 apps on your cloud PC, you may find yourself using the integrated apps (some of which are covered in Chapter 11) through Teams instead of trying to remember how to use them independently.

Getting Familiar with Teams Terminology

Just like every other software program out there, Microsoft Teams has its own specific terminology. And even though the list of terms is short, keeping the Teams terminology straight can be a challenge. For example, you will likely one day find yourself inviting one of your teammates to your Teams team. Or asking which Teams team your coworker is talking about. After you get used to it, however, the terminology will seem normal.

To get a jump on the terms, here are some quick definitions:

>> **Teams:** Use the term *Teams* (uppercase) to refer to the product itself.

>> **Team:** A *team* (lowercase) is a group of users. You can specify settings for teams and have multiple teams within Microsoft Teams. For example, you might want to create a team for accounting, a team for legal, and another team for external contacts.

>> **Channel:** A *channel* is a group chat within a team. A team can have multiple group chats with the idea being that you can create a chat for different topics.

>> **Thread:** A *thread* is a specific topic of discussion within a channel. For example, one person might start a new thread in the channel and then others can reply to that thread. You can have multiple threads going in a channel at the same time.

>> **External/guest user:** An *external* or *guest* user is a user who is not part of your organization. For example, you might be a consultant and need to communicate with the company's accountant. You can invite that person as a guest user to your team.

These are the basic terms to get you started. When you get familiar with the relationship between Teams, a team, a channel, and a thread, you have all the knowledge you need to dive in further and get productive.

Getting Started with the Teams App

Now that you have an idea of what makes Microsoft Teams a useful tool for online collaboration and communication, it's time to dive in and take a look at the app for yourself. It is already installed by default on your cloud PC.

Taking a Quick Spin around Teams

If you have been following along in this chapter, you may notice that Teams running on your cloud PC (refer to Figure 10-2) looks a lot like Teams running from within your web browser (see Figure 10-3). Microsoft did this on purpose. The design thinking is best practice, and we were glad to see Microsoft adopt it. This way, if you usually use Teams on your cloud PC and find yourself logging in to Teams using a web browser on your computer at home, you don't have to worry about learning a different interface. Of course, you could always just log into your cloud PC directly, too, and find the same Teams app you are used to using. Microsoft gives you options, though, by also offering Teams in any browser on any device.

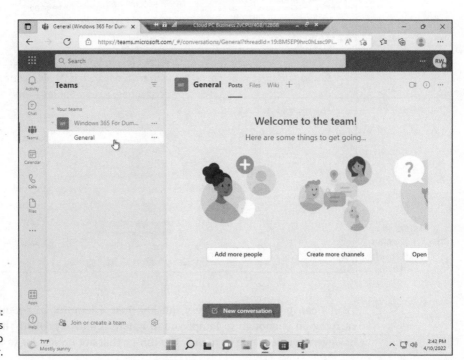

FIGURE 10-3:
Microsoft Teams running in a web browser.

Primary navigation appears on the left side of the screen and includes the following icons: Activity, Chat, Teams, Calendar, Calls, and Files, as shown in Figure 10-3. At the bottom of the screen on the left, you will find links to Apps (refer to Figure 10-2) and Help. Clicking one of these main options opens that associated screen in the main part of the app.

Activity

If you click the Activity icon in the navigation pane, you will see your feed. You can also see your activity by clicking the feed heading and selecting My Activity, as shown in Figure 10-4. In the Activity feed, you find notifications about things going on around Teams that you might find interesting. For example, if there is an unread message in a channel or if someone sends you a chat message, it will appear in your Activity feed. Think of it as your one-stop-shop for everything that has happened in Teams since you were last there.

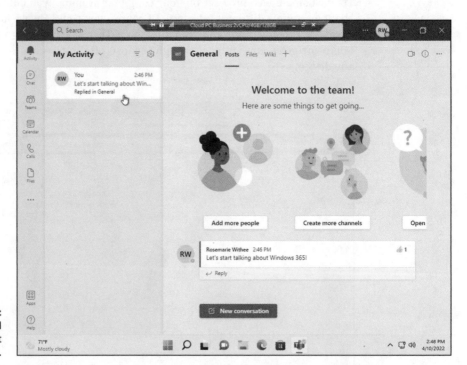

FIGURE 10-4: The Activity feed in Microsoft Teams.

Teams can get very noisy very quickly. Just a handful of people chatting and carrying on is enough to tempt you to ignore it entirely. Using the Activity feed, however, you can tune in to only the things that are important to you.

Chat

The Chat area is where you find all of your personal and group chats. There is a subtle difference between conversations in chats and conversations in channels. We like to think of chats as ad-hoc messages to one other person or a few other people. Chats come and go and are spontaneous, whereas a channel is a dedicated area that persists and where people can communicate about a particular topic. You will find channels within Teams as described in the next section.

TIP

You can have one-on-one chats with another person or group conversations with several people at the same time in the Chat area.

Teams

The navigational area where we seem to spend all our time, and likely you will too, is the Teams area. Yes, the product is called Teams and the navigation component is also called Teams (see the left side of Figure 10-5). And within the Teams navigation component you have individual teams called a *team*. Confused yet? We don't blame you! But don't worry; it will become clear shortly.

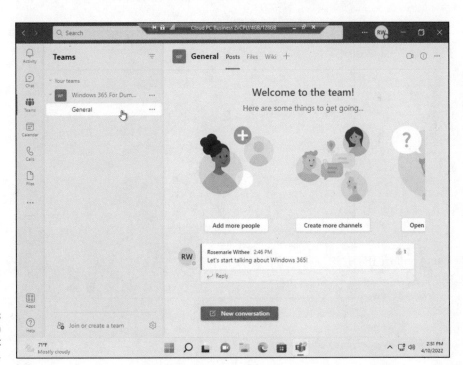

FIGURE 10-5: The Teams area of Microsoft Teams.

Clicking the Teams icon in the left navigation pane opens all the teams you are a member of. In Figure 10-5, you can see that we are only a member of one team: Windows 365 For Dummies. This is the team we created when we first set up Teams. Within the Windows 365 For Dummies team is a channel called General, which is the default channel created automatically when a new Team is created. If we click the General channel, we can see all of the chats going on in the channel. Right now, it is empty because Rosemarie is the only person in the team and in the channel.

Calendar

The Calendar area is focused on your calendar of events and meetings, as shown in Figure 10-6. If you have ever scheduled a meeting in Microsoft Outlook, then you will be familiar with working with your calendar in Teams. The calendar area is where you can have real-time meetings.

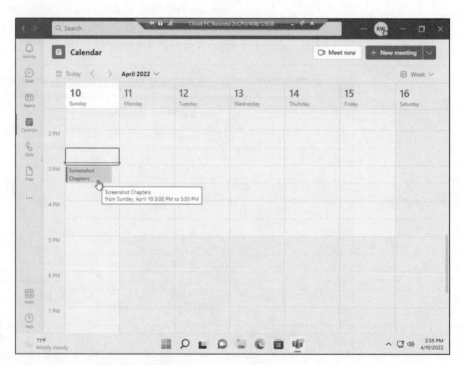

FIGURE 10-6:
The Calendar area of Teams.

Calls

The Calls area is where you can make and receive phone calls, as shown in Figure 10-7. If you have ever used Skype, then this area will feel familiar to you.

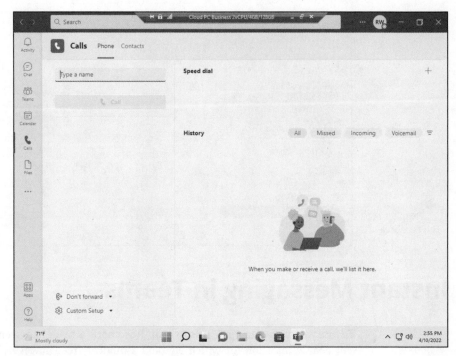

FIGURE 10-7:
The Calls area of
Teams.

Files

The Files area is where you can save and share digital files, as shown in Figure 10-8. If you have ever used SharePoint or OneDrive, then you will be happy to learn that you are already ahead of the game. Teams uses SharePoint and One-Drive behind the scenes of Teams, and at any point you can jump out of Teams and open the same files in the SharePoint or OneDrive applications.

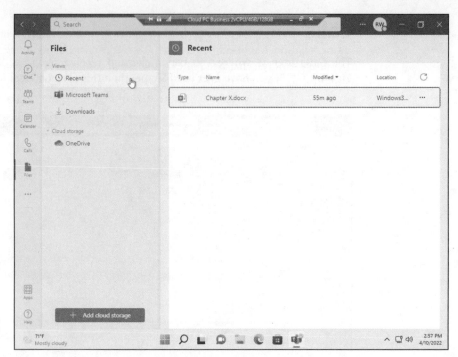

FIGURE 10-8:
The Files area of
Teams.

Instant Messaging in Teams

Before we started using Teams to chat, Rosemarie's team had been using a different chat application for which we paid a monthly fee. However, we also had an
Office 365 subscription (which included Teams). Teams was still brand new back
then, but we realized we could stop paying for the other chat program and use
Teams instead. It already came with Office 365, and unless it was terrible, it would
work just fine for sending instant communications.

Our story happened a few years ago when Teams had just been released. However,
based on our work with many clients, their stories (and perhaps your story) are very
similar to us. Teams might have already been included with your organization's
Microsoft 365 subscription, even though you hadn't used it before. You might need
to use Teams now because the coronavirus pandemic in 2020 forced everyone in
your office to start working from home, and you need a way to communicate virtually with your coworkers. Regardless of how you start using Teams, you will likely
spend your initial interactions sending messages to other people on your team.

Instant messages in Teams happen in channels. A channel is a place where people
can type messages, add files, and share links. We like to think of a channel like a
virtual water cooler. You go there to communicate with colleagues, learn and
share gossip, and generally stay in touch with your social circle.

A channel lives inside of a team, and a team can contain multiple channels. You can name a channel anything you want. We recommend using a name that describes the purpose of the channel. For example, you could name your channels channel01, channel02, channel03, and so on, but these titles aren't descriptive. Are you creating a channel that people in your team will use to discuss carpooling to and from work? Name the channel Carpooling. Or do you want to create a channel for accounting and another for human resources? Name them Accounting and Human Resources, respectively. Or perhaps a group of people want to discuss the new policy of allowing pets in the office. Create a channel called Pets. You get the point.

A channel can contain multiple conversations happening at the same time. To try to make these conversations easier to follow, Teams groups them together in what are known as threads. A thread is simply a topic of conversation. When someone types a brand-new message, it appears in the channel, and any replies to that original message are placed underneath. If someone else types a different message for a different topic, it will become its own thread and any responses to that message will be grouped under the original message.

In Figure 10-9, you can see that we are creating a brand-new topic of conversation in the General channel. If we want to reply to the existing topic, we click the Reply link at the bottom of the thread. If we want to start another new topic, we click the New Conversation button at the bottom of the message window to open the text box to begin a new conversation.

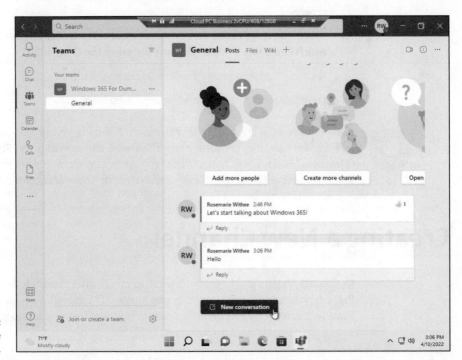

FIGURE 10-9:
A new topic in the General channel.

Sending Messages in Channels

Whenever you create a new team, a channel is created for that team automatically. Called *General*, this channel is perfectly acceptable to use to start chatting with others on the team.

To send a message in the General channel, follow these steps:

1. **Select the Teams icon in the left navigation pane to view all your teams.**

   Under each team, you will see a list of channels that are available to you. If this is a new team, you will only see the General channel until more channels are created.

   TIP

   In addition to the channels available to you, there may be other, private channels in the team that you don't have access to. There could also be channels that are public but that you have not joined. The list of channels you see under a team might not be inclusive of every channel that team contains. You will see channels that you have either joined or that the channel administrator has joined you to on your behalf.

2. **Select the General channel, as shown in Figure 10-9.**

   When you click a channel, it opens in the main part of the screen.

3. **Click the New Conversation button that appears at the bottom of the screen.**

4. **Type a message in the text box that appears and click the Send icon, which looks like a paper airplane (or press the Enter key).**

   Your message appears in the General channel screen.

   Congratulations! You are sending messages!

TIP

Notice above your message that Microsoft Teams is giving you some hints about adding more people, creating more channels, and opening the Frequently Asked Questions (FAQ). These buttons that appear in new channels are shortcuts for you. You can achieve these same tasks without using these shortcuts.

Creating a New Channel

As you use Teams more, you will want to create chat channels for other topics so that everything does not happen in one "general" channel. For example, you might want to create a channel for your team to discuss finances, another for carpooling, and another for team morale events. Team conversations can be organized in endless ways. The only thing that matters is what works for your team.

To create a new channel in your team, follow these steps:

1. **Select the Teams icon in the left navigation pane to view all your teams.**

2. **Click the ellipsis to the right of the team to which you wish to add a channel.**

The More Options drop-down menu appears.

3. **Choose Add Channel, as shown in Figure 10-10.**

WARNING

If this option isn't shown in the drop-down menu, you don't have permission to create a new channel. If you are a guest to a team, your ability to create teams and channels can be limited.

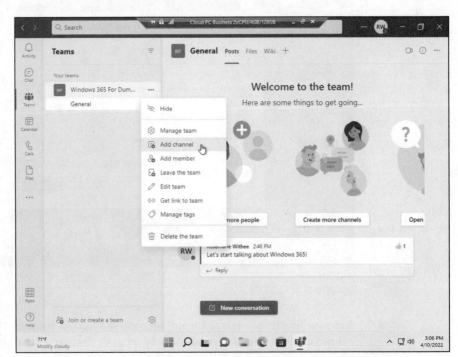

FIGURE 10-10: Choosing Add Channel from the settings menu for a team.

4. **Enter a name and description for the channel in the dialog box that appears and then click Add, as shown in Figure 10-11.**

The new channel appears under the team.

TIP

When you create a new channel, you can set a few options. First, you can set the privacy settings as shown in Figure 10-11. The options are standard and private. A standard channel is accessible to everyone on the team by default. A private channel is only accessible to a specific group of people. When you select Private, you then have the option on the next screen to add members to the channel. You can always add additional people to a private channel at any point in the future.

Second, you can also select the box to have this channel automatically show up for every person in the team. If you don't select this box, the channel will show up as hidden, and people will need to click a button to see it in the list of channels in the team.

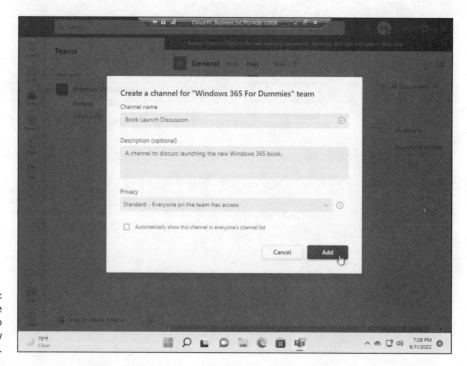

FIGURE 10-11:
Filling in the dialog box to create a new channel.

REMEMBER

A channel is part of a team. A team can contain multiple channels, and each channel can contain its own threads of conversation. You can create chat channels for any topic you want. We see teams have a lot of success breaking out work-related channels from non-work-related channels, such as morale events in one channel and budget discussions in a different channel.

Some things to keep in mind with channels are:

>> Each team can have a maximum of 200 standard channels.

>> Each team can have a maximum of 30 private channels with a maximum of 250 members each.

>> You can search using keywords in standard or private channels.

>> Guest users cannot create private channels.

Configuring a Channel

You can configure many different settings for a channel via the More Options drop-down menu. You access these additional options by clicking the ellipsis next to the channel name you wish to manage. Figure 10-12 shows the More Options drop-down menu that appears next to the new channel we created in the previous section. The options that appear for a channel you add include the following:

>> **Channel Notifications:** You can configure the notifications you receive for this channel. This is important as your organization's use of Teams increases. Teams can quickly become noisy with everyone chatting about all manner of topics. You can use this setting to turn down the noise for channels that are less important to you and turn up the volume for topics you need to pay close attention to.

>> **Pin:** Select this option to keep a channel at the top of your list of channels. You can pin multiple channels and arrange them in any order you want. Teams hides the Pinned area until you pin a channel. You can rearrange your pinned channels by dragging them up and down. And you can remove a pinned channel by choosing More Options and then selecting Unpin.

>> **Hide:** Select this option to hide the channel from the list of channels you have in the team. You can always unhide the channel at any time. You will see a little message that lets you know how many channels you have hidden, and you can click it to see those hidden channels.

>> **Manage Channel:** This option allows owners of the channel to manage the permissions for the channel, as shown in Figure 10-13. You can allow others to moderate the channel and control who can post new messages to the channel. See "Adding Moderators" later in this chapter for more on adding moderation to a channel.

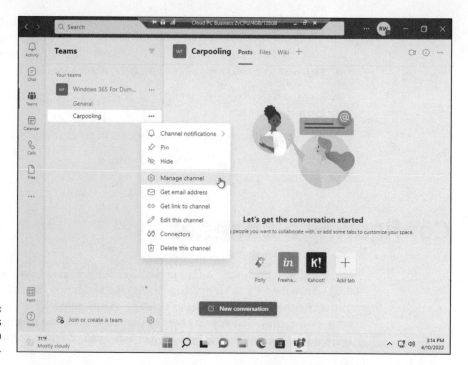

FIGURE 10-12:
The More Options
menu for a
team's channel.

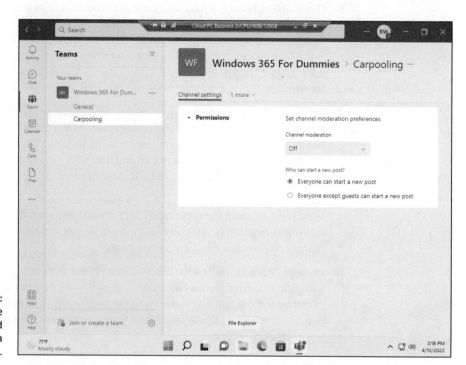

FIGURE 10-13:
Managing the
moderators and
permissions for a
channel.

>> **Get Email Address:** A cool feature we use all the time is the ability to send an email message directly to a channel. You can configure the channel so that if you send an email, the message appears in the channel. (We frequently send a copy of our email messages to our channels!) Figure 10-14 shows the email address for the private channel we created. Whenever we send an email message to this address, it appears in the channel.

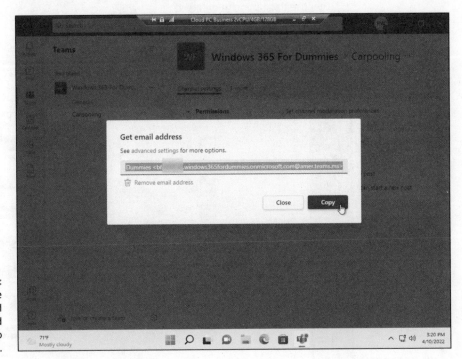

FIGURE 10-14:
Obtaining the dedicated email address to send email directly to the channel.

>> **Get Link to Channel:** You can quickly get overwhelmed with the number of teams and channels in your organization. When you want to tell people about a channel, you can send them a direct link to the channel. You can get the link by using this option.

>> **Edit This Channel:** When you first created the channel, you set the title and description. You can change those settings with this option.

>> **Connectors:** Connectors are add-on apps. Think of them as custom extensions to Teams that you can add to a channel in order to connect with other software services. They allow you to connect other apps to your channel. There are many types of connectors, as shown in Figure 10-15. For example, you can connect your channel to GitHub or Zendesk or seemingly any other app on the Internet.

>> **Delete This Channel:** When you are ready to remove a channel, you can choose this option to delete it.

Note which ellipsis you click to open the More Options drop-down menu. Figure 10-10 illustrates opening the menu for a team, whereas Figure 10-12 illustrates opening the menu for a channel. Channels appear underneath the team name, but it is easy to select the wrong ellipsis because they appear very close to each other.

Adding Moderators

One way to keep the team channel organized is to assign moderators. Moderators may only be assigned by team owners. With moderation, only an assigned moderator is able to start new posts and decide whether or not members are able to reply to posts. Using moderation allows you to leverage subject matter experts for a channel and ensure that their voices are heard. Think of a moderator as an air traffic controller. They can help things keep moving and avoid collisions.

The General channel and private channels do not have moderators by default. To turn on moderation for a standard channel, follow these steps:

1. **Click the ellipsis next to the channel name to which you want to add a moderator and choose Manage Channel.**

2. **On the Channel Settings tab, open the Channel Moderation drop-down menu and select On, as shown in Figure 10-16.**

3. **Click the Manage button to select who can be a moderator and then select which options require moderation.**

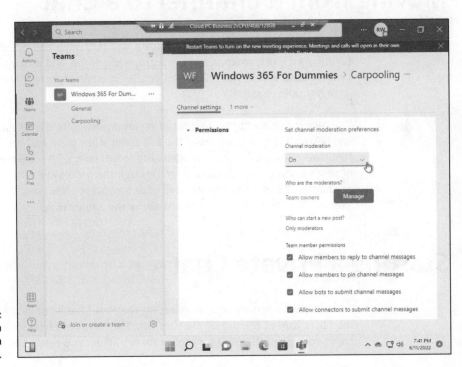

FIGURE 10-16:
Turning on moderation for a channel.

You can allow or disallow members to reply in the channel and bots or connectors to submit messages.

TIP

Your changes are saved as you make them so there is no need to click a Save button.

A team moderator can do the following:

>> **Start new posts:** Note that only moderators can start new posts when moderation is turned on.

>> **Add and remove team members as moderators to a channel:** Moderators, however, cannot remove a team owner as a moderator.

>> **Control whether team members can post replies to existing channel messages:** The moderator can also control whether bots and connectors can make changes as well.

Moving from a Channel to a Chat

The various ways you can communicate within Teams can quickly become confusing. As a quick recap, a *team* is a group of people, and a *channel* is an ongoing conversation within the team. You can be in multiple teams and each team can have multiple channels.

The nice thing about this system of communication is that it has structure. You can always select a team from the left navigation pane and see the channels in that team. However, you might also need to just chat with someone or with groups of people, and you don't want to go through the process of setting up a new team or channel. Teams has you covered with a concept called *chat*. You find the Chat icon in the left navigation pane just above the Teams icon.

Starting a Private Chat

You can start a private chat by selecting the New Chat icon, located to the right of the Filter icon at the top of the chat list. The New Chat icon looks like a piece of paper with a pencil on it (see Figure 10-17). When you select the icon, a new chat appears in the main pane of the Teams workspace. Type in the name of the person you want to send a chat message to in the To: field, and then click that person's name to add that person to the chat. After you have added the person to the chat, you can send a message just like you do in a channel. You type your message in the text box at the bottom of the chat area and press the Enter key on your keyboard or select the Send icon, which looks like a paper airplane.

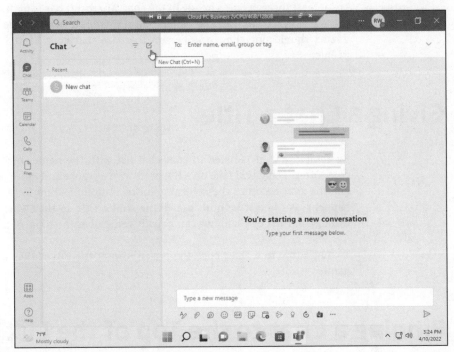

FIGURE 10-17:
Starting a new chat in Teams.

Adding Multiple People to a Chat

The previous section covers how to start a new chat. You can chat with multiple people by adding them in the To: line when you start the chat. However, you may find that you want to add more people to an existing chat.

To add more people to a chat that has already started, select the Add People icon that appears in the top-right corner of the chat window. Then, type in the names of the people you want to add in the Add dialog box. If you are chatting with only one person and you add another person, a new chat will appear with the three people in the chat. If you already have three people in a chat and you add a fourth person (or more), you will be presented with the option of including the chat history for the new people you are adding.

If you are chatting with one person, you cannot add another person to the same chat and share the history of the personal chat with the new third party. The feature of adding people and keeping the history of the chat only appears when there are at least three people already in the chat. Microsoft has said that this is done for privacy reasons and the expectation that if there is a one-on-one chat happening, Teams should not allow one person to share that confidential chat with other people.

Giving a Chat a Title

By default, a chat is listed in your chat list with the names of the people in the chat. Often a chat will take on a life of its own as more and more people are added, and the chat becomes the central point of communication for a topic. When this happens, we find it helpful to give the chat a title so that when we are looking through our list of chats, we can quickly remember the topic of that chat.

To add a title to a chat, click the pencil icon at the top of the chat and type in a name.

Pinning a Chat to the Top of the List

In addition to giving a title to a chat, you can also pin a chat so that it always appears at the top of the list. By default, chats are listed in order with the most recently used chat at the top. We like to pin a chat to the top of the list so that we can quickly get to that chat even if it has been a few days since anyone has added a message to it.

To pin a chat, select the ellipsis next to the chat in the left navigation pane and choose Pin from the More Options drop-down menu.

Sending More Than Text When Chatting

Entering text into a channel or chat is the most common way of sending your message to others on the team. However, you can send more than just text. You can send emojis, GIFs, stickers, and even attach files. These options appear at the bottom of the text box where you type in your message.

Adding a File

You add a file to the chat message. For example, you might be working on an Excel spreadsheet and you want to include it in the chat. You can add the file to your chat message using the paperclip icon. You can choose a recent file you have been working on, browse the files already uploaded to Teams, choose a file from One-Drive, or upload a file from your local computer.

TIP

When you attach a file to a channel, the file appears in the Files tab at the top of the channel. The Files tab is a SharePoint site behind the scenes. You can spot the Files tab at the top of Figure 10-9 in between the Posts tab and the Wiki tab.

» **Understanding SharePoint sites**

» **Adding content to SharePoint**

» **Using OneDrive**

Chapter **11**

Managing Content with SharePoint and OneDrive

SharePoint and OneDrive go hand-in-hand and have been a part of the Microsoft suite of content management products for a long time. You get SharePoint when you sign up for a Microsoft 365 subscription. OneDrive is a file management system that you use to sync your files between SharePoint and your cloud PC.

In this chapter, you first learn how to create a new SharePoint site. You learn how Teams acts as a front end to work with SharePoint and how SharePoint is behind the scenes of many aspects of Teams. Next you learn how to work with SharePoint directly. You learn how to create a new SharePoint site, get documents into your SharePoint site, share documents, and sync content with OneDrive. Finally, we walk through some guidance and strategies for storing documents in SharePoint.

Finding SharePoint in Microsoft 365

In Chapter 2 we walked through signing up for Microsoft 365 and Windows 365. When you sign up for Microsoft 365, you can choose a subscription option that includes SharePoint. After you have signed up for Microsoft 365, you can access your SharePoint site.

To access the SharePoint site in Microsoft 365, you must first sign into Microsoft 365 and then choose SharePoint from the available apps. Here's how:

1. **Open your web browser (on your cloud PC or physical computer, any browser will do for SharePoint but we recommend using your cloud PC so you maintain your sign in) and navigate to www.office.com.**

   If you have signed in before, your dashboard will load. If you have not yet signed in, you will need to sign in.

2. **Click the waffle icon in the top-left corner of the screen and then click SharePoint, as shown in Figure 11-1.**

   The Frequent Sites page appears, which lists your frequently visited SharePoint sites. If you have already visited some sites, then they will show up here and you can open them. If this is a new subscription, then you can create a site.

TIP

You can also click SharePoint from the left side of the main dashboard to access the Frequent Sites page. However, if you are in another app, such as Outlook, you can always get to SharePoint using the waffle icon in the top-left corner. Also be aware that Microsoft tends to change things fairly frequently so your screen might look slightly different.

To create a new SharePoint site, follow the same procedure above to access Share-Point. Here are the steps to do it:

1. **On the main SharePoint Frequent Sites page, click the Create Site button, as shown in Figure 11-2.**

2. **When you create a new SharePoint site, you can choose between a team site and a communications site. These are what are known as site templates. A site template creates a site based on specific scenarios.**

3. **Click the Team Site option, as shown in Figure 11-3.**

4. **Provide a name for the site and then click Next.**

5. **Add other members to the site if you want and then click Finish.**

   The site is created and loads in your browser as shown in Figure 11-4. Congratulations! You just created your first SharePoint site.

SharePoint

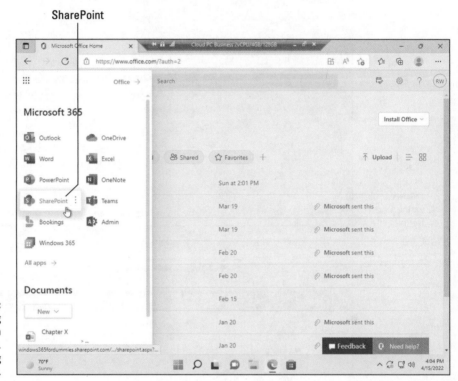

FIGURE 11-1:
Selecting
SharePoint from
the main office.
com landing
page.

TIP

The team site template for SharePoint is completely different than Microsoft Teams. This can be confusing because in Microsoft Teams you can create a new team. And when you create a new team in Microsoft Teams, a SharePoint site is created for you on the back end. It would make sense if the site that Teams creates is the same as the site you are creating now based on the Team template. Unfortunately, however, this is not the case: The two sites are different. Keep in mind that the team site template is different from a site created from a team in Teams. Makes complete sense, right? The way we remember it is that the team site template in SharePoint was introduced long before Microsoft Teams was even a product. Microsoft Teams came along and took over the name, but the team site template still persists.

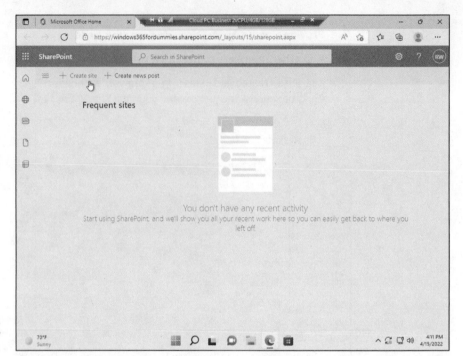

FIGURE 11-2:
Creating a new
SharePoint site.

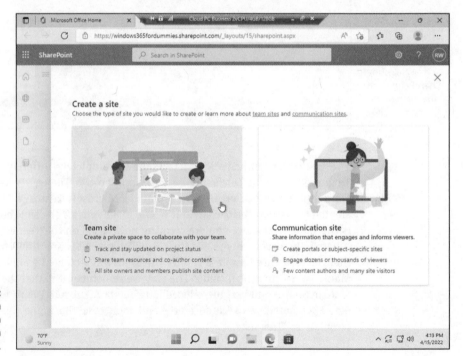

FIGURE 11-3:
Choosing a
template when
creating a
SharePoint site.

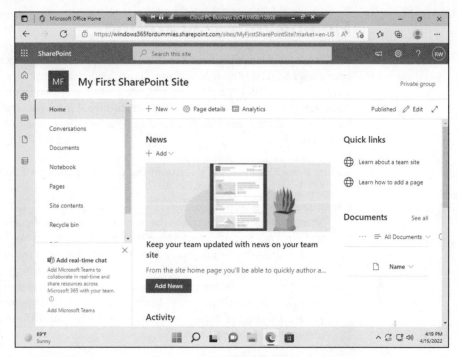

FIGURE 11-4:
A brand new
SharePoint site
based on the
team site
template.

Exploring Your SharePoint Team Site

Although you can choose from many different site templates when you create a SharePoint site, the most popular is the team site template, as it contains a number of useful features for teams to share content and apps and collaborate on projects.

When you first open your newly created team site, you can do a number of things right out of the gate. From the left-side navigation menu, you can partake in Conversations (which is an integration with Outlook), you can store your digital documents in the prebuilt Document Library app (Documents), you can open OneNote to keep shared notes (Notebook), and you can create new web pages (Pages).

The default page that appears when you first open your team site is the Home page, which is also always accessible by selecting Home from the navigation menu. The team site home page has lots of useful functionality. It includes sections for news, quick links, activity, documents, and site comments. You can also customize the home page sections to fit your own needs.

Finding your way around

All SharePoint team sites have the same features. If you're using a new team site, your site should be similar to the one shown earlier in Figure 11-4. If you are using a default communication site, you will see a site using that template designed for communications. If your site has been customized, it may look slightly different. Never fear: All the same features are there. You may just have to hunt a little bit to find them.

Almost every SharePoint site contains the following major sections:

>> **Header:** The header spans the entire top of the page. The header in a SharePoint page acts much like the menu in a traditional Windows application, such as Microsoft Word. SharePoint even features the ribbon in the page header, similar to the way the ribbon appears in the top of many Office applications. The header changes depending on what you are doing in SharePoint. If you refer back to Figure 11-4, a New button appears, allowing you to create new content as well as page details and analytic information. If you are working in a document library, then the header will have items related to that area of SharePoint.

>> **Left navigation pane:** The navigation pane provides quick access to the site's document libraries, lists, and discussion boards. You can even add links to content you create, such as documents and web pages. The navigation is fully customizable, and you can add any links you want. You can even add links to websites outside of SharePoint, such as a link to your partner website or any other favorite website.

>> **Page content:** The content displays in the body of the page. Microsoft has done a nice job of providing a good default page for the team site. You can add your own pages and also customize the default page.

Generally speaking, the header and left navigation pane stay fairly consistent, whereas the body of the page changes to display the content of the web page. This is very similar to how most websites work. However, some sites have different layouts. For example, the Communication site includes navigation across the top and then large tiles and sections that are geared toward distributing information to an organization.

TIP

Microsoft has spent a lot of money on usability research to determine how best to lay out the pages in SharePoint. We highly encourage you to use the layouts provided by Microsoft instead of creating your own custom layouts. We have seen more than one site turn into a never-ending journey of changes and edits that end up causing confusion for people that land on the site.

Uploading documents

On a default team site (see Figure 11-4), the section in the lower-right part of the page is called Documents. This seemingly innocuous little section is actually an example of SharePoint at its finest.

TIP

A link to the Documents section also appears in the navigation menu. This is a common theme in SharePoint. There are seemingly endless ways to do any one task in SharePoint, which can make for some interesting breakroom chatter. One person might insist on how to do something in SharePoint whereas another person might insist on a different way. In SharePoint both ways can be correct!

In a nutshell, Documents is a digital repository to store your files. Adding a new file, such as a Microsoft Word document, to Documents is as simple as clicking the ellipsis link in the Documents header and then clicking New, as shown in Figure 11-5. If your screen is wide enough, you might not see the ellipsis and will see the New button directly on the Ribbon. After a document is located in SharePoint, you have all the content management functionality right at your fingertips, such as check-in/check-out, versioning, security, and workflow.

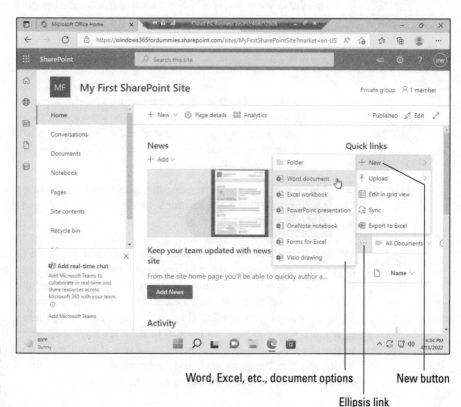

FIGURE 11-5:
Adding a new document to a SharePoint team site.

Word, Excel, etc., document options

New button

Ellipsis link

Sharing your team site

A site without any users is a bit pointless. You can share your SharePoint team site in a number of different ways. The easiest way to share is to invite users to the site. When you share a site, the people you are sharing with receive an email with all the information they need to access the site.

To share your SharePoint site using your web browser, follow these steps:

1. **Open your web browser and navigate to the SharePoint team site you want to share.**

2. **Click the gear icon in the upper-right corner and select Site Permissions.**

   The Permissions pane opens.

3. **Click the Add Members button and choose either to add members to the group of users who can access the site or to share the site only.**

   In this example, we chose to share the site only, as shown in Figure 11-6.

TIP

   If you choose to add members to the group, you will be presented with a list of users who are already part of your Microsoft 365 subscription. If you are following along with the book, you will only see a single user (unless you have added more along the way).

4. **Enter the email address of the person with whom you want to share the site.**

WARNING

   If the person is outside of your organization, a message that alerts you to that fact appears. This notice is important, as you want to be careful not to share information outside of your organization if it shouldn't be shared. If you are an administrator, you can turn off the ability to share with people outside of the organization completely.

5. **Type a message to the person with whom you are sharing the site, confirm that the check box for Send Email is selected, and then click Add (see Figure 11-7).**

TIP

In SharePoint, Microsoft lets you choose between using an older user interface experience or a newer user interface experience. The older user interface is called the classic experience. If you are using the classic SharePoint experience, your interface will be different than we describe here. For example, in the past, a Share button would be displayed at the top of a site. However, there could be a number of reasons why you may not see this button. We have seen where it doesn't appear in the Chrome browser but appears in others. We outlined the procedure to share a site via the Permissions window because this method works regardless of whether you see a Share button at the top of your screen.

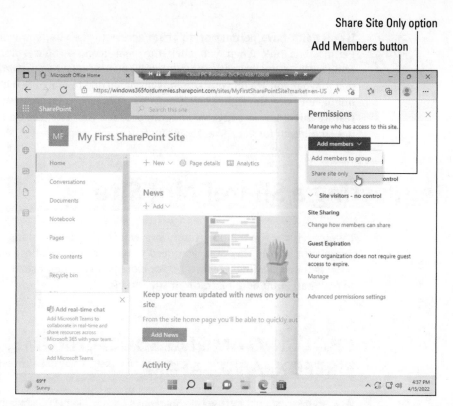

Share Site Only option

Add Members button

FIGURE 11-6:
Inviting people to
a SharePoint site.

FIGURE 11-7:
Sharing a
SharePoint site by
sending an email.

REMEMBER

If you don't have permission to share access to the site, you won't see the Site Permissions link when you click the gear icon — SharePoint automatically removes it. In general with SharePoint, if you read about something and it doesn't match what you see on your site, it is probably due to one of two issues: First, you might not have the right permissions for that particular feature; or second, the feature might not be activated or configured for your site. For example, if email is not configured for your SharePoint instance, you won't see the Share button.

Requesting a SharePoint Site

If you aren't a site administrator, you won't have permissions to create a new SharePoint site. In this case, you need to request one. Most organizations have a process for requesting a team site. For example, you might send an email request to the SharePoint administrator or fill out a form.

CHOOSING AMONG EDGE, CHROME, FIREFOX, AND SAFARI

Which browser should you use with SharePoint on your cloud PC? Firefox, Chrome, and Edge browsers have some differences; for instance, some pages look better in Firefox or Chrome than in Edge. After you create a SharePoint site you can access it from outside of your cloud PC too. Because Chrome and Firefox were designed to be OS-agnostic, they support Mac and Linux users as well as Windows users and Microsoft Edge supports Windows, macOS and Linux. Microsoft has worked hard to make the SharePoint experience the same in all mainstream browsers; however, you might find a scenario where something doesn't work as expected in all browsers. The bottom line is that if you think something should work and it isn't currently working, try the same thing in a different browser, then choose the browser that works the best and is speedy. We recommend using Edge in your cloud PC. The new Edge browser is very similar to Chrome and uses the same underlying technology. Microsoft is actively improving Edge and adding features to make life in your cloud PC easier than ever.

Getting Your Documents into SharePoint

There are many ways to upload your documents into SharePoint. You can upload them one at a time, or add a whole bunch in one swoop. You can even upload template files so that you can use them to create new documents within SharePoint based on the template. SharePoint doesn't care whether you are uploading from within your cloud PC or from a physical computer.

Uploading files has become quite easy and intuitive with modern web technologies. If you are using your web browser, you can drag and drop them right into the web browser window. If you are using Microsoft Office, you can save them right into SharePoint without even leaving your Office application.

TIP

We cover getting files onto your cloud PC using File Explorer in Chapter 8. Another approach could be to upload your files from your physical computer using your web browser and SharePoint. In SharePoint, you can access your files from your cloud PC.

Uploading a single document

When you have a single document to upload into SharePoint, you can do so easily through a web browser. The easiest way is to simply drag the file onto the Share-Point app and drop it, as shown in Figure 11-8. Dragging and dropping the file into the web browser uploads it automatically to the SharePoint library. In this example we are adding a file from our cloud PC onto our SharePoint site. We could just as easily open SharePoint on our physical computer and drag a file into SharePoint that way, too.

TIP

You can also upload documents from directly within the SharePoint Mobile App. We have found this to be useful when we need to upload a document from another file-sharing service such as Dropbox into SharePoint so that we can work on it.

To upload a file using the SharePoint Mobile App, you first need to navigate to the site you want to store the document. On the team site, there is a web part that shows this on the main page. A web part is a special container in SharePoint that contains functionality. Scroll down the page to see the Documents section and then tap the small ellipsis that shows up next to the name of that location. (The Document Library called Documents, in this case.)

Uploading multiple documents

There may be times when you have multiple documents to upload. You can drag and drop multiple documents into SharePoint in the same way you do a single document. To select multiple documents, click the first document then, hold down the Ctrl key as you click additional documents to select as many as you want.

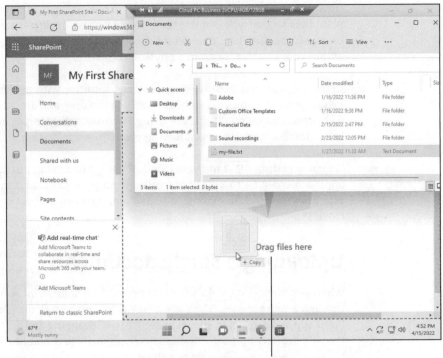

FIGURE 11-8:
Dragging and dropping a document into SharePoint.

Drag and drop files right into the web browser and they automatically upload to the SharePoint library.

If you want to upload an entire folder of documents, choose the Folder option from the Upload tab and simply select the folder you wish to upload. All the files in that folder are uploaded to SharePoint. This makes it pretty nice when you want to get your content into SharePoint quickly.

TIP

Uploading multiple documents saves you time getting the documents into your app, but you still need to go into the properties for each document and set the properties for that particular document. Unfortunately, you can't batch-upload properties. To learn about how to update properties for documents you upload, see the coverage of the Edit in Grid View option in the next section. Another option: If you have a developer on hand and need to work with documents in batches, then you can ask the developer to work with the SharePoint Application Programming Interface (API) and create a script to make the changes through code.

REMEMBER

Your SharePoint administrator can block the upload of certain file types, such as executable (.exe) files. The reason is to prevent a malicious person from uploading a virus to SharePoint, because any user who clicked the virus file would run the virus. If you try to upload a blocked file type, you see a message letting you know that the administrator has blocked the file from uploading.

Sharing Your Documents

You're probably familiar with network file shares: the file systems that enable people to upload files to a shared network drive so that other people can access and use them. File shares, when they were invented, revolutionized the ability of organizations to keep files in relatively secure locations and manage who had access. But SharePoint has done the file-sharing process one (okay, a whole bunch) better.

SharePoint apps based on libraries let you store and share files securely, and they also add features that help you manage things such as document workflow (the processes that let people edit, comment on, and approve documents) and version histories (what happened to a file, and who did what). And although file shares give you one path through folders to your document, SharePoint Library apps give you other paths to expose content. You can access documents directly through the browser, you can display them in Web Parts, and you can sort and filter them by their metadata and content types. And with Library apps, you can expose files by their title, not just their filename.

To share your document with others, they must know where to find the document. One way to do so is to send them the web address of the SharePoint site. You can also send them a link directly to the document itself.

To obtain the URL to a document in SharePoint, follow these steps:

1. **Click the ellipsis next to the document to view the pop-up menu.**

   The document options are displayed.

2. **Click the Share option and provide the person's email address or name. You can also copy the URL link to the document on this dialog, too.**

   Alternatively, click the Copy Link option to copy a direct link to the document into your clipboard. You can then paste it into an email or chat so the person receives it. As long as your team members have network access and permissions to the document, they can click the link and open the file.

Recovering Deleted Documents

It is often said that SharePoint delivers on the promise of making people more productive through software. Although that's not always true, one feature of SharePoint that truly delivers is the Recycle Bin. When you delete a document from an app, it isn't gone forever. Nope. The document just moves to a holding place in your site — the Recycle Bin.

Go ahead and try it. Go to an app and delete a document. You can use the ellipsis menu to access the Delete command. You can also select the document and then use the Delete button in the ribbon. Either way, you're prompted to confirm the deletion, and then your document appears in the Recycle Bin.

TIP

The Recycle Bin works for items in lists as well. A list is like a document library but instead of adding documents to it you add new items. For example, you might create a list of lunch spots nearby and then add new places you and your coworkers find to the list. When you delete a list item it appears in the Recycle Bin and you can restore it if needed.

Follow these steps to restore a document from the Recycle Bin to its original location:

1. **Go to the Recycle Bin by clicking the Settings gear icon and choosing Site Contents.**

   The Site Contents page is displayed.

2. **Click the Recycle Bin button in the upper-right corner to display the Recycle Bin.**

   TIP

   This process works for any SharePoint template. If you are using the team site and following along with this chapter, then you can also just click the Recycle Bin in the left navigation.

3. **Select the deleted document and then click the Restore link, as shown in Figure 11-9.**

You can click the Delete link in the Recycle Bin to remove the file from your Recycle Bin. Doing so, however, doesn't permanently delete the file. Instead, the file is moved to another Recycle Bin that can be accessed by the site collection administrator.

If you are a site collection administrator, you will see a link at the bottom of the Recycle Bin called Second-Stage Recycle Bin. If you click that, you will see the Recycle Bin for all the SharePoint sites in the collection. This is a feature of SharePoint that gives additional power to site collection administrators. So if a regular user accidentally deletes something and then goes into the Recycle Bin and accidentally deletes it from the Recycle Bin, a site collection administrator can still get the content back.

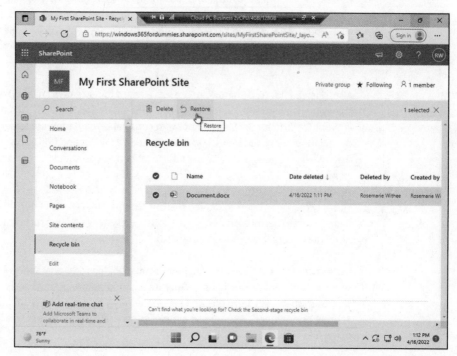

FIGURE 11-9:
Restoring a document from the Recycle Bin.

Files remain in the Second-Stage Recycle Bin for a period of 30 days or until they're deleted by the administrator, whichever comes first. When removed from the Recycle Bin, the fate of your documents depends on your company's business continuity management plan. That's a fancy way to say, how does your IT team back up data? SharePoint stores your documents in databases. An administrator can connect to a backed-up copy of the database and select individual documents to restore.

Uploading Documents into a Folder

You can use folders within your SharePoint apps as a means to organize your documents. We show you how to create a folder and upload files into it, but we urge you to first read the sidebar, "Why folders in SharePoint are evil."

REMEMBER

WHY FOLDERS IN SHAREPOINT ARE EVIL

Resist the urge to use folders in your SharePoint apps; this file-share paradigm generally causes nothing but problems. One reason to use SharePoint instead of a file share to begin with is so that you can add properties to describe your documents. Properties allow you to view your documents in different ways. If you dump your files into folders just like they were arranged on the file share, ignoring properties, you probably won't be very satisfied with your SharePoint experience.

Also, nested folders in SharePoint are just as hard to navigate as nested folders in file shares (and nested URLs in folders inside apps get unwieldy quickly). Instead of replicating your file structure in SharePoint, we recommend you flatten the folder hierarchies by replacing them with views. If you decide to use folders and find yourself going more than two layers deep, stop and ask yourself whether you should create another app instead.

The only reason to use a folder in an app is to separate a group of documents to give them separate permissions. For pretty much everything else, we recommend you use properties to organize your documents.

Perhaps you have an app and you have a subset of files that only supervisors should see. You could put those files in a separate app and set the permissions on it. But suppose you already have one app set up the way you like, and it seems silly to create another one. Instead, you can use a folder to separate the restricted files from the rest of the files in the app.

SharePoint apps can be confusing. An app based on a list is designed to store data in columns. An app based on a library is designed to store documents and data about those documents in columns. SharePoint tries to simplify the whole discussion of list and library and just calls everything an app. When you create the app, you give it a name and choose an app template. From that point on, you just call your app by its name. For example, you might create the Sales Pitch app. The app is designed to hold sales-pitch documents. Because the app holds documents, it uses the Document Library app template. After your app is created, you wouldn't call it the "Sales Pitch app based on the Document Library App template." That would be a mouthful! If you're a seasoned SharePoint user, this new app stuff might take you a while to get your head around. It did us! But when you realize that most users don't think in terms of lists and libraries, and instead think about what a list or library does, it really is much easier to just call everything an app.

Saving Stuff with OneDrive

Your personal storage location, known as OneDrive, is designed as a place to store, organize, and share your documents, such as a carpool list you're working on or a potluck spreadsheet. You might also be working on business documents that don't really fit into any specific app in SharePoint. Your OneDrive is the catch-all place you can store it.

Think of your OneDrive as your personal Documents folder on your computer. The difference is that the personal Documents folder on your computer is only on that single computer. If you're using a different computer, you can't access those documents. In addition, if your computer crashes and you have not backed up your Documents folder, then those files are lost. OneDrive is designed to be a secure and safe place to store all your documents. What if your device crashes or is stolen? With your documents stored in OneDrive, you just sign in again from a different device and continue working on your documents.

TIP

Your OneDrive files are only secure and backed up if your IT team sets up the infrastructure that way. If you're using SharePoint Online, then you can be assured that Microsoft is doing this for you. If your local IT team is running SharePoint for you, then check with them to make sure they back up and secure your OneDrive documents. This is because SharePoint Online is hosted and run by Microsoft, whereas SharePoint On-Premises is hosted and run by your internal IT team.

Your OneDrive is designed to live in the cloud and to be accessible by any device you happen to be working on. For example, if you start a document at work and then have to stop working on it when you leave to pick up your kids, you can sign in and continue working on the document when you get home. And if you later have to take your mother-in-law to the doctor, and you take your tablet with you, you can sign in from your tablet while you're waiting in the doctor's office. Finally, if you drop off your mother-in-law and make a quick stop at the grocery store, and you get an email on your smartphone asking about a detail in the document you have been working on, you can connect to your OneDrive on your smartphone and view the document so you can respond to the inquiry. Being this connected isn't always the best way to spend your off-time, but OneDrive enables you to decide when and where you want to work. The idea behind OneDrive is that when you need your documents, you can access them as long as you can connect to the Internet.

TIP

OneDrive has been a source of confusion in the past because there was a separate OneDrive for business and a OneDrive for personal use. Microsoft has been making changes to try to reduce this confusion. Now, when you sign up for a Microsoft 365 subscription, you can choose either a home- based subscription or a business- based subscription. And OneDrive is included with all of the available subscriptions available. There is even a free Microsoft 365 subscription called Basic, which includes 5GB of OneDrive storage. The OneDrive discussed in this chapter is called OneDrive for Business, and it is designed for organizations and is part of SharePoint. A consumer version of OneDrive is also available at `https://onedrive.live.com`, but it is not part of SharePoint. It is a completely separate offering designed for general consumers, not organizations and business. When using the consumer version, your files are stored in the cloud on Microsoft servers. The consumer version of OneDrive is similar to other cloud storage services such as Dropbox and Google Drive.

Creating or Uploading Documents in Your OneDrive

When you first land on your OneDrive page, you are presented with a notice letting you know some tips about OneDrive such as accessing recent documents. OneDrive for Business is a place to store, sync, and share your documents. You can add documents to OneDrive by following these steps:

1. Navigate to your OneDrive page by clicking the waffle icon in the top-left corner of your screen and choosing OneDrive from the menu (refer to Figure 11-1).

2. Click the New link at the top of the page and select the type of document you want to create, as shown in Figure 11-10.

3. The blank document opens, ready for you to add content.

4. On the other hand, if you want to upload an existing document, click the Upload button instead of the New button and then choose Files or Folder (Step 2), browse to the document you want to add to OneDrive, and click OK to add the file.

You can choose to overwrite the document if a document with the same name already exists. If versioning is turned on, a new version of the document will be created and the existing document will become the previous version. If versioning is turned off, then overwriting will result in the loss of the existing document with the same name.

The OneDrive site contains a number of ways to sort your document. You can sort the documents by things like the type, name, modified date, modified by user, and file size. You can also choose to do the sort in ascending or descending order. In addition, you can view the documents as a list, a compact list, or as tiles. You can find these options in the top-right corner of the screen. You can see all the documents you have recently worked on and all of the documents that are shared with you. You access these views by clicking the links in the left navigation pane (refer to Figure 11-10).

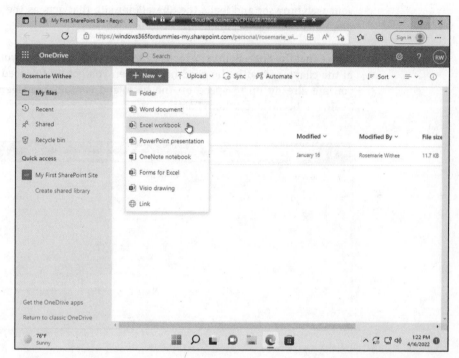

FIGURE 11-10:
Creating a new document in OneDrive.

This chapter provides a brief overview of SharePoint and OneDrive. These topics have a lot of depth and require a book unto themselves, and we have written just such a book. If you want to go deeper in this area, then check out *SharePoint For Dummies* (Wiley) in which we go through all aspects of SharePoint in detail.

Discovering How SharePoint and Teams Work Together

Chapter 10 covered Microsoft Teams. Whenever you create a new team in Microsoft Teams you are also creating a new SharePoint site. When you select a team and then click the Files tab or Wiki tab at the top of the team you are viewing the contents of the back-end SharePoint site. Teams essentially becomes the front-end interface for using SharePoint. Teams even provides a menu item to open a document directly in the back-end SharePoint site.

To open a document in the SharePoint site, select the ellipsis next to the document and then select Open in SharePoint, as shown in Figure 11-11. The action opens your web browser and loads the SharePoint site that acts as the content storage mechanism for the Teams team.

Notice that the SharePoint site looks nearly identical to the site you created earlier in the chapter. That is the good news: When you get up to speed on SharePoint, you are already up to speed on the back-end content management system of Teams — because it *is* SharePoint!

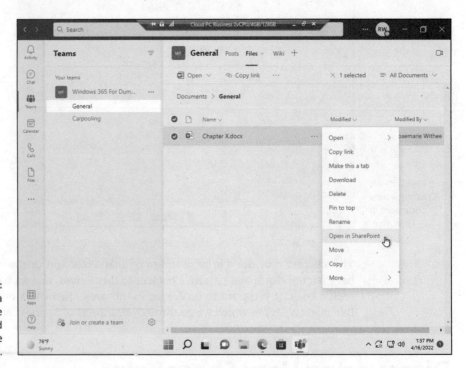

FIGURE 11-11:
Opening a document in the back-end SharePoint site from Teams.

IN THIS CHAPTER

Chapter **12**

Getting the Most Out of Microsoft 365

As you learned in Chapter 1, you must have a Microsoft 365 subscription in order to obtain Windows 365. Because you already have Microsoft 365, you might as well get the most out of your subscription.

In this chapter, you learn about your Microsoft 365 subscription. You learn about some of the most popular apps including Microsoft Office. You also learn about some of the lesser known apps such as Bookings, Lists, To-Do, Whiteboard, and Stream. Finally you learn about one of the most important apps, which is actually a platform for building your own apps, called Power Platform. We consider the Power Platform a game changer; the topic requires a book unto itself, but we cover some of the key aspects here to get you started.

Taking a Spin around Your Microsoft 365 Subscription

Microsoft 365 is a marketing term that encompasses many other services with the most prominent being Office 365. As we mentioned in Chapter 1, Office 365 is the cloud version of the traditional Office product. Several years ago, Microsoft moved Office to the cloud in the form of Office 365 and thus began a cloud first suite of software products. Over the last decade Microsoft has continued to build Office 365 and it is now a dominant product within the Microsoft offerings. Microsoft is now doing the same with Windows in the form of Windows 365. We expect that Windows 365 will now take the baton from Windows and be the primary operating system that Microsoft invests in and that organizations move toward going forward.

With all of that said, you can think of Microsoft 365 as an umbrella term that encompasses many different services and products. Microsoft moved Office 365 into the Microsoft 365 umbrella in order to try to simplify the branding and terminology. However, when you hear Microsoft 365 you can also think of it as a synonym for Office 365.

TIP

Office 365 and Microsoft 365 are branding terms. When you hear Office 365 and Microsoft 365 you can think of the branding terms nearly interchangeably. We still hear most of the people we work with use the term Office 365 even though Microsoft has changed the name to Microsoft 365.

To learn about the latest Microsoft 365 and Office 365 products you point your web browser to `https://www.office.com`. Microsoft segments the offerings into four primary categories: Home, Business, Enterprise, and Education.

TIP

Some versions of Office are even free. You can find a link to the free version of Office on the website office.com.

In Chapter 2, you learned how to sign up for Microsoft 365 in order to sign up for Windows 365. As a refresher, scroll down on the `https://www.office.com/` website and click For Business. All of the available Microsoft 365 subscriptions appear here. The subscription types include different apps. For example, the Business Standard plan includes the desktop versions of the Office apps whereas the Business Basic subscription only includes the web versions of Office. And the Business Premium plan includes advanced services such as Intune and advanced security and cyberthreat features such as Defender for Office 365. You can also find a detailed list of apps and what is available with each subscription type by scrolling down the page and expanding each feature, as shown in Figure 12-1.

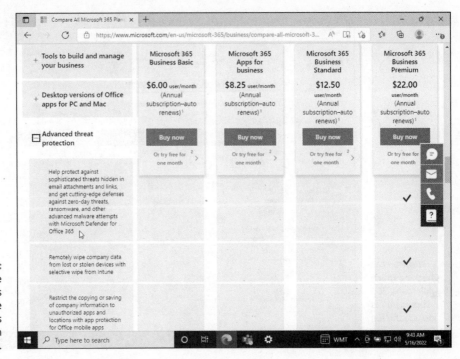

	Microsoft 365 Business Basic	Microsoft 365 Apps for business	Microsoft 365 Business Standard	Microsoft 365 Business Premium
+ Tools to build and manage your business	$6.00 user/month (Annual subscription–auto renews)[1]	$8.25 user/month (Annual subscription–auto renews)[1]	$12.50 user/month (Annual subscription–auto renews)[1]	$22.00 user/month (Annual subscription–auto renews)[1]
+ Desktop versions of Office apps for PC and Mac	Buy now	Buy now	Buy now	Buy now
☐ Advanced threat protection	Or try free for[2] one month >	Or try free for[2] one month >	Or try free for[2] one month >	Or try free for one month
Help protect against sophisticated threats hidden in email attachments and links, and get cutting-edge defenses against zero-day threats, ransomware, and other advanced malware attempts with Microsoft Defender for Office 365				✓
Remotely wipe company data from lost or stolen devices with selective wipe from Intune				✓
Restrict the copying or saving of company information to unauthorized apps and locations with app protection for Office mobile apps				✓

TIP

For large organizations, Microsoft offers Enterprise subscriptions. These subscriptions are designed for the largest organizations. You can learn more about them by clicking the For Enterprises link on the www.office.com website.

Rediscovering an Old Friend in Microsoft Office

We have used Microsoft Office on our computers for years and feel at home with the software. Sure, new web-based productivity tools have been released including Google Apps and the new web-based Office products, however, we still prefer installing and using Office on our actual computer. We have embraced using a cloud PC and even though our cloud PC is in the cloud, we still prefer installing the Office products directly on our cloud PC.

When you sign up for Microsoft 365 you can choose whether you want access to the Office software that can be installed on your computer. At the time of this writing, the Microsoft 365 Business Basic subscription does not include the Office software. You must sign up for one of the higher subscriptions, as shown in Figure 12-2.

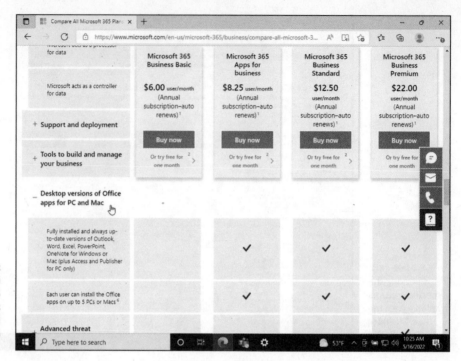

FIGURE 12-2:
Checking which
Microsoft 365
subscriptions
include the full
Office desktop
clients.

The Office products, such as Word, Excel, and PowerPoint, are only available to install on your cloud PC with specific Microsoft 365 subscriptions. If you want to use this software on your cloud PC, make sure to check which subscription includes it when you sign up for Microsoft 365.

TIP

We cover finding and opening the Office apps on your cloud PC in Chapter 8.

Learning about Common Microsoft 365 Apps

Microsoft is continually adding apps to the Microsoft 365 subscriptions. Some of the apps are very simple and easy to use and others are more advanced and require a bit of time to get the hang of. You find the Microsoft 365 apps on the app launcher. Open your web browser and navigate to any of the Microsoft 365 apps and you see the app launcher in the upper-left of the page. For example, you can navigate to the administrative site at `https://admin.microsoft.com` and then click on the app launcher to open the Bookings app, as shown in Figure 12-3.

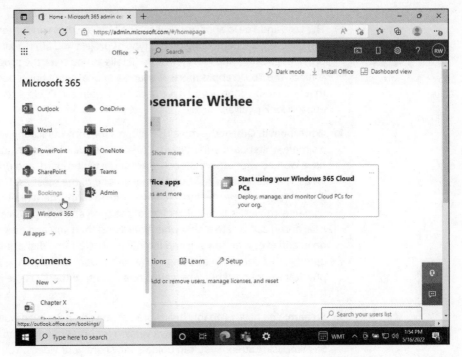

FIGURE 12-3:
Opening the
Bookings app
from the app
launcher on the
Microsoft 365
administration
site.

A handful of the most prominent apps are:

>> **Bookings:** A meeting setting app that customers can use to set appointments with your organization. For example, you might run a dog grooming business and want your customers to be able to schedule and track appointments, and have them appointments added to your calendar and their calendar. The Bookings app lets you do this through a web-based interface.

>> **Lists:** An app designed to create and share lists of information. We find this app incredibly useful because it is so simple and straightforward to under-stand and use. We like to use lists to manage our daily routines, tasks, and chores. The Lists app lets us do this and share our lists with other people and stay in sync.

>> **To-Do:** Keeping track of things you and your team need to do is one of the most basic needs of any organization. The To-Do app is a simple app you use to keep track of things you need to get done. You can use the app on the web and through a mobile device. You can create and share To-Do lists with others so that everyone is on the same page with what needs to get done and what is already done.

The Lists and To-Do apps are similar. The Lists app has various templates you can choose from depending on the type of project you are working on. It provides columns and rows for more details as you track the progress of the project. The To-Do app is more of your traditional set of bullet points of items that need to be done. If you have used To-Do items in Outlook, then the To-Do app will look familiar.

>> **Whiteboard:** One of the most useful tools for communicating with others is a simple whiteboard and markers. We can't tell you how many times we have worked with others, standing around a whiteboard, and drawing out ideas. A whiteboard is right up there with one of the most useful ways for people to communicate and exchange information. The Whiteboard app, as its name implies, is a digital version of the tried and true physical whiteboard. You can create a new whiteboard and then you and others can draw on it, and everyone can see and interact with the same digital surface. In our opinion, this doesn't beat being in the same room and standing around a physical whiteboard but when everyone is remote then it is the next best thing.

>> **Stream:** You have probably heard of YouTube and have even watched some videos there. Microsoft has its own version for organizations, and it is called Stream. Using Stream you can upload and share your videos. You can embed them in other areas and track metrics that relate to them. Stream uses SharePoint behind the scenes, and if you are familiar with SharePoint, you know the value it can provide. We cover SharePoint in further detail in Chapter 11 and have even written an entire book on the technology called *SharePoint For Dummies* (Wiley).

Finding Control with the Power Platform

The Microsoft Power Platform is a series of apps and services that have been brought together under the same marketing umbrella. The Power Platform includes Power Business Intelligence (Power BI), Power Apps, Power Automate, and Power Virtual Agents.

Power BI is a tool you can use to pull in data from many different sources and then create visualizations in order to analyze and understand it. We like to think of Power BI as an Excel spreadsheet with all sorts of super powers. We use Power BI all of the time for large and small projects and we see even the largest organizations utilizing it to run even their largest businesses.

Power Virtual Agents is an area of the Power Platform designed to create chat bots. Using artificial intelligence and machine learning you can create, train, and deploy agents that can provide information to customers in the form of chats. The technology is getting better all the time — we even found ourselves asking someone on a support chat service whether they were a human or an AI. Just the fact that we had to ask says a lot about how far the technology has come and where it is headed.

The other two areas of the Power Platform are Power Apps and Power Automate. We think these are two of the most impactful tools in the Power Platform. Let's explore them in some detail.

Creating Apps across the Microsoft Cloud with Power Apps

Microsoft Power Apps is a service that spans many different products. The idea of Power Apps is to provide a platform for non-developers to build apps that people can use on their smartphones and other computing devices. Power Apps is designed for business needs and thus, fits in nicely with SharePoint and your Windows 365 cloud PCs.

Introducing Power Apps

When we first started using Power Apps, we were excited. It seemed like a platform designed specifically for SharePoint. The Power Apps we built we made available to all types of users on their mobile phones. All of a sudden, people started using SharePoint and had no idea they were using SharePoint. They just used an app on their phones and knew that it solved a specific business problem. So we initially thought of Power Apps as a mobile app platform, and we used it almost exclusively with SharePoint. Now that we have some experience under our belts, we realize that Power Apps is more than just making SharePoint apps available on a mobile device (though this is still the biggest value in our opinion).

TIP

Even though we think of Power Apps as primarily a mobile experience, you can also add the Power Apps you build to SharePoint pages as well.

Signing into Power Apps

The easiest way to access Power Apps is by clicking the Microsoft 365 app launcher menu and then selecting Power Apps. If you don't see it right away, then you may need to select All Apps.

You can also access Power Apps by opening your web browser and navigating to the site directly. The Power Apps site is located at `https://powerapps.microsoft.com`. When you sign into the Power Apps site, you use your Microsoft 365 credentials just like you use to sign into your cloud PC.

Getting familiar with Power Apps

The Microsoft Power Apps service uses your web browser as a development tool for building apps. The development environment is shown in Figure 12-4.

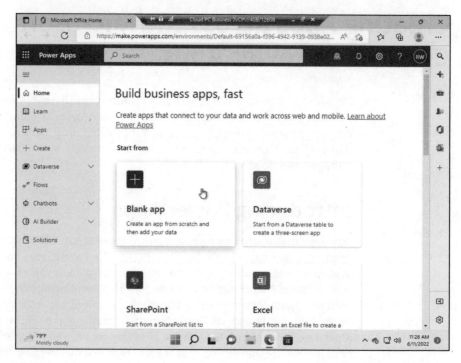

FIGURE 12-4:
The main Power
Apps page.

Notice along the left side of the page you have the following navigation options: Home, Learn, Apps, Create, Dataverse, Flows, Chatbots, AI Builder, and Solutions.

The Home navigational link is your friend that always takes you back to the beginning if you get lost. The Power Apps home page includes overview information and is always a good place to start when you are developing Power Apps.

Next up is the Learn link. The Learn link includes guided learning, help topics, and a Power Apps community.

When you first get started with Power Apps, make sure to spend some time going through the Guided Learning experience found on the Learn page. It is time well spent and saves you lots of frustration and headaches down the road.

The Apps link takes you to a location that shows you all your Power Apps. There you can find the recent apps you have developed, apps that have been shared with you, apps you have permissions to edit, and apps that are part of your organization.

After the Apps link is the Create link. The Create link is where you go to create a new PowerApp. You use this in the next section when you create your first Power-App. After the Create link is the Dataverse link. The Dataverse link expands and includes links for Tables, Azure Synapse Link, Connections, Custom Connectors, and Gateways. This is where you can create connections and manage the data you are using in your Power Apps. Data is at the heart of a business app, so you will spend a lot of time here after you get comfortable with building and customizing Power Apps.

After the Dataverse link is the Flows navigational link, which lets you integrate your Microsoft Power Automate workflows directly into your Power Apps. We cover Microsoft Power Automate in the next section.

Microsoft often changes the names of navigational items. If you don't see the exact names we mention then they have likely changed. As we were writing this book, for example, the Data link changed to Dataverse even though the functionality remains nearly the same. Just something to keep in mind when using Microsoft 365 apps.

The Chatbots link is where you can create virtual agents that respond in chats. Think of a chatbot as an automated response system that people can use to interact and have guided conversations.

The AI Builder is covered further in the next section on Power Automate. AI Builder is an advanced feature that lets you enhance your apps with common AI models.

Last in the list is the Solutions navigational link. Solutions is a relatively new feature of Power Apps (Microsoft is adding new functionality all the time). Solutions is beyond the scope of this book, but in a nutshell, a *Solution* allows you to encapsulate a group of Power Apps and move them all at once to another environment instead of one at a time. Imagine a Power Apps solution for a finance team that includes apps used by financial departments. This is the idea behind Solutions.

Building your first Power App

A very simple, but incredibly powerful, use for Power Apps is to let users work with a custom SharePoint List-based app using their mobile phones or tablets. Just about everyone has a smartphone now, and building an app that lets your users interact with a SharePoint list brings your intranet to their mobile devices.

Let's build a Power App so that users can work with a SharePoint list from their mobile devices.

To build a Power App for working with a SharePoint list:

1. Open your web browser and navigate to the SharePoint list.

This assumes you already have a SharePoint list in mind. If you don't already have a SharePoint list, you can create one before proceeding. Refer to Chapter 11 for more information on SharePoint.

2. Click the ellipsis in the Ribbon, choose Integrate, and then on the Power Apps fly-out menu select Create an App, as shown in Figure 12-5.

TIP

If your screen is wide enough you might not see the ellipsis and will instead see the direct options such as Automate and Integrate.

A dialog displays where you can enter a name for the app.

3. Enter a name and click Create, as shown in Figure 12-6.

Your browser redirects you to the Power Apps development environment called Power Apps Studio.

Power Apps Studio might sound impressive, but it is really just a web page with a lot of functionality for building apps. All you need is your web browser to work with it and build Power Apps. Because we started with an existing SharePoint list, the heavy lifting of creating the Power App was already done for us.

4. Click the play button, displayed in the top-right corner of the page, to display the app in a preview window.

The preview shows you what the app will look like when viewed on a mobile phone.

The SharePoint list that contains the data for this app doesn't have any items in it yet, so let's create one.

5. Click the plus (+) sign in the top-right corner of the screen.

A form that represents the columns in the SharePoint list appears.

6. **Enter information into the form to create a new list item and then click the check mark in the upper-right corner of the app to create a new item, as shown in Figure 12-7.**

A new list item is added and the main app page reloads. Let's head back over to our SharePoint list in our web browser to confirm the item was created.

7. **Open the Power Apps Example list in our browser and confirm the new item has been created from the Power App, as shown in Figure 12-8.**

Next, let's create a new item in the SharePoint list in our web browser and then confirm it appears in the Power App.

8. **Click the plus (+) sign to create a new item in the SharePoint list, then head over to the Power App preview and click the refresh icon (it looks like a circular arrow).**

Our new item is pulled into the Power App. We can now work with a SharePoint list from a Power App.

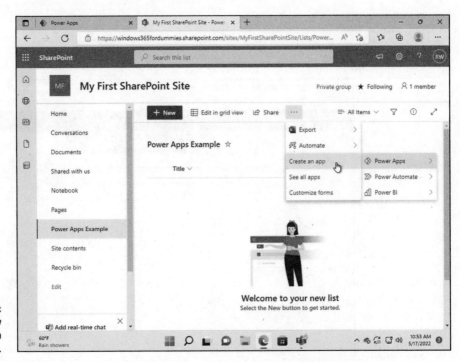

FIGURE 12-5:
Creating a new
PowerApp for a
SharePoint list.

TIP

Power Apps can be integrated with Microsoft Power Automate. This combination lets you take SharePoint to the mobile world and also incorporate your workflow at the same time. In our view, this is a game changer in the technology world.

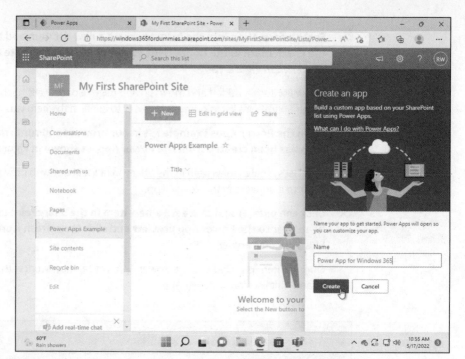

FIGURE 12-6:
Providing a name
for a PowerApp.

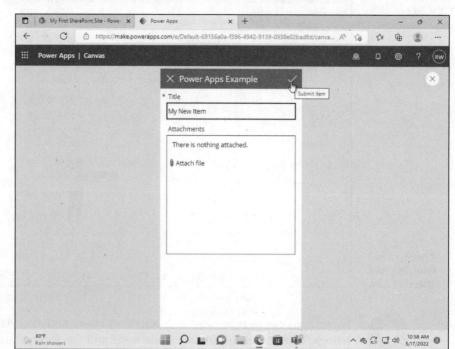

FIGURE 12-7:
When a new
PowerApp is
created from a
SharePoint list,
we can preview it.

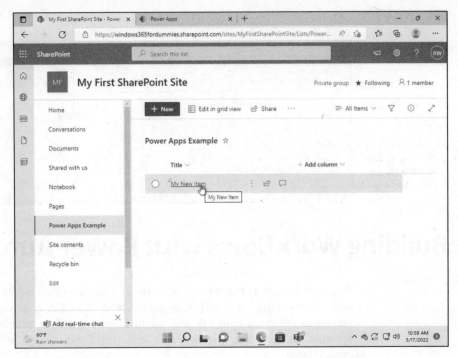

FIGURE 12-8:
Create a new
SharePoint list
item from a
PowerApp.

TIP

Power Apps Studio is a complex development environment. It takes some time to get a feel for customizing and creating new Power Apps. Remember to check out the Learn navigational link at `https://powerapps.microsoft.com` to see hands-on training guides and videos.

Sharing your PowerApp

Now that you have a working Power App, the last step is to share your app so that it is available to use. To share a Power App:

1. **Open the Power App you want to share in Power Apps Studio.**

   If you followed the previous procedure, you are already viewing the app created for the SharePoint list.

2. **Click the File tab, shown at the left in Figure 12-9, and then click the Share button, shown at the right in Figure 12-9.**

3. **Enter the name or email addresses of the people you want to be able to use the app and then click Share.**

   An email is sent with instructions on how to access the app.

File tab   Share button

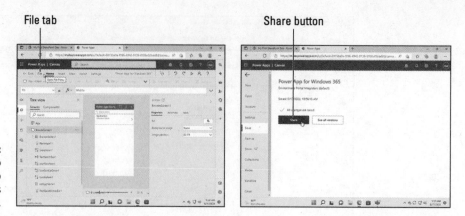

FIGURE 12-9:
Sharing an app
from the File tab
in Power Apps
Studio.

Building Workflows with Power Automate

Any organization is made up of processes. Some processes might be very simple, such as checking an email, responding, and then filing it in a folder. Other processes are more complex and might involve multiple people and computer systems. In any case, processes — and workflows — are at the core of an organization.

Understanding Workflow

A workflow can be used to manage a human-centric process or a computer-centric process. For example, you might have a process that involves five people working partly in parallel and partly in sequence. If these five people are all in the same room and accomplish the process in one sitting, then using a workflow to coordinate their activities wouldn't make much sense. If the people are dispersed in different offices or cubicles, or if the process takes place over a period of time, then a workflow can be used to coordinate and keep the process on track.

In addition, a process might interact with other computer systems. For example, you might have a process that needs to pull customer data from a Customer Relationship Management (CRM) system. Or you might want to pull data into SharePoint from Twitter and the CRM so that a workflow is triggered whenever someone complains publicly about your company or product on Twitter. Just about anything you can dream up can be built into a workflow.

Introducing Microsoft Power Automate

Microsoft Power Automate is the next generation of workflow. It was born in the cloud and designed from the ground up to interact with Microsoft 365 products as well as third-party products (external to Microsoft) such as Dropbox, Amazon, Twitter, Facebook, and nearly any other online service in the world. It enables employees to create and automate workflows across multiple applications. When you think of Microsoft Power Automate, think of an online workflow engine that is available to the Internet — not just to Microsoft products.

TIP

Microsoft Power Automate is a rebranding of Microsoft Flow. If you are reading about workflow in Microsoft 365 and see articles outlining Microsoft Flow, you can think of Power Automate now instead. Microsoft has a culture of changing the names of things all the time so don't worry if you see a new name. Chances are good that the technology is not brand new, just the name.

Signing into Microsoft Power Automate

Microsoft Power Automate is accessed in one of two ways. You can select the Power Automate icon in the Apps menu from within any Microsoft 365 service (such as SharePoint) as described earlier. Alternatively, you can go to the Microsoft Power Automate web page at `https://powerautomate.microsoft.com`.

Getting familiar with Power Automate

The Microsoft Power Automate service uses your web browser as a design tool for building out automated workflows called *flows*. The design environment is shown in Figure 12-10. Notice the navigation options that appear along the left side of the page: Home, Action Items, My Flows, Create, Templates, Connectors, Data, Monitor, AI Builder, Process Advisor, Solutions, and Learn.

The Home navigational link always takes you back to your start page if you ever get lost. The start page includes overview information and is always a good place to return to when working with Power Automate.

The Action Items menu provides a place for approvals and business process flows. The Approvals link takes you to the approvals page, as shown in Figure 12-11, where you can build a new approval workflow or interact with approvals that you have sent or received. You can even see the history of the approvals on this page.

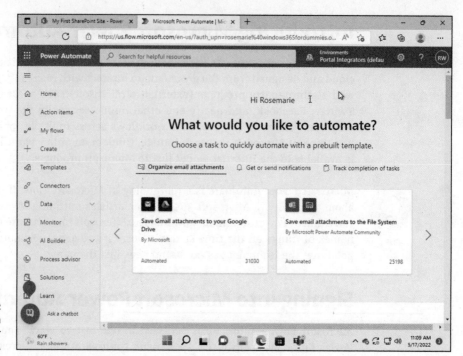

FIGURE 12-10:
The main Microsoft Power Automate page.

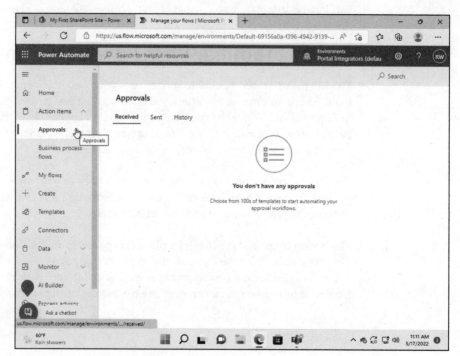

FIGURE 12-11:
The Approvals page for Microsoft Flow.

The heart of the Power Automate interface is the My Flows page. When you click this navigational link, you see all your flows and the flows for your team. There you find tabs to group flows by Cloud flows, Desktop flows, Business Process flows, and Shared With Me flows:

>> **Cloud flows** are workflows that are triggered automatically, instantly, or via a schedule based on events that happen in the cloud.

>> **Desktop flows** are workflows for repetitive things that you do on your local computer. For example, organizing your documents and folders or pulling data into an Excel file from the same source each day.

>> **Business Process flows** are designed for human workflows in that the person follows the same steps each time. For example, when someone opens a new account they should always follow the new account workflow.

>> **The Shared With Me flows** are flows that others have created and shared with you.

The Create navigation item lets you start a new workflow. The next item is the Templates link that takes you to the Templates library. Templates are prepackaged flows you can use and customize for specific scenarios. For example, there is a flow to send yourself a reminder in 10 minutes or start an approval when a new item is added to SharePoint or Outlook. An incredible number of templates are available, and new ones are added all the time. Chances are, if you already have a workflow in mind, someone has created a template for it.

Next up on the navigational menu is Connectors. Connectors are where Power Automate gets its power. Connectors, well, connect Power Automate to all types of services and products. This is where you can build workflows that interact with popular sites and products. Remember when we mentioned Dropbox, Amazon, Twitter, and Facebook? This is where you find connectors for those products, as well as nearly any other online service or product in the world.

TIP

Keep in mind that some services require a premium subscription in order to connect to them.

The Data navigational link is where you can pull data into your flows so that it can be analyzed and decisions in the workflow process can be made. After you get up to speed with Power Automate, you will spend a lot of time in this area.

The Monitor option is where you monitor things regarding your flows. Here you see things like notifications, failures, and alerts.

The AI Builder option lets you enhance your workflows with common AI models. For example, you might train a model to look at incoming invoices and pull out key information. As the model learns it can adapt to new invoice formats without human interaction. You can use many different AI models with Power Automate.

Next up is Process Advisor which you can think of as an automated way to visualize your workflows. You can then review the visualizations and figure out how to improve your workflows.

The Solutions navigational link is where you can bundle flows into a single deployable unit. The deployable unit is called a solution and you can group related flows together for ease of deployment and maintenance. Solutions can be very useful in extremely large organizations that have a lot of flows.

Finally, the Learn navigational link is where you can find step-by-step learning guidance from Microsoft.

Building your first flow

A basic, but useful, workflow is to send an approval email when a new item is added to your SharePoint site. For example, imagine a ticketing app you have built using a SharePoint List (see Chapter 11 for more about creating List-based apps). Whenever someone adds a new item to the app, you want to fire off an approval email to a group of people so that they know a new ticket has been added and someone can approve it. Let's build this workflow using Power Automate.

To build a workflow to send an approval email when a new item is added to your SharePoint List app follow these steps:

1. **In SharePoint, click the Microsoft 365 apps menu in the upper-left corner and select Power Automate.**

   A new tab opens on your web browser and the Microsoft Power Automate page loads.

2. **Click the Templates navigational link on the left side of the page.**

3. **Type** sharepoint **into the search box and press Enter to display the templates that relate to SharePoint, as shown in Figure 12-12.**

   A template is already available to do exactly what we are trying to do.

4. **Click the "Send approval email when a new item is added" template (shown as the last template in the third row in Figure 12-12).**

   The page for this template appears and provides a visual for how the workflow flows. (Pun intended.) You can see in Figure 12-13 that the workflow originates in SharePoint and then moves to Microsoft 365 and Office 365 Outlook (email).

The arrow pointing to the right indicates the direction the data is sent. Farther down the page are the permissions that are required for this email (see Figure 12-14).

Something we appreciate about Microsoft services is that authentication is handled for us automatically. If you look at the permissions required for this workflow (Figure 12-14), you will see it actually crosses services. Because our user is part of Microsoft 365, we don't need to set up any extra permissions. It "just works" after we sign into each service from within the flow.

A "gotcha" with connectors is that Microsoft Outlook and Office 365 Outlook are different email services. Microsoft Outlook is for personal email addresses and Office 365 Outlook is for work and organization email addresses. If you try to setup an email connector in a flow and receive an error that the account doesn't exist, then you might be using the wrong email service for the type of account you are signed in with. We ran into this with the connector that sends an email notification when a new item is added to a SharePoint list. The connector wants the personal Outlook.com email service and we were trying to use the Office 365 Outlook service.

5. **Make sure to click the "sign-in" next to either SharePoint or Office 365 Outlook and then click Continue. Next, click the SharePoint Site Address drop-down menu and choose the SharePoint site where your List-based app resides.**

In our example we chose our Windows 365 For Dummies site that we created in Chapter 11.

6. **Click the SharePoint List Name drop-down menu and select the List-based app the workflow will use.**

In our example, we chose the Power Apps Example list from earlier in the chapter, as shown in Figure 12-15.

It can take a little time for a SharePoint site or List-based app to appear in these drop-down menus. If you just created something and it is not showing up, go grab a coffee and check back later.

7. **Fill in the approval details and then click Save to create the workflow and attach it to your SharePoint List-based app.**

Now whenever a new item is added to the list, an approval email will be sent as a notification. You can customize the workflow with the destination email, email message, and timing by editing the flow. You can find it on the My Flows page.

Using Microsoft Power Automate, you can build workflows that integrate SharePoint with just about any other software you can imagine. Spend some time exploring the templates and when you are feeling comfortable, start customizing the templates to suit your own needs and then move into building your own custom flows from scratch.

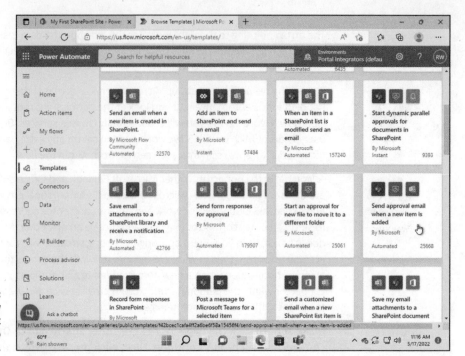

FIGURE 12-12:
The Flow
templates that
relate to
SharePoint.

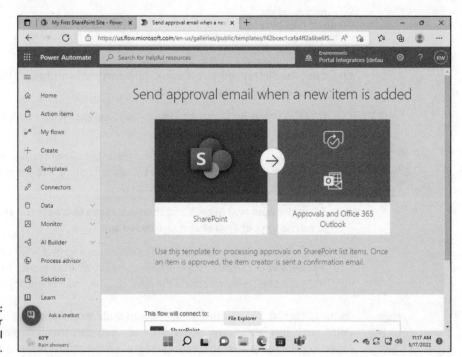

FIGURE 12-13:
The data flow for
a custom email
workflow.

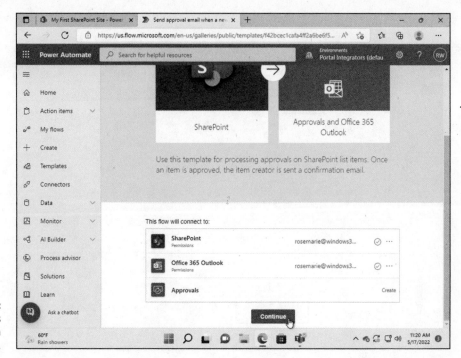

FIGURE 12-14:
The permissions
for a custom
email workflow.

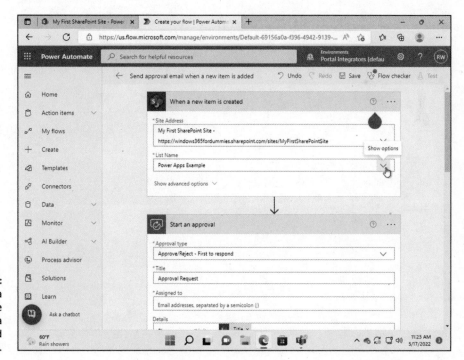

FIGURE 12-15:
Selecting a
SharePoint site
and List app for a
flow-based
workflow.

4

Maintaining Your System

» Figuring out how to update all Microsoft software

» Getting familiar with the Windows Insider program

» Finding out how to keep all software apps updated

Chapter **13**

Keeping Your System and Apps Up to Date

O ne of the most important things you can do to ensure your computer security is keeping your system and software apps up-to-date. Most Microsoft software does a great job of keeping itself up to date through a mechanism known as Windows Update.

In this chapter, we cover the primary update mechanism on your cloud PC called *Windows Update*. We walk you through the various options and advanced options and then cover the Windows Insider program. Finally, we discuss how to keep the software on your cloud PC that was developed by someone other than Microsoft up to date.

Learning Your Way around Windows Update

Windows Update is part of the Settings application, and you can use it to keep your Microsoft software up to date.

To open Windows Update, follow these steps:

1. **Make sure you are working on your cloud PC and then click the Start button.**

   The Start menu appears.

2. **Click the Settings app (if it is visible) or type** settings **in the search box.**

   The Settings app appears.

3. **Click Windows Update in the left navigation area of the Settings app. It appears at the very bottom of the list.**

   The Windows Update page opens, as shown in Figure 13-1.

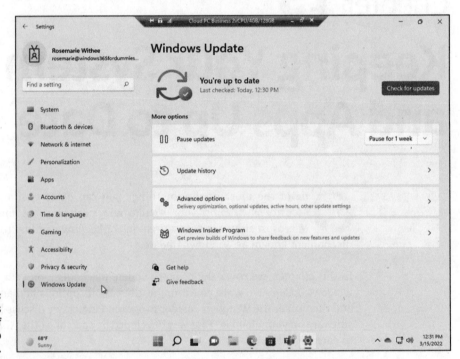

FIGURE 13-1:
The Windows Update area of the Settings app on a cloud PC.

TIP

You can open apps on your Windows 365 cloud PC in the same way you open apps on your physical computer running Windows. Just make sure you are working on your cloud PC so that the work you do happens where you expect.

Windows Update provides a status area at the top of the screen, and you can click the blue Check for Updates button to see whether any updates are available. Below the status area you find and the More Options area. In this area, you can configure how Windows Update works with your cloud PC. The options include the ability to pause updates, review update history, configure advanced options, and join the Windows Insider program.

Pausing updates might sound counterintuitive because you really want to make sure your cloud PC is always updated. However, you also don't want Windows Update hogging your system resources at the most inopportune time. We remember seeing a viral video of a live weather report where Windows stated it was performing updates. Perhaps the weather person should have paused the updates before going live on the air! You can pause updates from anywhere between 1 and 5 weeks. When the time has elapsed, the updates will continue again.

It can also be helpful to view the history of your system and see exactly what updates have been applied and when. When you click the option to view update history, you can see every update installed on the system along with the date it happened and a status of whether it was successful. We rarely look at this information; however, if you need to track down specific functionality regarding an update, you will find the information incredibly useful.

The next two items are for configuring advanced options and joining the Windows Insider program, and we cover them next.

Diving into Advanced Options

The advanced options page provides settings to fine tune the Windows Update process. Here you can configure settings to update all Microsoft software (not just Windows), set update notifications, and set active hours when you are working and might not want to be bothered with updates. In addition, there are options to configure optional updates, optimize how updates are delivered, setup recovery and restart options, and configure policies. *Policies* are a mechanism that can be set for an entire organization. For example, your organization can set a policy that every computer updates automatically. The Advanced Options screen is shown in Figure 13-2.

Keeping all Microsoft software updated

Windows Update keeps your Microsoft cloud PC operating system up to date by default. But what about the rest of the Microsoft software installed on your system? Windows Update can be configured to update all the Microsoft software on your system. The setting is a toggle switch located in the Advanced Options section of Windows Update. When you enable this option, the Windows Update checks your system to see what Microsoft software you have installed and then provides updates to it directly from Microsoft. The toggle is off by default; you can toggle it on by clicking it.

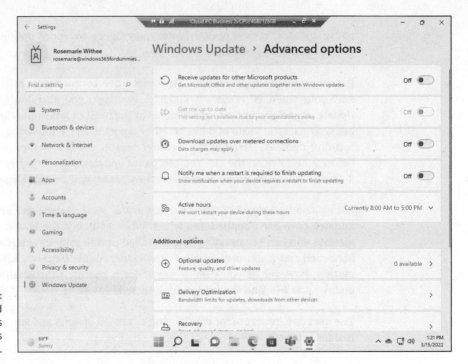

FIGURE 13-2:
The advanced
options settings
in Windows
Update.

TIP

We highly recommend using Windows Update to keep all the Microsoft software on your cloud PC system up to date. You can find the option in the Advanced Options section of Windows Update.

On the Advanced Options page, some options appear that aren't relevant for your cloud PC system. For example, the Keep Me Up to Date option is grayed out because it is not relevant to a cloud PC. Another example: the Download Updates over Metered Connections option — which isn't grayed-out —isn't relevant because your cloud PC lives in a Microsoft data center and is always connected to the Internet via an ultra-fast connection.

When Windows Update has downloaded and installed updates it often needs you to reboot your system before the updates take effect. You can toggle an option to receive a notification that will appear on your cloud PC screen when such a reboot is required.

We have all experienced a surprise reboot in the middle of our work. The way to avoid this is to let your cloud PC know when you are usually active on your computer. Your active hours are set to "automatically" by default, which means Windows learns from your behavior and sets the active hours for you automatically. During your 'active hours' Windows won't automatically reboot. You can also override the default and set these active hours manually.

TIP

We expect that Microsoft will start to tailor Windows 365 to the cloud-first world. All we must do is look back at Microsoft Office to get a glimpse into the future. Office became Office 365 and then Microsoft began building features specifically for the always on and always connected nature of the Internet. Eventually Office 365 became something barely recognizable as the traditional Office. The product morphed and adapted. Microsoft did this over time and continues to release new features. We cover this topic further in Chapter 1.

Taking a look at additional options

Many of the updates Microsoft sends to your cloud PC through Windows Update are very important and should be installed right away. However, there are also sometimes updates that are optional. Examples of optional updates include features that you might want to try, quality updates that might be helpful, and driver updates to help improve performance of devices. You can view and install optional updates by selecting the option as shown in Figure 13-3. The screen shows how many optional updates are available. In our case we like to keep all updates installed so we have 0 available.

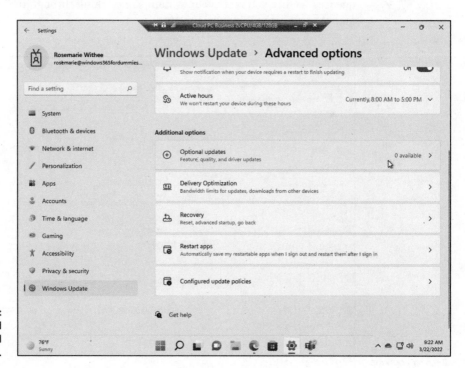

FIGURE 13-3:
Viewing and installing optional updates.

The delivery optimization section is one of those areas that is a holdover from Windows on a physical computer. The option allows you to set updates to download from other computers on your network or even other computers on the Internet, too. You can limit the amount of network bandwidth updates take so your network is not overwhelmed, and you can monitor the updates as they happen. In the case of your cloud PC, you get the updates directly from Microsoft data centers and your cloud PC is already on the Microsoft network. So we recommend sticking the default options.

Most everyone has experienced a time when their computer is not behaving, and they need to recover to a working system again. In the old days, if you wanted to start over with your computer, you would need to reinstall the operating system (or perhaps just throw in the towel and go buy a new one). The Recovery screen, shown in Figure 13-4, guides you in troubleshooting your system and if that doesn't work then in resetting back to a fresh state. If you decide to reset your system, it is like starting over from the beginning with your cloud PC. Be very careful before performing this option because it can have dramatic effects.

TIP

Resetting your system back to a brand-new state can have unintended consequences. Before you reset your system, try working through the troubleshooting guides provided in Windows Update.

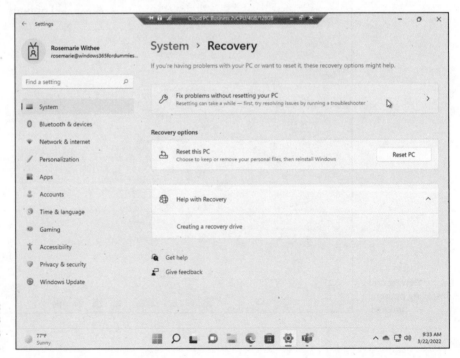

FIGURE 13-4:
Recovery options in Windows Update.

As with many things in Windows, many user interface navigation paths take you to the same task. Microsoft does this to try to make your life easier. For example, clicking the Restart Apps option, which you can see in Figure 13-3, in the Advanced Options section of Windows Update loads a screen in which you can configure sign-in options, as shown in Figure 13-5. Notice in Figure 13-5 that the navigation in the Settings app changed on the left side and it now says you are in the Accounts area. This is because the option in Windows Update was a link to the Accounts area of Settings where you can configure settings that relate to restarting apps. This jumping around can be confusing at first and can make for a maddening experience. On the other hand, when you get used to it, it can make the user interfaces in Windows feel more streamlined and connected. In this case, you can select the toggle to save the state of your apps when you restart your cloud PC and Windows 365 will automatically start the apps for you again when you sign back in.

WARNING

The Windows 365 user interface often has multiple ways to navigate to the same settings. This can easily turn into a confusing situation. Keep in mind that navigational items are often linked to other areas. For example, if you are in the Advanced options of the Windows Update section in Settings and click Restart Apps, then you are instantly transported to the Accounts area of Settings. When you realize what is going on, then the way things work begins to make sense. Make sure to keep an eye on the navigation to understand where you are in Windows 365 settings.

TIP

In the Settings app, you can click the "back" button (hint — it looks like an arrow pointing to the left) in the upper-left screen of the app to go back to the pages of the app you previously visited. This way you don't have to click through the navigation to try to find your way back to settings you were just looking at.

There are many settings that are controlled in a bulk fashion on your cloud PC. In large organizations many settings are usually controlled by your IT team and administrators. The settings are controlled through policies, and you can view the policies that relate to updates in the Configured Update Policy section. Several policies appear already configured for your cloud PC, as shown in Figure 13-6. Microsoft has configured these policies as part of Windows 365 and their duties in managing your cloud PC.

"Back" button

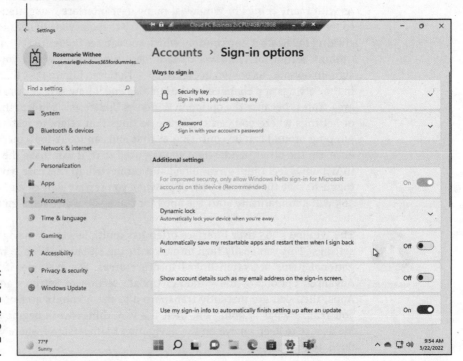

FIGURE 13-5:
Restart apps
option in
Windows Update
takes you to
Sign-in options in
Accounts.

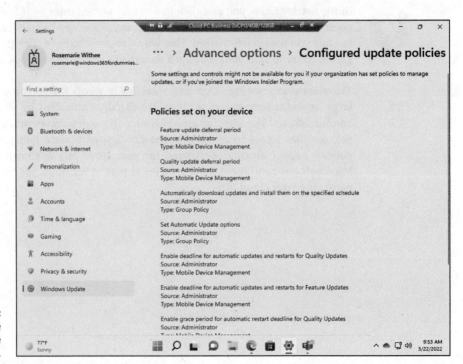

FIGURE 13-6:
Reviewing update
policies for the
cloud PC.

Understanding the Windows Insider Program

The Windows Update screen includes a section for joining the insider program. The Windows Insider Program gives you access to preview builds and provides a mechanism to share feedback on any new features and updates that are planning to be released. You can see the Windows Insider Program option in Windows Update in Figure 13-1. This option was used for Windows 10 and, at the time of this writing, is not currently available for Windows 365. In the future, we this will be a primary mechanism for Microsoft to gather feedback from Windows 365 users and make improvements and updates. Keep an eye on this area to see if it is available if you are interested in helping shape the future of Windows 365.

Until the insider program is available for Windows 365, you can still help the Microsoft team by turning on diagnostic updates as shown in Figure 13-7. When you turn on diagnostic updates, your cloud PC sends information back to Microsoft on how you are using your system. Microsoft then uses this data to make decisions on how they move the product forward.

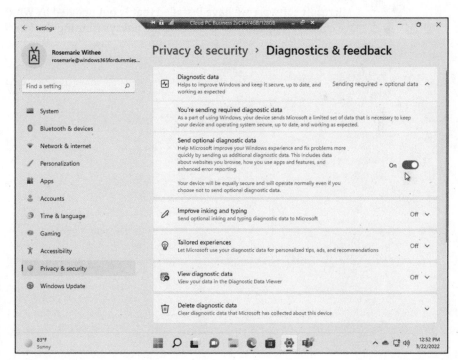

FIGURE 13-7: Turning on diagnostic updates to send data back to Microsoft.

TIP

You can turn on diagnostic updates to send data back to Microsoft so they can use it to help improve the Windows 365 product. Not everyone is comfortable, or willing, to send data to Microsoft and thus the option is disabled by default. In other words, you must opt into sending your optional data. You will find this option in the Privacy and Security section of the Settings application.

Keeping All Your Software Apps Updated

Software can be updated in many ways. Sometimes a pop-up appears when you open the app; other times, the app updates itself automatically. Keeping software up to date is critically important because updates include security fixes. When someone discovers a problem with software that can be abused, then a bad actor can use it to steal your data. This is often referred to as an exploit or vulnerability. Software companies fix these vulnerabilities and send the fixes to you through updates.

TIP

It is important to keep all your software up to date. Problems, such as security exploits and vulnerabilities, are fixed through updates. We catalog all the non-Microsoft software we have installed that is not updated by Windows Update, and we check it frequently to ensure we are always running the latest versions.

Chapter **14**

Staying Safe in a Virtual World

S ecurity has always been important but now it's more important than ever. In the old days, you had a form of physical protection because your computer was in your office. You had to go into a building to access your computer and get work done. Now, with everything in the cloud, everything is always accessible and available to you and from anywhere in the world. Unfortunately, this also means the same cloud PC is also available for someone to hack at any time and from anywhere in the world. For this reason, it is important to think about security as a top priority.

In this chapter, you learn about the credentials you use to access your cloud PC. You learn about Credential Manager and the Windows Security app that are preinstalled and ready to use. Next, you learn about the importance of having multiple steps to signing into your cloud PC. These multiple steps are called multifactor authentication and you learn how to set it up and start using it. Finally, you learn about other aspects of security such as encryption, physical security, and the difference between security on your physical device versus your cloud PC. This chapter also includes some security best practices you can follow to get a jump-start on staying safe in a cloud-based world.

Keeping Track of Your Account and Credentials

Your identity in Windows 365 comes from your Microsoft 365 account. In Chapter 1, we signed up for Microsoft 365 and created credentials (username and password) we use to sign into our Windows 365 computer. Microsoft often refers to this as your "work or school" account. This account is different from a personal account that you get when you sign up for a personal service. For example, you would get a personal account when you sign up for a new personal email address at outlook.com or Hotmail or when you sign up for Skype or Xbox.

TIP

Your Microsoft 365 account is already tied into your Windows 365 cloud PC. You don't have to set anything up. You just sign in with it.

Finding your account settings

Your account settings are located within the Settings app. We covered opening the Settings app in Chapter 13. As a reminder, you can click the Start button and type **settings** and then open the app. On the Settings app, Accounts appears in the left navigation, as shown in Figure 14-1.

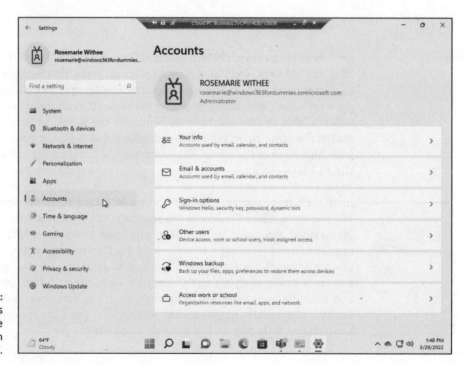

FIGURE 14-1:
The Accounts area of the Settings app on your cloud PC.

On the Accounts screen are settings related to the accounts and security on your cloud PC.

TIP

Some of the settings on your cloud PC are geared toward Windows on a physical computer and cannot be changed. We expect that in the future the settings throughout your cloud PC will shift toward a cloud first operating system and settings for physical devices will be removed.

Table 14-1 outlines the options on the Accounts settings screen:

TABLE 14-1 **Accounts Settings**

Option	Description
Your info	Change your photo icon and find related links and help info. We walk you through how to do this in a later section.
Email & accounts	Add and manage accounts used by email, calendars, contacts, and other apps. This area is where you manage all of these. We show you how to add an additional Microsoft 365 account in the next section.
Sign-in options	Set up a security key to add an additional security mechanism. The section below on security best practices outlines additional information about multi-factor authentication. You will also find additional sign-in settings such as using sign-in information to automatically finish setting things up after an update. Note you will also see options that are not relevant for a cloud PC.
Other users	Your Windows 365 computer is already pre-configured for your Microsoft 365 account. We are keeping an eye on the Windows 365 roadmap for the ability to add additional users to a cloud PC. For now, think of your cloud PC as locked to only your user.
Windows backup	Backup options are not relevant to your cloud PC because it is hosted and managed by Microsoft. These backup settings are geared toward physical devices whose loss means you lose everything. With your cloud PC, if can lose a physical device you can grab another one and reconnect to your cloud PC. Your cloud PC is always available in the cloud and not attached to any physical device.
Access work or school	Here you can see that your cloud PC is already preconfigured with your Microsoft 365 organization. We set this up from scratch in Chapter 1. Depending on your organization, this might have already been set up for you or you might have followed along in Chapter 1 and set it up yourself.

TIP

Because the account you use to sign into your cloud PC is your Microsoft 365 account, you won't need to adjust many settings. This is a good example of how Windows 365 has evolved. We saw the same thing with Office moving to Office 365. In the beginning we wondered whether Office 365 was just another name for Office. And then Microsoft put the development hammer down and the product quickly diverged from its legacy roots. Windows 365 is currently quite similar to

Windows 11. Soon, you can expect Microsoft to rapidly update the cloud PC operating system with cloud-first features and remove legacy features that only made sense when operating systems were for physical devices.

Adding an additional Microsoft 365 account to your cloud PC

Within the account settings on your cloud PC, you can add additional accounts. Microsoft refers to Microsoft 365 subscription accounts as "work or school accounts" and others as "Microsoft accounts." You can think of a "Microsoft account" as a personal account you get when you sign up for an email service like outlook.com, hotmail.com, or live.com. In Figure 14-2 you can see both account types. The "work or school" account is the account we created in Chapter 1 when we signed up for Microsoft 365 and Windows 365. The "Microsoft account" is one of our personal @outlook.com email addresses we have added to our cloud PC.

A common use case is that you are a member of multiple Microsoft 365 organizations, and you want to sign into various resources as those other accounts. You can add those credentials to your cloud PC.

To add a Microsoft 365 account to your cloud PC:

1. **Click the Start button and then type** settings **in the search box.**

The list of apps filters down and the Settings app becomes visible.

2. **Click Settings to open the app.**

The Settings app opens, and the settings options for your cloud PC appear.

3. **In the left navigation, click Accounts and then click Email & Accounts.**

4. **In the Add accounts section click Add a New Work or School Account.**

A sign-in screen opens, and you can enter your username and password for the new account as shown in Figure 14-3.

5. **Enter your username and password for the account.**

The credentials are validated and then the account is added to your cloud PC as shown in Figure 14-4. We find this incredibly useful as we bounce around between various SharePoint and Teams sites.

TIP

You remove a Microsoft 365 account in a different area of the Settings app than where you added it. To remove an account, go back to the Settings app, click Accounts, and this time click the Access Work or School button. Click the account you want to remove and then click Disconnect.

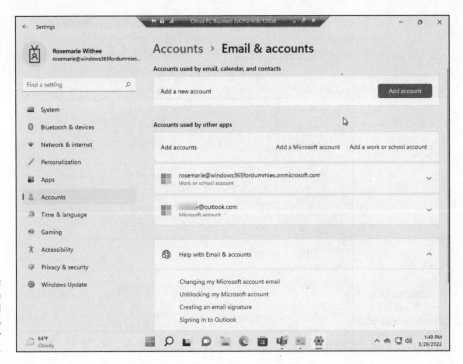

FIGURE 14-2:
Adding an
additional
Microsoft 365
account to your
cloud PC.

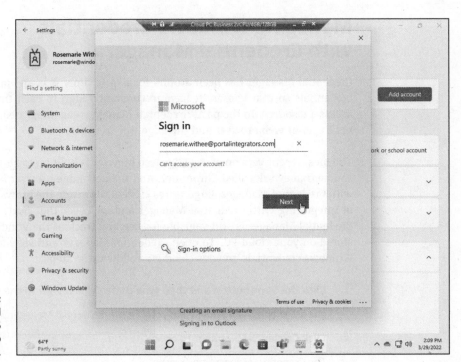

FIGURE 14-3:
An additional
Microsoft 365
account added to
our cloud PC.

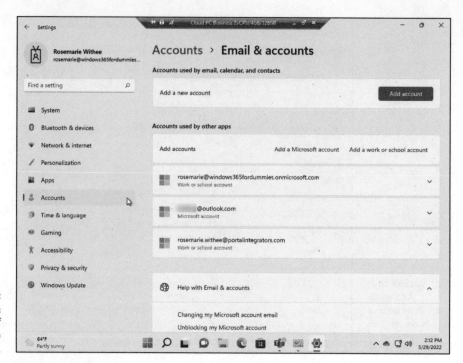

Managing Windows Credentials with Credential Manager

Credential Manager has been around for a long time. It is an app that can store credentials so that you don't have to constantly sign in each time you want to access a resource. In the past, Credential Manager was integrated with the Internet Explorer web browser and the Edge web browser.

The most recent version of the Edge web browser is built on top of Google's open-source framework called Chromium. And the new Edge browser is not integrated with Credential Manager. Edge stores credentials inside the browser itself instead of integrating with Credential Manager and we cover that next. With that said, Credential Manager is still valuable for keeping track of the Windows credentials stored on your cloud PC. To open Credential Manager and view and manage the Windows credentials on your cloud PC, follow these steps:

1. **Click the Start button and then type** credential manager **in the search box.**

   The list of apps filters down and you can see Credential Manager.

2. **Click Credential Manager to open the app.**

   The Credential Manager app opens.

3. **Click Windows Credentials to see credentials for resources on your cloud PC.**

   Credential Manager stores all types of credentials and not all of them are usernames and passwords. Credentials can also take the form of certificates. Certificates are similar to passwords but much, much longer. Think of a certificate credential as a long password that uses math and encryption to let you into a resource somewhere. Similar to how passwords work but geared toward computers to authenticate with each other instead of for humans to enter a username and password. The Windows Credentials on our cloud PC are shown in Figure 14-5.

4. **Click a credential to expand it and learn more about it.**

   You can see the details of a credential. You can edit it or remove it.

FIGURE 14-5: View credential information in Credential Manager.

Credentials in your web browser

There are many web browsers to choose from when browsing the web. Your Windows 365 cloud PC comes preinstalled with the Microsoft Edge web browser. You can install additional web browsers on your cloud PC, and we walk you through how to do that in Chapter 7.

Whichever web browser you use will store credentials for you so you don't have to repeatedly enter your sign-in credentials each time you visit the site.

TIP

It used to be very difficult on your cloud PC to change your default web browser. Microsoft recently made headlines by making the option as easy as a single click of the mouse. You can change your default web browser by going into the Settings app, selecting Apps, and then selecting Default Apps. Find the web browser you want to set as your default, click the button to display the app's screen, and then click the Set Default button on the 'Make <browser> your default browser'.

To view and edit the credentials in the Edge web browser on your cloud PC:

1. **Make sure you are on your cloud PC and open the Edge web browser app.**

   The web browser opens, and your default web pages appear.

2. **Click ellipsis in the upper right corner and then select Settings from the drop-down menu.**

   The Settings page loads.

3. **Click Passwords from the list of settings categories.**

   The Passwords page loads, as shown in Figure 14-6. You can choose how Edge will save your web passwords. By default, Edge is set to save your passwords automatically. You can change the option to require your cloud PC credentials to be entered first, to prompt for a custom primary password, or disable the option all together by toggling it off.

4. **Scroll down the page and view any saved passwords.**

   You can view and edit saved passwords. Edge also provides information about the password including the health of the password. The health of the password is a new feature that lets you see whether the password you use for a site has ever been hacked and leaked and the weakness or strength of the password. These are features that were previously only available in dedicated password managers.

Credentials on your physical device versus your cloud PC

We found that switching to a cloud PC is a giant paradigm shift, and it took us a long time to get our heads around it. When you are sitting at your physical computer, you might be working on your physical computer, or you might be working on your cloud PC. You are using the same physical keyboard and mouse and monitor regardless of where you are working. This can take some time to get used to, and we covered some tips we have found helpful in Chapter 5.

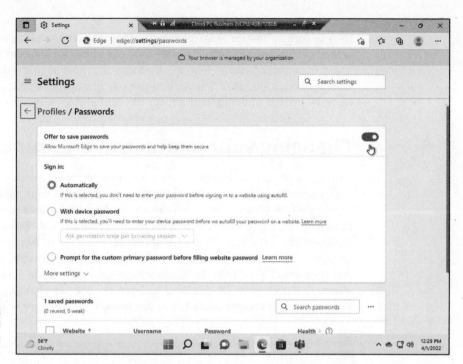

One area where the difference between your physical computer and cloud PC is particularly important is credentials. The credentials (username and password) you use to sign into your physical computer are different from those you use to sign into your cloud PC.

REMEMBER

It is important to keep in mind that the account you use to sign into your cloud PC is your Microsoft 365 account. We covered setting up your Microsoft 365 account in Chapter 1. You manage this account on the Microsoft 365 administration site, which is found at `https://admin.microsoft365.com`.

When you are working on your cloud PC, you sometimes also need to sign in to other computers, services, and websites. Your cloud PC can manage these accounts for you so that you don't have to sign in each time you need to access a resource. We covered ways you can manage credentials previously. Where we have found ourselves getting confused is when we float back and forth between working on our physical computer and our cloud PC. If you are working in a browser on your physical computer, then any credentials you save in the browser will be on your physical computer. If you move to a different physical computer, then your browser won't have those credentials. If you are using a browser on your cloud PC, then it doesn't matter what physical computer you are using because the web browser is installed on your cloud PC, and the physical computer is just acting as a way to connect to your cloud PC. To make the most of this paradigm shift, we embraced our cloud PC for work and use our physical devices to connect to our cloud PC instead of doing work on our physical devices directly.

Changing your photo icon on your cloud PC

As mentioned previously, most of your information for your main cloud PC account comes from Microsoft 365. One thing you can change is your photo icon. As with many things in Windows 365, you can access the screen where you do this in multiple ways. The fastest way is to click the Start button and then click the icon on the lower left of the Start Menu that shows your name. On the pop-up menu select Change Account Settings. Alternatively, open the Settings app, select Accounts, and then select Your Info. Both procedures take you to the Your Info screen as shown in Figure 14-7. On the Your Info screen, you can change your photo icon. You can take an instant selfie or you can browse for a picture to use.

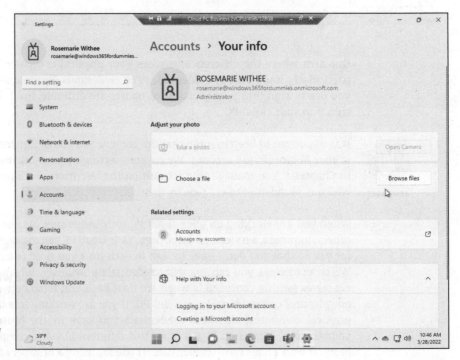

Using the Windows Security App

The Windows Security app is a one-stop shop for security issues on your cloud PC. The Windows Security app, shown in Figure 14-8, includes features for viruses and malware scanning, account protection, firewall and network protection, app and browser control, device security, device performance and health, family options, and protection history.

To open the Windows Security app and address any security issues, follow these steps:

1. **Click the Start button and then type** windows security **in the search box.**

2. **In the results, click the Windows Security app to open it.**

    The Windows Security app opens.

3. **The app opens to show a Security at a Glance screen and provides icons to show any potential problems. Scroll down through the cards and address any warnings.**

    Notice in Figure 14-8 that a warning is displayed on the App & Browser Control card. Turning on this feature lets your cloud PC protect you against apps and websites that have a bad reputation when it comes to security.

TIP

There are multiple ways to achieve the same goal in Windows 365. Another way to open the Windows Security app is through the Settings app: In the Settings app, select Privacy & Security in the left navigation and then view an overview of the security settings. On the overview page, click the Open Windows Security button. This opens the Windows Security app, which is exactly what you did by searching for it on the Start menu in this procedure.

Using the Windows Security app, you can scan your computer for viruses and malware. The app that does the scan is called Windows Defender. By default, these settings are configured to err on the side of caution. In other words, the settings protect your cloud PC in real-time. There are times though when we like to scan our cloud PC beyond the default settings. You can start a scan, or configure scan options, by clicking the "Virus & threat protection" card on the Windows Security app. From there you can start a quick scan, which scans the most likely places a virus would be found, or you can click Scan Options and perform a full scan or customize a scan to individual files or folders. Performing a scan using the quick scan button is shown in Figure 14-9.

TIP

The viruses and malware that your cloud PC is checked for comes from a list that is updated when you run Windows Update. It is one of the reasons we recommend keeping your cloud PC updated with the latest updates from Microsoft. We covered Windows Update in Chapter 13.

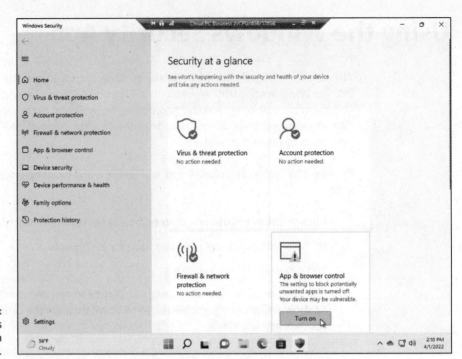

FIGURE 14-8:
The Windows
Security app on
your cloud PC.

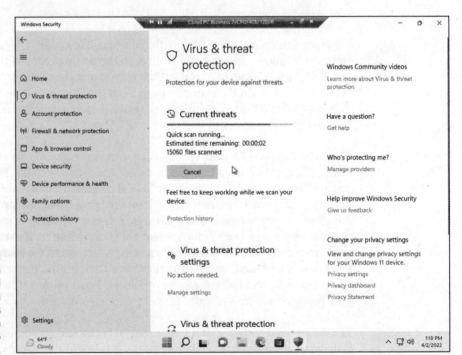

FIGURE 14-9:
Performing a
virus and
malware scan
using Windows
Defender on a
Windows 365
cloud PC.

There are many security options available and depending on your organization, these might already be configured for you. In general, we recommend making sure the Windows Security app doesn't warn about any problems and doing a full scan on your cloud PC regularly.

TIP

The Virus & Threat Protection area of the Windows Security app also includes a section to help protect against ransomware. Ransomware is a form of malware that encrypts your files and holds them for ransom until you pay to have them unencrypted.

Getting Familiar with Security Best Practices

There are some tried and true best practices when it comes to online security. We have outlined some of the most important here.

» **Keep your software updated.** All software has bugs and exploits that might provide attackers a way into your system. Some bugs are known, and others are not yet known. The best way to keep an attacker from exploiting a software application is by not installing it if you are not using it. The second-best way is to make sure you regularly update any software you download. One of the big value propositions with your cloud PC is that Microsoft keeps their software up to date and secure for you. Unfortunately, when it comes to software you install yourself from companies other than Microsoft, you are on your own. Each software application has its own way of staying up to date. When a new bug or security problem surfaces, software companies create updates to patch and fix the problem. Keeping your software up to date is critical in making sure you fix known problems. We covered updating your system in Chapter 13.

» **Use a password manager such as LastPass.** A password manager has several benefits including ensuring that every account has its own unique password and that every password is a long random string of characters. For example, it might be easy to remember your password if the password is the name of your dog, but it only takes minutes for a hacker to figure out the password, too. When you use a password manager the password field can be generated automatically and then filled in for you when you need to sign in.

» **Using multiple authentication factors.** Using multiple ways to identify yourself is a best practice. In the old days, you would only use your username and password to identify yourself. This is a single factor for proving you are you. Modern identity management systems use multiple factors for authentication. Windows 365 uses Microsoft 365 and Azure behind the scenes and multiple factors are available. For example, you might set up a second factor of authentication to text your mobile phone a code or get a code from an app on your mobile phone. After you set this up, you need to sign in using your username and password along with the code from your mobile phone. Using multiple factors like these to prove your identity is called *multi-factor authentication*.

>> **Keep your physical security in mind when you are in a public or accessible location.** For example, it might not be the best idea to leave your laptop with a stranger in a coffee shop while you are in the bathroom. At the same time, when you step away from your computer, make sure to lock it so somebody cannot sit down at the keyboard and pretend to be you. It only takes seconds for someone to lean over your physical computer, type in a URL to download malware, and then close the tab. In those few seconds, the bad actor can completely control your computer remotely. Game over.

Just like in real life, we can always be more conscious and observant of our safety and security. When you dive into the computer security industry, like we have, it is easy to become paranoid very quickly. Not everyone needs to be paranoid, but everyone can follow some basic best practices when it comes to both physical safety and computer safety.

Staying in Sync with Backups

If you are using a physical computer, then backups can be your best friend. The reason for this is because the files often reside on the hard drive on your physical computer. So, if you haven't backed up those files and lose or destroy your computer or experience a crash, then your files are gone. Windows on a physical computer still has backup mechanisms you can use, such as backing up to external drives, however Windows 365 is built for the cloud and doesn't have a need for physical drives. All your files live on your cloud PC, which Microsoft backs up for you. One area where you could still lose files is when you accidentally delete them. To avoid losing files, and to maintain multiple backups, you can use SharePoint and OneDrive.

The current version of Windows 365 uses Windows 11. We expect Windows 365 to start diverging from the Windows designed to run physical computers. We saw the same thing happen when Microsoft moved Office to the cloud with Office 365. Backing up files is a good example. For Windows on a physical computer, you might want to back up your files to an external drive. On your cloud PC there is no need. Your cloud PC, and files, are already backed up by Microsoft.

WARNING

Microsoft keeps your cloud PC, and files, safe and secure from hardware failures. If someone obtains your sign-in credentials and signs into your cloud PC as you, then they have full run of your computer. They could even delete important apps and files or reset your cloud PC entirely.

For backups on your cloud PC, we recommend using SharePoint and OneDrive. OneDrive is already installed by default on your cloud PC. We covered SharePoint and OneDrive in Chapter 11.

Advanced Security with Windows 365 Enterprise

We have primarily covered the Windows 365 Business offering throughout the book. In addition to this, Microsoft also offers Windows 365 Enterprise. The enterprise offering is designed for large organizations that have teams of IT experts managing a large amount of cloud PCs. We cover Windows 365 Enterprise further in Chapter 17.

One of the major value propositions of Windows 365 Enterprise revolves around security. If your organization has hundreds, thousands, or tens of thousands of cloud PCs, then managing them all requires scaled systems. Large enterprises already use these scaled systems for management and security. They include products like Microsoft Endpoint Manager, Conditional Access Policies in Azure Active Directory, and Microsoft Intune. Each of these areas deserves, and has, multiple books dedicated to them, so we won't try to cover them here. Just keep in mind that cloud PCs can be scaled to tens of thousands of computers just like physical computers in the largest of organizations.

» Checking out connection issues and how to resolve them

» Seeing how to reset your cloud PC

» Looking into crashes in apps and your system

Chapter **15**

Troubleshooting When Windows Won't Cooperate

Whenever you work with any new product it can take time to get things figured out. Perhaps your problems are with the way the product works or perhaps they're with the way you use the product. Windows 365 is no exception. Sometimes things just won't work out the way you expect them to, and frustration will set in.

In this chapter, we look at some of the main issues you will experience with your Windows 365 cloud PC and how to resolve them. First, we look at issues related to setting up your cloud PC and then dive into problems with connecting to it after it is set up. Finally, we look at some general issues you might experience with crashes and how to reset your cloud PC when you want to start over.

Working through Problems with the Setup Process

In Chapter 1 you learned how to get set up with Windows 365. The process can require some patience when things don't go smoothly. We remember when Office 365 was initially introduced and the pain and suffering we had to go through to sign up and use the product. Windows 365 is a much more streamlined experience than Office 365 was over a decade ago, but it is still a brand-new product.

When we signed up for Microsoft 365 in Chapter 1 and then added Windows 365 the process went smoothly. We didn't experience any issues. However, if you are adding Windows 365 to an existing Microsoft 365 subscription, then there are some things to watch out for.

Azure Active Directory limits adding new devices

Azure Active Directory is the backbone for managing users and devices in the Microsoft cloud. If you use Microsoft 365, then you are using Azure Active Directory. It sits behind the scenes, but you should know about it and how to access it to solve certain problems.

You may run into issues with the settings in your Azure Active Directory tenant. For example, Azure Active Directory has settings to restrict or limit users adding new devices to the tenant. A cloud PC is just another device in the eyes of Azure Active Directory; if your tenant won't allow you to add a device, then you won't be able to create your cloud PC. You can find these settings by signing into the Azure portal at https://portal.azure.com, selecting Azure Active Directory, and then selecting Devices, as shown in Figure 15-1.

Multifactor authentication causes problems

Another feature that can cause problems is multi-factor authentication. Multifactor authentication is critically important for security and yet Microsoft recommends turning it off to set up your cloud PC. We find this incredibly unfortunate and hope that soon Windows 365 will have features that support multifactor authentication. Azure Active Directory has a setting to require multi-factor authentication in order to add a new device. If this is turned on, then you won't be able to add your cloud PC because it is considered a device. These settings appear in the Azure portal along with the device settings mentioned in the previous section.

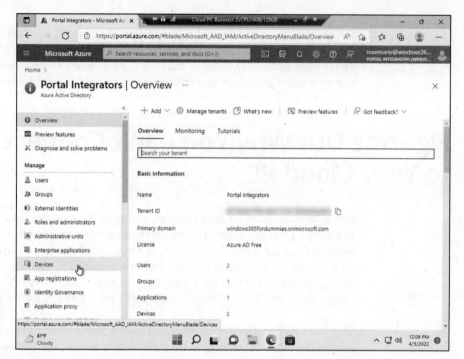

FIGURE 15-1:
Managing devices in your Azure Active Directory tenant.

TIP

Another area to check for problems is the Mobility section of Azure Active Directory. Microsoft recommends various paths to fix these problems depending on whether you want to use Microsoft Intune to manage your cloud PCs.

Troubleshooting the setup process for your Windows 365 cloud PCs is an ever-changing target. Microsoft continually fixes problems and adds new features that result in new problems. We have covered a couple of the top issues we have seen, and you can stay up to date with new guidance on troubleshooting on the Microsoft Docs website. The troubleshooting links are

>> **Business Subscriptions:** https://docs.microsoft.com/windows-365/business/troubleshoot-windows-365-business

>> **Enterprise Subscriptions:** https://docs.microsoft.com/windows-365/enterprise/troubleshooting

TIP

We see extremely smart people spending massive amounts of time trying to solve problems in the Microsoft ecosystem. When you use Windows 365 you are also using Microsoft 365. Microsoft 365 provides a mechanism for opening a *service request*, also known as a *support ticket*, for someone to help you through your problems. We recommend opening a support ticket if the issue you are experiencing is not obvious. The Microsoft support engineers are smart and helpful, and they spend their entire day in and day out solving issues. As a result, it is likely they have seen the exact problem you are experiencing before and know exactly how to handle it. Your time is incredibly valuable and to make the most of it we recommend opening a service ticket as soon as you run into a problem that isn't obvious to resolve.

Figuring Out Why You Can't Connect to Your Cloud PC

Before you can work on your cloud PC you must first connect to it. As we covered in Chapter 3 you can connect using a web browser or, preferably, the Windows 365 Remote Desktop client. To connect to your cloud PC, you must use a physical device and you must have a stable Internet connection. Although this process is straightforward, after you get things set up and in a groove, it can be frustrating when things don't work. When things don't work you can start with the basics.

The first thing to check is whether you have a stable Internet connection. It is not always obvious that a simple Internet connection is the problem as shown in Figure 15-2. When there is no Internet access, a message appears saying that you cannot connect to the service. Another error message that threw us for a loop is shown in Figure 15-3. The message is complaining about connecting to a specific server; however, the root cause was that our physical computer had its network cable unplugged. This reminds us of the time we spent an hour trying to get a scanner to work on our computer and finally realized it wasn't plugged in, had no power, and thus our computer couldn't add it. Sometimes it pays to start with the simplest things first and work toward the outliers.

You can check for Internet connectivity by browsing to well-known websites and checking Microsoft connectivity by browsing to a site such as `https://docs.microsoft.com`.

If your network connection is solid, then the next thing to check is whether the Windows 365 Remote Desktop client is installed and working correctly. Follow the steps in Chapter 2 to get setup if you haven't yet done it. In particular, you must subscribe to your cloud PC in the Remote Desktop client so that it knows how and where to connect.

If you are connecting using your web browser, then there are many more factors to consider. Every web browser handles things slightly different. One immediate step to try is to use a different browser. For example, if you are using the security-focused Brave web browser and things aren't working, then try using Edge or Chrome. We have also had problems with web browser add-ons that are designed to block trackers and ads. These add-ons can usually be configured to allow specific sites, and you might need to add the `https://windows365.microsoft.com` site to get things working.

FIGURE 15-2:
Windows 365
Remote
Desktop client
complaining it
cannot connect to
a service.

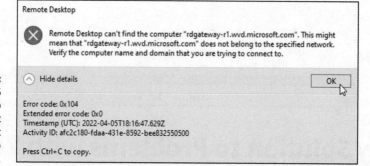

FIGURE 15-3:
Windows 365
Remote Desktop
client
complaining it
cannot connect to
a server.

TIP

Web browsers store information in what is known as a cache. The idea of a cache is that the browser can load information from the cache faster than it can over the network. Unfortunately, the cache can also create problems when you want fresh information instead of the information from the cache. Every web browser has a way to clear the cache. In addition, every browser also includes a way to open a window that ignores the cache. The window is called InPrivate in the Edge browser and Incognito in the Chrome browser. You can open one of these windows by clicking the ellipsis in the upper right corner of the browser.

If you can load your cloud PC and are presented with a sign-in prompt, then you are close to solving your problem. When you sign into your cloud PC you are using your Microsoft 365 credentials. We walked through how to set these up in Chapter 2. To check your Microsoft 365 credentials, you point your web browser to `https://admin.microsoft.com`. If you can't sign in and you are an administrator, then click the Can't Access Your Account? link, as shown in Figure 15-4. When you have your credentials working, you can use them to sign in to your cloud PC.

FIGURE 15-4:
Sign-in page for
Microsoft 365
with a link to
access account.

An Easy Solution to Problems with Your Physical Device

Your cloud PC is always on and always available. Of course, you need a physical device such as a desktop computer, laptop, tablet, or phone to connect to it and use it. If you experience a crash or problem with your physical device, then the fastest way to get back to work on your cloud PC is to simply switch to a different device.

We have done this multiple times and have even used old computers that we thought were long beyond their life. Because the old computer only acts as a gateway to the cloud PC, we didn't have a problem. The only limitation is to make sure the physical device meets the minimum requirements, and we cover those in Chapter 2.

TIP

A tablet or phone will work to connect to your cloud PC in a pinch, but we find we are most productive when we have a full keyboard, monitor, and mouse. The physical computer might be the most inexpensive thing you can find, and it still works great to get work done on your cloud PC. Assuming it meets the minimum requirements, of course.

Keeping Up to Date with Known Issues

As we mentioned, Windows 365 is a brand-new product, and it is bound to have problems. Some of these problems are known even if they are not yet fixed. We like to keep an eye on the known issues so that we don't go down the road of chasing a problem resolution when none exists. Microsoft maintains a "known issues" list on the documentation site. You can find it at the following locations:

>> **Business Subscriptions:** https://docs.microsoft.com/windows-365/business/known-issues

>> **Enterprise Subscriptions:** https://docs.microsoft.com/windows-365/enterprise/known-issues-enterprise

Recovering Deleted Files

Files, such as Word documents, Excel spreadsheets, PowerPoint presentations, OneNote notes, and countless others, are critical to storing information and getting things done. Microsoft keeps your cloud PC backed up and secure, however, there is nothing to stop you, or someone that uses your cloud PC, from accidentally deleting files. The good news is that there are multiple safeguards in place to help you recover deleted files.

If you are using a content management system, such as SharePoint and OneDrive then you have a powerful technology helping you keep things organized. When you delete a file from SharePoint you can view it in the recycle bin in SharePoint. We cover SharePoint in Chapter 11. And we love SharePoint so much we have written an entire book on the subject. If you want to dive deep on SharePoint, then check out *SharePoint For Dummies* (Wiley).

TIP

If you use Teams to store files, then you are using SharePoint behind the scenes. To view the files for a team you click on the team's name and then click on the Files tab. We cover Teams in Chapter 10.

TIP

In SharePoint, you can turn on versioning so that every time you save a file a new version is created. You can turn on major and minor versioning. We find this feature incredibly helpful when we want to look back over previous versions and see what has changed.

TIP

Using a physical computer to access and use a virtual computer can often lead to confusion when it comes to deleted files and recovering those files. For example, you might have a file on your virtual computer and then look for it on your physical computer. It might initially seem like the file was deleted or "disappeared" when in actuality it is just in another location.

Even if you don't use one of the powerful content management technologies we discussed previously, some features built into your cloud PC will help you recover deleted files. When you delete a file on your cloud PC, it is not really deleted right away. Instead, it is moved to the Recycle Bin. The Recycle Bin is a special folder that you can browse to see deleted files. By default, the Recycle Bin shows up as an icon on your desktop as shown in Figure 15-5. You can add or remove the Recycle Bin, and other icons, from your desktop.

TIP

To restore a file from the Recycle Bin, double-click the Recycle Bin icon on your desktop, and then right-click a file and select Restore.

To add or remove the Recycle Bin icon from your desktop:

1. **Click the Start button and then type** settings.

   The Start menu appears, and the options are filtered to show the Settings app.

2. **Click the Settings app to open it.**

3. **Select Personalization from the left navigation.**

   The personalization screen appears.

4. **Scroll down and select Themes.**

   The Themes options appear.

5. **Scroll down, click Desktop Icon Settings, and then select which icons you want to show on the desktop, as shown in Figure 15-6. Then click Apply.**

6. **Click Apply to save the settings.**

   The Recycle Bin icon now appears (or is hidden) on the desktop of your cloud PC.

Recycle Bin

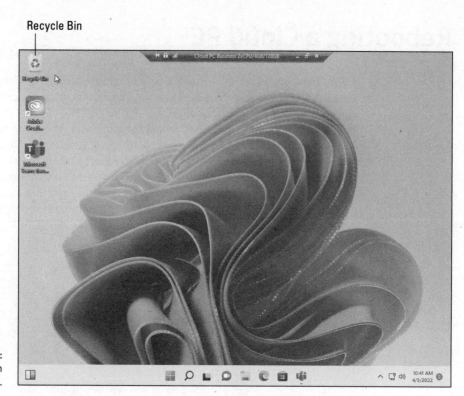

FIGURE 15-5:
The Recycle Bin
on a cloud PC.

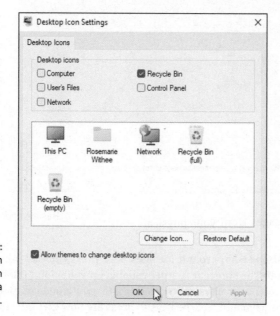

FIGURE 15-6:
Choosing which
icons to show on
the desktop of a
cloud PC.

Rebooting a Cloud PC

A Windows 365 cloud PC is always on and always available. However, it is still running Windows, and there comes a time when rebooting your virtual computer can be beneficial to problems you might be facing. The old joke in technical support is that step one is always to reboot the computer. The same adage holds true in the virtual world. If you are running into problems, try rebooting your cloud PC. You reboot your cloud PC by clicking the Start button and then selecting the power icon and choosing Restart as shown in Figure 15-7. Alternatively, you can restart your cloud PC from the administration page at `https://windows365. microsoft.com`. To reset the PC, sign in to the administration page, click the settings icon on the cloud PC, and then select Restart as shown in Figure 15-8.

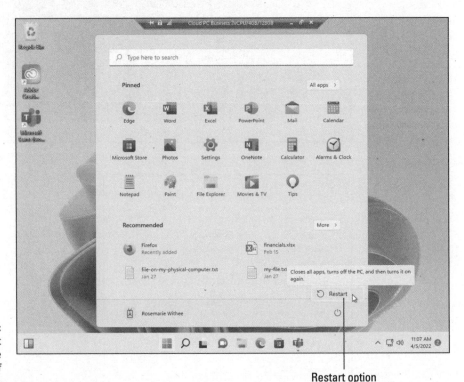

FIGURE 15-7:
The Restart option on the Start Menu of your cloud PC.

Restart option

TIP

A shortcut that has been around for ages is to press the Ctrl-Alt-Delete keys to bring up a menu. The shortcut is still available on your cloud PC; however, to differentiate between your physical computer and your cloud computer, you use the End key on your keyboard. So, the keys to press are now Ctrl-Alt-End and then the same menu you would see on a physical computer is shown on your cloud PC.

FIGURE 15-8:
The Restart option on the Windows 365 administration page.

Restart option

Finding Help within Your Cloud PC

Windows has had a shortcut to finding help information for ages. The shortcut is the F1 key on your keyboard. The result is a help window based on the app you are using when you press it or for Windows in general. For the most part, this shortcut still works on your cloud PC. Though in our experience Microsoft is moving away from this integrated help feature. We are still in the habit of pressing F1 on our keyboard though the result now is that a web browser opens to a help page. We have had better luck opening a web browser and searching Google for the problem we are experiencing.

TIP

Some keyboards have a function key you must press and hold before you press the key labeled F1 on your keyboard. In our case, the F1 key on our keyboard acts as the volume key by default. To trigger the F1 key, we must press and hold the function key, labeled *Fn*, and then press the F1 key.

As we have mentioned throughout the book, it is easy to get confused between your physical computer and your cloud PC. If you are entering a keyboard shortcut, like F1 for help, make sure you are working in your cloud PC and that the window is active. We have experienced times when we didn't have our cloud PC window at full screen and even though we could see our cloud PC on the screen the window wasn't active. So, when we pressed F1 for help, we were presented with help from our physical computer.

Crashing in the Cloud

Crashes are a fact of life when working with software. Applications crash, web sites crash, and entire operating systems crash. When working on your cloud PC you will experience the same types of crashes as you do on your physical computer.

When your physical device crashes you can restart it and reconnect to your cloud PC. If your physical device can't recover from the crash, then the easiest thing to do is just grab another device and use it to connect back to your cloud PC. Your cloud PC is always on and always available, and it doesn't matter what physical device you use to connect to it.

If one of your applications on your cloud PC crashes, then you can potentially lose data. It is important to keep in mind that your cloud PC is very similar to a physical computer in the way applications run on it. For example, if you are working in Notepad and Notepad crashes before you remember to save your file, then all your data in that Notepad document is likely gone.

Depending on the application you are using when the app crashes, there are some possible solutions. When you are using Office, a crash file is created so the next time you open the Office application you will receive a message that the app crashed recently and a message asking if you want to recover the crashed document. If you are using Office and saving your files to SharePoint and OneDrive, then your files will have the auto-save feature turned on. If you aren't using SharePoint and OneDrive, then you will need to remember to save the file every so often, so you don't lose it.

Keep in mind that the term *cloud* is just another way to talk about software running in a data center somewhere that you connect to over the Internet. If your Internet connection goes down, then the cloud is down for you. Your cloud PC is still running and waiting for you to connect, but without an Internet connection you won't be able to connect to it as shown in Figure 15-9. Therefore, a stable

Internet connection is critical in the modern world and especially when working on a cloud PC. We cover network requirements and recommendations in Chapter 16.

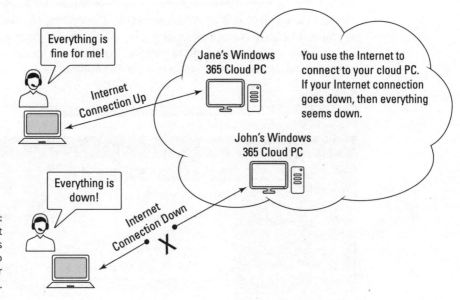

Microsoft has announced new Windows 365 features that allow you to work offline on your cloud PC and then sync the changes the next time you are connected to the Internet. We expect Windows 365 features like this to come fast and furious in the near future.

TIP

Resetting Your Cloud PC

We can't tell you how many times we have reinstalled the operating systems on our computers. The number must be in the hundreds. We have reinstalled everything from Windows, to Mac, to Linux, and just about everything in between. Reinstalling an operating system is an extreme option. Many people would say it is a nuclear option because going through with it means you have completely obliterated your old operating system.

You can lose data when you reset your cloud PC. Use extreme caution and make sure you are prepared by making sure all your files, data, and settings are backed up.

WARNING

Because your cloud PC is not a physical computer, there is nothing to reinstall. What you can do instead is reset your computer back to an initial state. The process to reset your cloud PC can be found on the Windows 365 administration page. Earlier in the chapter you saw the option to restart your cloud PC on the same administration page. Refer to Figure 15-8. Just below the Restart option is an option to Reset the cloud PC. When you select this option, you receive a warning, as shown in Figure 15-10. Performing this task reinstalls Windows on your cloud PC, removes your personal files, removes changes you made in settings, and removes your apps. Like we said, it is a nuclear option.

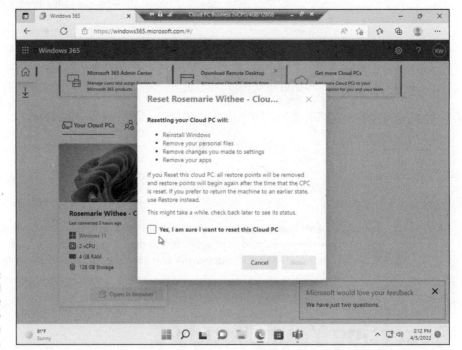

FIGURE 15-10: Resetting a cloud PC from the Windows 365 administration page.

Restoring Your Cloud PC to an Earlier State

A brand-new feature that is less destructive than resetting your cloud PC is *restoring*. The Restore option, which is still in preview, is like a time machine. It transports your cloud PC back (back to the future?) to a previous point in time, as shown in Figure 15-11. For example, let's say a week ago you installed the Firefox browser and then created two new Word documents. If you now restore your cloud PC to that point in time two weeks ago, all the changes you made in the last week vanish. It's like the last two weeks never existed. We love this feature because we can rewind the clock to a time before we thought it would be a good idea to start installing some wacky software on our cloud PC. Then *poof*, the crazy idea to install every browser known to civilization is erased and we are back to just the standard web browsers.

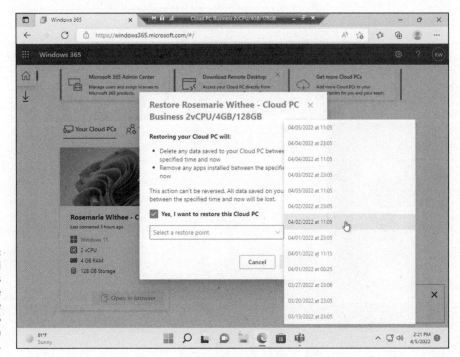

FIGURE 15-11:
Restoring a cloud
PC to a previous
point in time
from the
Windows 365
administration
page.

5

Implementation and Administration for Organizations

Chapter **16**

Getting Comfortable with Networking in a Cloud-First World

Your cloud PC is, well, in the cloud. Which means that in order to connect to it and use it you must use a network. In fact, you must use the mother of all networks, the Internet. Because the network is so critical to using a cloud PC, it is worth gaining knowledge about how networks work, or at least taking a refresher.

In this chapter, you learn about computer networks and how your cloud PC works with them. You learn how local computer networks work and how the network of networks, known as the Internet, works. You learn how your cloud PC can talk to things on your local network, like printers, and the Windows 365 Remote Desktop client is recommended. Finally, we take a look at how Microsoft networking works and how it is the home network of your cloud PC.

Getting Familiar with Computer Networks

Networks come in many shapes and sizes. For example, you might set up your home network by plugging in a cable modem and router and then wirelessly connecting your devices, your smart appliances, and so on. Similarly, a coffee shop might do the same and offer its wireless network to its customers to browse the web on their phones and maybe get some work done.

At the other end of networking you have large enterprise networks where computers and devices in entire office buildings are connected. Managing these networks is a career unto itself and one of your authors once worked a graveyard shift in a Network Operations Center (NOC) keeping an eye on massive networks before finally moving to become a full-fledged network engineer that could keep daylight hours.

TIP

At the end of the day the fundamentals of a network are the same regardless of the size of the network. A home network has more in common with a massive enterprise network than you might imagine.

Networking is all about sending messages

The complexity of modern computers can make many concepts opaque and difficult to understand. To make matters worse, buzzwords come along that are used in numerous ways and take on a life of their own, often detached from any technical reality.

To understand networks at the basic level let's take a look at sending messages. A fantastic book that we highly recommend is called *The Victorian Internet: The Remarkable Story of the Telegraph and the Nineteenth Century's On-line Pioneers* by Tom Standage (Bloomsbury). The book title says it all. The Victorian Internet. An Internet back before we even had computers! The telegram was, in essence, an Internet because it consisted of sending messages from place to place. In other words, there were groups, or networks, of telegraphers who would send messages and route them to their final destinations.

The modern Internet is really not that different. Instead of telegraphers tapping like mad sending electrical pulses down copper wires, we now have computers sending the electrical pulses. Computers are massive orders of magnitude faster than humans so the messages can be scaled to unimaginable levels. However, the fundamentals of the message passing are the same. The electrical signals move through copper wires at the speed of light.

Over the years, electrical signals in copper wire have been replaced with light signals on glass wires, known as fiber optic cable, but the fact that a message is being passed between two places has not changed. And many places, likely including your home network, still use good old electrical signals on copper wire instead of light pulses on glass fiber cable! For convenience's sake many messages are now passed wirelessly using radio signals. Again, the medium of passing the messages is different but the fundamental of passing messages is the same.

The most common mediums for passing messages between devices are as follows:

>> **Electrical signals sent through copper wires.** If you have any "Ethernet" cables around your house, then you are using copper wires.

>> **Light signals sent through glass fiber-optic cables.** If you are lucky and live in an area that has fiber, then congratulations! Most people in the world don't have access to fiber optic because it is expensive to put those glass cables in the ground. Even if you have fiber to your neighborhood, you likely have regular old copper wires running the last way into and around your home.

>> **Wireless signals sent using radio waves.** Just like listening to the radio, messages can be sent between two places wirelessly. This includes your cell phone and any wireless Internet connection you happen to use.

Making messages reliable

The beauty of the Internet is that it was created to be a reliable way to pass messages. So the way the messages are passed doesn't matter and when you send an email your message is likely passed in multiple ways. For example, when you hit Send on an email message from your laptop at a coffee shop in Seattle it might be passed wirelessly to an access point at the coffee shop. The access point at the coffee shop might then pass the message using electrical signals down a copper wire attached to a nearby phone company building. The phone company building might then pass the message using pulses of light down a fiber optic cable to your email provider on the other side of the world. The message might sit there waiting until the recipient opens their laptop at a coffee shop, let's say in Amsterdam, and then the same process might happen in reverse until the message arrives on their computer. Now scale this process billions and trillions of times, and you can get a picture of how the Internet works. Figure 16-1 shows the example.

If one of those wires happens to be dug up by an excavator or if an ocean liner drags their anchor and breaks one of the fiber cables in the ocean, then the messages are designed to find another route. In this way, the messages flying around the Internet are reliable because they can take many different routes to reach their destinations.

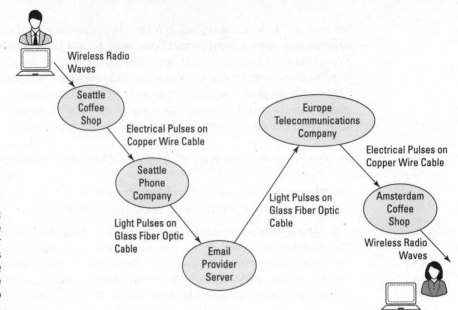

FIGURE 16-1:
A message passing over many mediums between a coffee shop in Seattle and a coffee shop in Amsterdam.

TIP

A computer network is nothing more than devices passing messages back and forth to each other. The way the messages are passed can be using electrical signals through copper wire, light pulses through glass fiber optic cable, wireless signals using radio waves, or even carrier pigeons. The only real difference is the speed and formatting of the messages. At the end of the day all are simply passing messages.

Sending and receiving messages to and from your cloud PC

We have used a simple example of sending an email message to someone on the other side of the world. So how does this relate to your cloud PC? The answer is because everything you do on the Internet, including connecting to your cloud PC, is nothing more complicated than sending messages. In the example in Figure 16-1 you could replace your friend in a coffee shop in Amsterdam with your cloud PC in a Microsoft data center in California. You are sending messages, lots, and lots of messages, between your laptop in the coffee shop in Seattle and your cloud PC in a Microsoft data center. The data center location doesn't matter very much but in our mind we like to think of a physical data center to get our mind around how this stuff works.

Of course, all of these messages happen behind the scenes and we don't need to spend much time thinking about them. Unless something doesn't work, and we can't send or receive messages. Then our cloud PC appears to be down. We cover some ways to troubleshoot connectivity to your cloud PC in Chapter 15.

From your point of view you just double-click your cloud PC in the Windows 365 Remote Desktop client and then start working. Behind the scenes a massive number of messages are flying over the networks to make things happen.

Creating a Local Network

Let's bring networking back from the big picture and into your home. If you buy a computer and then buy a printer, you want the two devices to be able to exchange messages so that you can print a document. The simplest way to connect the two devices would be to plug the printer directly into your computer. Now suppose you have a second laptop, and you also want to be able to print with it. You could unplug the printer from one laptop and into the other and pass messages that way. Or you could create a local network and connect each device to the local network so that they could all send messages to each other.

Younger people might not believe it but this is how computer networks were set up before the Internet. They were all local and devices on the network could send messages to other devices on the network but there was no concept of external networks. Not a ton has changed in terms of local networking with one big exception. The Internet is a network of networks and allows your local network to send messages to computers on other networks. That's it! And what a simple concept it is. And what a game changer, as we explore in the next section. This network of networks is called the Internet.

Peering into the Internet

When you buy Internet service through your phone company or cable company or some other provider you are really just buying a connection from your local network to their network. And they have agreements with other big companies to connect their network to their peer companies network, which are connected to other networks, and on and on. And through the magic of message routing, you are able to send messages from devices on your local network to other devices on other local networks on the other side of the world.

Remember the coffee shop example? Each coffee shop was its own local network and those local networks had connections to other networks and through the linking of all the networks a message can be sent. This network of networks is called the Internet. The big *I*. Or simply *the cloud*. Why the cloud? Because the network of networks is so complicated it would be nearly impossible to draw a diagram of how it connects. So to simplify things, we just say it is a cloud of networks.

Taking a Look at the Microsoft Network

Imagine you buy a bunch of computers, put them on shelves in your garage, and add them to your local network. What you have done is created a data center. A place where many computers are stored and all networked together. Many hobbyists and nerds, your authors included, have done this same thing multiple times over the years. Large companies, like Microsoft, do this, too, and on an entirely different level.

Open your favorite web browser and search engine and look for *Microsoft data centers* and browse through the pictures. The size of these behemoths is astounding. Your cloud PC lives in one of these places (with backups in other locations for redundancy), and you are connecting to it over the Internet.

Companies like Microsoft, Google, and others don't stop with just their data centers. They also put their own fiber optic cables in the ground and under the ocean to connect their data centers to each other. The end result is a massive network of data centers where Microsoft manages and maintains the infrastructure. Because your cloud PC lives within this network, it is very convenient for it to send messages to other cloud PCs and also to other Microsoft services like Teams, SharePoint, OneDrive, and Office 365, as we cover throughout the book. The communication is mind numbingly fast and the number of messages that can be sent is incomprehensible to mere mortals. From your cloud PC's point of view the world is scorchingly fast to things within the Microsoft network. Which leaves the connection your physical device uses to connect to the Microsoft network. Your network connection might go through many other networks before it gets to Microsoft's network, or it might be right next door. The speed you get from your network and any problems you experience with your cloud PC connection can be mostly narrowed down to this process of sending messages from your physical device to the Microsoft network.

Viewing Networking from Your Cloud PC Point of View

As described in the previous section, your cloud PC sits inside the Microsoft network in a data center. When you connect to your cloud PC, you are sending messages back and forth between your physical device and the cloud PC. Your cloud PC has a limited view of your local network and obtains this view based on the client you are using to connect (we cover connecting to your cloud PC in Chapter 3). For example, if your physical device knows about a printer on your local network then it can share this information with your cloud PC by sending it a message, as shown in Figure 16-2.

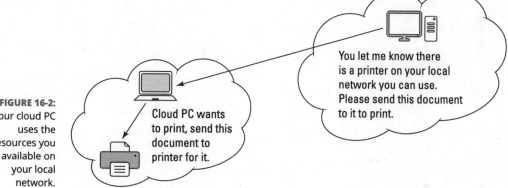

FIGURE 16-2:
Your cloud PC uses the resources you have available on your local network.

You let me know there is a printer on your local network you can use. Please send this document to it to print.

Cloud PC wants to print, send this document to printer for it.

If your cloud PC needs to print, then it can send a message to your device and your device can pass the message on to your printer. As you can see, your physical device acts as a central point of communication between the physical devices and peripherals on your local network and your cloud PC. We cover peripherals further in Chapter 7.

TIP

We recommend using the Windows 365 Remote Desktop client to connect to your cloud PC. The reason for this is that it is specifically designed to pass the messages back and forth between your physical computer and your cloud PC. You can use your web browser in a pinch but the web browser is a multi-purpose tool. Your web browser can do a lot of general things whereas the Remote Desktop client is designed with a single purpose, to connect to your cloud PC.

It can take some time to get your mind around this concept of a remote computer interacting with your local resources. The key to this understanding is to first understand how messages work in networks and then to understand that your Remote Desktop client acts as a message interpreter for your cloud PC. The result is that your cloud PC can send messages to your Remote Desktop client and it can pass along those messages on behalf of your cloud PC. With the end result being that your cloud PC can magically print to your local printer or use your Bluetooth headset or be controlled by your physical mouse and keyboard. All of this interaction happens by sending messages between your physical computer and your cloud PC and is controlled by your Remote Desktop client (or web browser if you happen to be using it to connect to your cloud PC).

Chapter **17**

Moving Forward into the Future of Windows

O ut of the gate, Microsoft has targeted Windows 365 squarely at large and small businesses and other organizations such as schools and non-profits. We expect that in the future you will also be able to sign up for a personal cloud PC that you can use for home. We can't wait because we still use a regular physical computer at home for most of our computing needs. What we like about using our cloud PC for business is that it is a clear separation between our work and personal lives. We have everything work related on our cloud PC and for home use mostly our phones, tablets, and a laptop computer. Whenever we sign into our cloud PC we are in "work mode" and everything on our cloud PC is geared to our work. If we could have a cloud PC for home use and a cloud PC for work use (separate cloud PCs), then we would be even happier.

Businesses and other organizations come in many shapes and sizes. Some are tiny and consist of only a solo person doing consulting work and others are hundreds of thousands of people located all around the globe. Setting up a plan for such a wide variety of implementations can be a challenge and so in this chapter we provide some general guidance for small and medium business and a few things to keep in mind for large organizations. We have spent over a decade working with organizations of all sizes implementing software and, in this chapter, we guide you on what we think you need to know to get up to speed with Windows 365.

In this chapter, you learn about implementing Windows 365 in your organization. We first look at the Scrum methodology and then see exactly how it can be used to get your organization up and using cloud PCs as quickly and efficiently as possible. Finally, the chapter closes with some tips for large enterprise organizations that need to manage PCs on a massive scale.

Deciding Whether Embracing a Cloud PC Strategy Is Right for Your Organization

A cloud PC is infinitely scalable in that you can use one for a business with just one person, and you can use them for everyone in a business with tens of thousands of people. Regardless of the size of your organization, you want to make sure the technology is right for your organization before you jump in because cloud PCs are powerful but not inexpensive. And you want to make sure you, and your organization, get the most out of this new technology.

The main question we like to ask people considering a cloud PC strategy is: Is everyone in the organization working in the office? If so, then perhaps it is better to stick with a local computer that your IT department already manages. On the other hand, if people in your organization are often remote and working from various locations, then a cloud PC might be the ticket. A cloud PC provides the centralized management and control that IT departments crave and at the same time offers the flexibility and convenience that makes modern workers so productive.

When you determine if moving to a cloud PC is the right choice, then the next step is to move your organization onto Windows 365.

Sprinting into Windows 365

We are big fans of the Scrum methodology in software development, and we think it can be used in just about every process. Scrum advocates a flexible path that accommodates shifting priorities. In essence, Scrum ensures that you and your organization are always focused on the most important thing instead of unimportant things that still might need to be done but are not as important. In our experience, every implementation or development process is filled with unknowns, dead ends, and other seemingly innocuous things that in hindsight end up being the most important. We haven't found a perfect system for implementing technology, but what we learned when we worked for Jeff Sutherland (one of the Scrum founders) is about as close to optimal as we have seen.

You can find the official Scrum Guide at: https://scrumguides.org and in this section we break down our tips and tricks on how to use Scrum to make the shift to Windows 365 and a cloud-based PC.

Determining your goals

At the heart of any project is the goal of achieving some particular outcome. In Scrum this is called the *project goal*. Let's set the project goal as follows:

Project goal: Everyone in the organization is up and running and doing their work on their Windows 365 cloud PC.

Of course, this goal requires the completion of some tasks, tasks that are captured in what Scrum calls a *product backlog*. The product backlog is a prioritized list of items (called *product backlog items* or PBI for short) that need to be accomplished. The list is prioritized with an order of the most important down to the least important including "nice to haves." Because some specific requirements are needed for Windows 365, we can capture those in our product backlog, as follows:

>> Obtain any approvals needed, including budgeting for subscription licenses.

>> Confirm that everyone has a physical device that they can use to connect to their cloud PC.

>> Confirm that everyone has an acceptable Internet connection for Windows 365.

>> Check whether the organization is already using Microsoft 365; if not, sign up for Microsoft 365 because it is required for Windows 365.

>> Obtain licenses for everyone that will have a cloud PC.

>> Create everyone's cloud PC and assign their license.

>> Log into cloud PCs and make sure they are fully updated and patched.

>> Change the look and feel to make environments less confusing.

>> Move files from local computers to cloud PCs.

>> Keep an eye out for new features.

Now that we have our product backlog, the next step is to start sprinting. If your organization is small enough, then we think you can get through the entire process in a one-week sprint. If your organization is large, then it might take several sprints and you might need to refine the product backlog further.

TIP

Product backlog refinement is the process of breaking large and ambiguous tasks into smaller and more manageable tasks. Every product backlog item (PBI) should have been written so that everyone can easily understand what it is and how to achieve the work it contains. Product backlog refinement also includes updating the order of the PBI to make sure that the most important work is always at the top of the list and being worked on as soon as the next sprint starts.

To start the sprint, you first need create a plan. Scrum calls this event *sprint planning*. During the sprint planning event you look through the Product Backlog and determine what you can complete during the weeklong sprint. The items you think you can complete you break off the product backlog and those become your sprint backlog. In our experience, Microsoft has made the process smooth in setting up and using Windows 365. We assume a small organization size and estimate that you should be able to get through the entire product backlog in a one-week sprint. In this case, the *sprint backlog* will be equal to the product backlog. If your organization is giant and the process to get budget approval is complicated, then you would need to break the first product backlog Item up further into smaller tasks that can be achieved and then bring those into the sprint backlog. In this way, Scrum is infinitely flexible and can be used for solo practitioners or massive multi-national organizations.

With the sprint backlog set, it is time to start sprinting!

Gathering any required approvals

The first task requires getting approvals and budgets and administrative bureaucracies out of the way. In the case of a small and nimble organization, this is just a matter of a few minutes discussion to determine whether using a cloud PC is worth it. In large organizations, well, each bureaucracy is different, and we leave that navigation up to you.

Confirming requirements for physical devices

The next task is to make sure that everyone using a cloud PC has a physical device that they can use to connect to, and use, their cloud PC. Because the physical device is essentially only acting as a gateway into the cloud PC, the requirements are minimal. Even a phone or tablet will work; however, we recommend a good keyboard, monitor, and mouse. We regularly use our MacBook Air at home or when traveling to connect to our cloud PC because we really like the form factor. Just about any computer will do, though, and we provide the specific requirements in Chapter 16.

Microsoft has released new features in Windows 11 that are specifically designed for working with Windows 365 cloud PCs. One of these features makes switching between the physical computer and the cloud PC as simple as switching between apps running on the same computer. Another feature, and one we are particularly excited about, is booting the physical computer directly into the connection to the cloud PC. The result is that the cloud PC feels just like a regular computer from the moment it is powered on. Of course, if the physical computer crashes, then there is no effect on the cloud PC, and another physical computer can be substituted in immediately. This feature is exciting because it showcases the power of the entire computer, a cloud PC, running in Microsoft's data center. Microsoft is responsible for the cloud PC infrastructure, and you are just responsible for paying for it and for your physical device you use to connect to it.

If you find that it takes more than one sprint to implement Windows 365 then make sure to do a *sprint retrospective* after each sprint so you and your organization can figure out what went right, what went wrong, and how to improve.

Checking everyone's Internet connectivity

We recently lost power in our apartment for several hours and quickly came to the realization that Internet connectivity has become about as important as the power grid these days. With a cloud PC, the most important requirement is a good Internet connection because you are using the Internet to connect to and work on your cloud PC. The good news is that the Internet is improving and, at least in downtown Seattle, is about as stable as our power company.

When visiting relatives in Montana we use to feel like we were "off the grid" (even though they are connected to the power grid) because the Internet was dismal. Even a picture in an email would not load. The area has recently adopted the new Starlink Internet from the SpaceX company and the bandwidth they get is twice what we get in Seattle and the speed (latency) is the same as our wired connection. We think Starlink is a game changer for the world. Imagine your dream location without any limitations on your Internet connection and work? An interesting future indeed!

Microsoft has some basic Internet bandwidth and speed requirements that we outline in Chapter 16. The requirements depend on how you are using your cloud PC with the primary factor being whether you plan to have online video meetings using Teams. In a nutshell, Microsoft recommends at the minimum 1.5 megabits per second (Mbps) bandwidth (both upload and download) for light loads and 15 Mbps for heavy loads.

When we recently checked our bandwidth on Starlink we were getting 150 to 200 Mbps, and at home in Seattle we generally clock 70 to 100 Mbps. We have never had any problem with our Seattle connection but wonder what our experience would be like down in the 1.5 Mbps that Microsoft recommends as a minimum.

We were once on a call using Teams and heard the person on the other end yelling at their teenager to stop streaming because they were having a call. If your bandwidth is high enough your whole family can utilize the Internet without bothering each other.

Checking the status of Microsoft 365 in your organization

In Chapter 1, we discussed how Microsoft transitioned Office into a cloud-based product with Office 365. That was over a decade ago and many organizations made the switch to Office 365 during that time. Recently, Microsoft rebranded Office 365 and started calling it Microsoft 365. Microsoft 365 includes some additional things beyond the traditional Office 365 products and some subscriptions are stilled referred to as Office 365. In short, you can think of Office 365 and Microsoft 365 as the same thing.

To sign up and use Windows 365, your organization must first have an Office 365/Microsoft 365 subscription. So, before you sign up, see whether your organization already has this subscription in place. If they do, then you can skip the whole process of setting up Office 365/Microsoft 365 and move straight into the Windows 365 cloud PC world. We covered signing up for Microsoft 365 and then signing up for Windows 365 in Chapter 2.

Figuring out licensing

Each Windows 365 license is tied to one user, which means no sharing unlike your Netflix account. Take note that you need a Microsoft 365 license to avail yourself of a Windows 365 license.

The big question you need to answer is between a Business subscription, shown in Figure 17-1, and an Enterprise subscription, shown in Figure 17-2. If your organization is big enough that they buy computers and distribute them through a corporate program, then you will likely need an Enterprise subscription. If, on the other hand, your organization buys computers directly from manufacturers like Dell or Lenovo or from your local Best Buy or other computer store, then the Business subscription will probably work just fine.

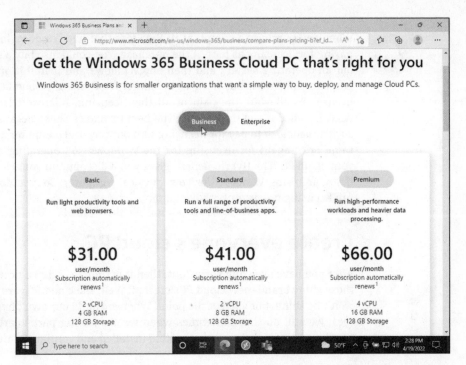

FIGURE 17-1:
The options when choosing a Windows 365 Business subscription.

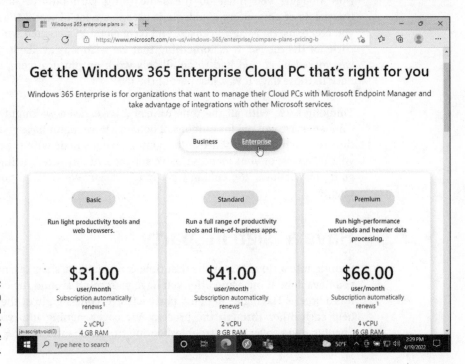

FIGURE 17-2:
The options when choosing a Windows 365 Enterprise subscription.

TIP

When you purchase a computer in the store that has Windows installed, you are paying for licensing as part of the purchase. You could also buy a computer without an operating system and then buy Windows and install it on the computer. Large organizations buy licenses in bulk. A Windows 365 cloud PC also requires a license. To alleviate the pain of all this licensing, Microsoft has implemented what is called a Hybrid Benefit. The benefit makes sense because it seems like such a roadblock to pay for licensing for your physical computer and then pay the same price again for licensing for the Windows 365 operating system running your cloud PC. The Hybrid Benefit gives you a discount on your cloud PC licensing if you are using Windows for your physical computer. So, you don't have to pay full licensing prices for both computers.

Create everyone's cloud PC

After you have licensing sorted out, then it is time to assign a license and have all those shiny brand-new cloud PCs created. Well, the cloud PCs are virtual, so they won't be shiny, but you get the point. When we build our own physical computers (yes, we still do that sometimes when we are feeling particularly geeky) it can take hours to get the operating system installed and configured and things set up.

Now imagine you must do the same thing with tens or hundreds or even thousands of computers. Suddenly it becomes a lot of work! With Windows 365 you create users, assign licenses, and have cloud PCs created with literally a few clicks of the mouse. It is something that we wish was available years ago when we worked in IT and had to do all this work on physical computers manually. Back in those days it was just part of the job.

Thinking back, with all the time we could have saved we might have saved the companies we worked for millions of dollars. Or we might have just used the saved time to watch more cat videos. The point is, what you do with the time you save is your business, or your manager's, we suppose. At any rate, getting the cloud PC's going in Windows 365 couldn't get much easier. We covered how to do this in Chapter 2.

Have a "sign in" party

Signing into a cloud PC for the first time can feel like a steep learning curve. After you have done it once and after you have your mind around the concepts — then it is a breeze. Having a "sign in" party lets everyone sign in at the same time and help each other through the process. We cover signing into your cloud PC in Chapter 3 and cover some troubleshooting tips in Chapter 15.

Luckily, there isn't a lot of required training, and everyone can jump on a video and screen sharing call using Teams, Skype, Zoom, or whatever they choose to use, and talk through the process in real-time.

Change the look and feel to make environments less confusing

If your team has used Windows before, then they will feel right at home on their new Windows 365 cloud PC. The main thing to get across is that the cloud PC is running in the cloud, and you use a physical computer to connect to it.

The number one speedbump we see with people adopting a cloud PC is getting confused between which PC they are working on, their physical computer or their cloud PC. We have even made this mistake ourselves! And we came up with some tips and tricks to make the distinction clear. We covered these in the look and feel section in Chapter 6.

Move everyone into their new cloud PC

After everyone has signed in and is familiar with their cloud PC then the next step is moving files and installing any required apps. Moving files is relatively easy when you use the Windows 365 Remote Desktop client. The drives on the local computer show up as drives on the cloud PC and you can drag and drop files between the two. We cover how to do this in Chapter 9.

TIP

We highly recommend using a content management system for your files and other content. The content system we prefer is called SharePoint and it is likely already part of your Microsoft 365 subscription. We cover SharePoint in further detail in Chapter 11 and we go even deeper in an entire book we wrote called *SharePoint For Dummies*.

Keeping an eye on new features

It can take some time to get used to a PC that is in the cloud and that is always available from any device you want to use to connect to it. When you get into a rhythm and get your head around it then it is hard to ever think of using a regular old physical computer again. Gone are the days when you must "run into the office to do something" because it is only available on your work computer. Your work computer becomes virtual, and you can connect to it from anywhere.

Now that everyone is up to speed and using their cloud PCs the only thing left is to keep an eye on new features that Microsoft is releasing. Microsoft seems to be on a breakneck pace adding new features to Windows 365. We recently even saw announcements from Satya about future plans, and were really excited by what is coming.

To keep an eye on new features, be sure to follow https://docs.microsoft.com/windows-365/business/whats-new for features that are released for the Business offering and https://docs.microsoft.com/windows-365/enterprise/whats-new for features for the Enterprise plan.

TIP

All organizations are different and if a one-week, one-sprint implementation is not feasible, then you will need to break up the steps further in a way that matches your organization. Review the Scrum Guide we mentioned earlier and focus on the most important pieces first. Continue to iterate until everyone is on board with using their cloud PC for work, forget about any overhead related to your computing environment, and focus on things that matter to your organization.

Some Tips for Enterprises

Information technology (IT) in large enterprises is a career and specialty unto itself. We are always impressed with corporate IT departments and how they must juggle and manage so many disparate tasks. If you are one of these people, then we commend you!

Managing large numbers of computers in an organization is a thankless job but we offer up some tips to consider when it comes to Windows 365. In a nutshell, everything you do with onsite computers can be done with cloud PC computers. The key is that you need to make sure you use the Enterprise license. With the Enterprise license in place, you can use tools such as Microsoft Endpoint Manager to keep a handle on all the cloud PCs in your organization.

TIP

If you have an existing endpoint management and infrastructure, determine whether Windows 365 will be included in it.

TIP

Windows Intune is now called Endpoint Manager. It is a tool used to manage lots of PCs in bulk. The people that manage your organization's PCs can also use it to manage cloud PCs. To do that you need to have an Enterprise subscription, though.

Chapter **18**

Unleashing Your Inner Administrator

S ome aspects of being an IT administrator can require specialized degrees, years of experience, and constant training. Large enterprise organizations need to administer massive amounts of resources and specializing becomes a requirement due to the sheer number of tools and technologies used. This level of expertise is still required for large enterprises but for small and medium organizations the administrative duties have become much simpler. Microsoft has done a reasonable job of making administration of their online services intuitive and understandable. Some things can still be confusing, but overall, we give the experience a thumbs up.

In this chapter, you learn about administration for Windows 365 and all the associated Microsoft services you need to administer, too. We start with a general overview of the administrative landscape for Windows 365. We then go into specific aspects including administration for Windows 365, Microsoft 365, Azure, SharePoint, and Teams. Finally, we walk through some ways to get help when you need it and provide help to others in your organization, too.

Getting a Handle on Cloud PC Management

You need to be aware of multiple administration websites when managing your cloud PC and the cloud PCs of your organization. The main reason for this is that Windows 365 is intimately tied in with Office 365/Microsoft 365 services and all Microsoft products are intimately tied in with Azure services. In addition, various services have their own administration websites, too! The good news is that Microsoft has tried to provide links between the various websites to make your life in finding them easier. In other words, you don't have to memorize the web addresses for each admin site.

Finding and exploring the Windows 365 administration center

The Windows 365 administration center is where you can remotely manage your organization's cloud PCs. Think of this administrator site as providing you with the ability to reach into all the cloud PCs in your organization and perform some actions on them. For example, you can change the user account on a cloud PC from a standard user to an administrator or vice versa. You can also rename the cloud PC, restart it, and even reset it back to an initial state, which is similar to reinstalling the operating system. We covered the Windows 365 administration dashboard further in Chapter 3.

You can find the Windows 365 administration website by opening your web browser and enter the address `https://windows365.microsoft.com`. Make sure you are signed in with your Microsoft 365 credentials. The Windows 365 administration site is shown in Figure 18-1.

To administer Windows 365 cloud PCs for your organization you must have permissions to do so. The permissions required can be set in multiple admin locations. For example, you can set the permissions in the Windows 365 admin center, the Microsoft 365 admin center, and in the Azure administration site on the Azure Active Directory user settings page. The permissions you need are in the form of a role. A *role* is a concept that allows permissions to perform various actions throughout the Microsoft services. To manage cloud PCs you need either the Windows 365 Administrator role or the all-powerful Global Administrator role.

TIP

If you are the one that originally signed up for your Microsoft 365 subscription, which we outlined in Chapter 2, then you have the Global Administrator role by default. You can also assign roles to other users. If someone else signed your organization up, they need to assign one of the roles to your user before you can be an administrator.

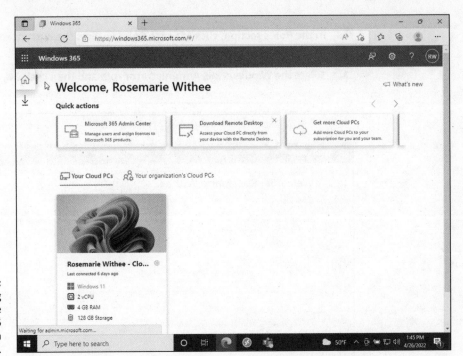

FIGURE 18-1:
The main landing
page of the
Windows 365
administration
site.

To give someone the Window 365 Administrator role so that they can administer cloud PCs in your organization:

1. **Open your favorite web browser and go to** `https://windows365.microsoft.com`.

The main landing page appears, as shown in Figure 18-1.

2. **Click the tab to view your organization's cloud PCs, as shown in Figure 18-2.**

The page to manage the cloud PCs in your organization loads. On this page you can add users, reset passwords, and update your organizations settings.

3. **Click the name of the person who you want to give the Windows 365 Administrator role.**

A dialog appears on the right side of the page as shown in Figure 18-3.

TIP

You can also block and unblock a user on this screen. If you suspect a user has had their password compromised or if you need to deactivate a person from signing in, you can block their sign-ins to the cloud PC. If the user is currently signed in, they will be signed out and won't be able to sign in again.

4. In the Roles section, click Manage Roles to view the current roles for the user.

5. Select the Windows 365 Administrator role and then click OK.

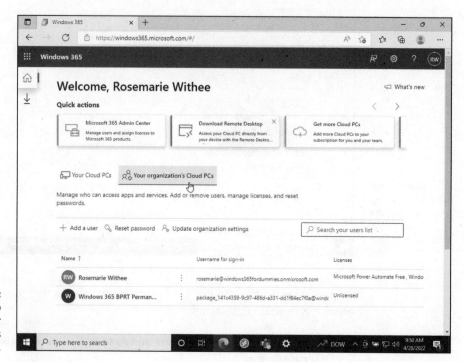

FIGURE 18-2:
Selecting the tab
to manage your
organization's
cloud PCs.

Within the cloud PC a user can be a standard user or an administrator. By default, a user is a standard user in their cloud PC. If they need to install software other than from the Microsoft store and do other administration, then you can change the type of user account on the cloud PC to an administrator.

REMEMBER

We recommend staying with the standard user type as much as possible. This reduces security concerns because only software that has been validated and vetted through the Microsoft store can be installed. Many organizations follow a best-practice policy that every user must be a standard user and any software installed beyond the Microsoft store must be checked by an IT department to reduce the risk of malware.

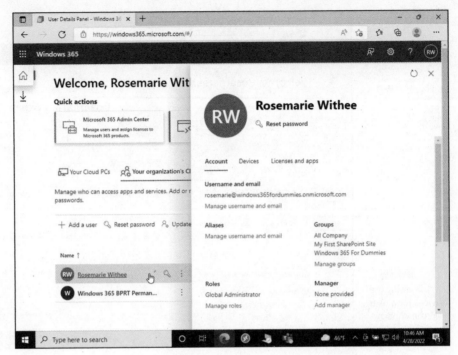

FIGURE 18-3:
Dialog for a specific cloud PC user.

To change the account type of a user on their cloud PC:

1. **Open your favorite web browser and go to** `https://windows365.microsoft.com`.

   The main landing page appears, as shown in Figure 18-1.

2. **Click the tab to view your organization's cloud PCs as shown in Figure 18-2.**

3. **Click the name of the person whose account type you want to change for their cloud PC.**

   A dialog appears on the right side of the page, as shown in Figure 18-3.

4. **Click on the Devices tab and then click Change Account Type, as shown in Figure 18-4.**

5. **Select either Standard user (recommended) or Local Administrator account and then click Confirm.**

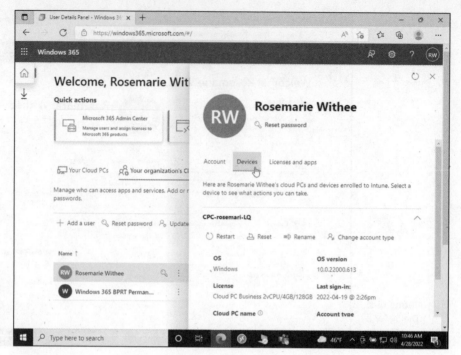

FIGURE 18-4:
Viewing the
devices for a user
in the Windows
365 admin
center.

Taking a look at the Microsoft 365 administration center

As discussed in Chapter 1, Microsoft launched Office 365 as a cloud first version of the traditional Office software. A cloud version of anything needs a place to manage it and the Office 365 admin center was born. Since then, Microsoft has rebranded parts of Office 365 to Microsoft 365. And the admin center has gone through, and continues to go through, many iterations and changes. You can find the latest version of the Microsoft 365 admin center at `https://admin. microsoft.com`.

Microsoft 365 and Windows 365 are closely tied together. The credentials you use to sign into your Windows 365 cloud PC come directly from the user you set up in Microsoft 365. The Microsoft 365 admin center is shown in Figure 18-5.

One of the main things you use the Microsoft 365 admin center for is managing users and subscriptions. You can add new users to your subscription and then purchase and assign them licenses, such as a Windows 365 license or license for the Office apps.

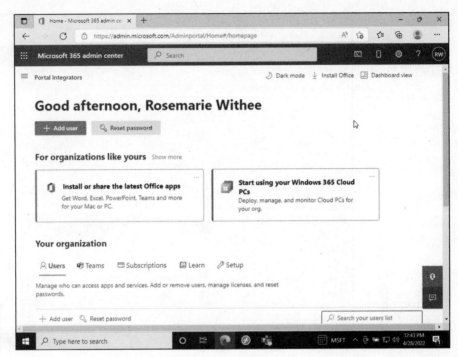

FIGURE 18-5:
The Microsoft 365 administration center.

TIP

We covered using the Microsoft 365 admin center to sign up for a Microsoft 365 subscription and then a Windows 365 subscription in Chapter 2. To add additional user and additional cloud PCs you must be an administrator for your organization.

Digging into the heart of Microsoft services with Azure administration

Azure is at the center of all Microsoft products and services. Azure provides a computing platform that companies can build on and Microsoft uses the same platform to build products like Office 365 and Windows 365. You might never need to sign into the Azure administration site but you should know that it exists and that it is where you administer all things related to Azure. You can find the site at `https://portal.azure.com` and you use your Microsoft 365 credentials to sign in. The identity portion of Azure is where users and roles are managed, and you can find that by clicking on Azure Active Directory in the left navigation.

The Azure administration portal is shown in Figure 18-6.

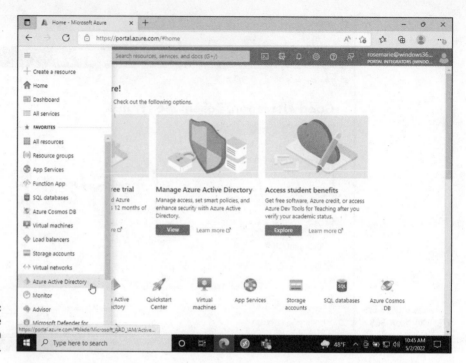

FIGURE 18-6:
The Azure
administration
center.

Discovering administration centers for SharePoint and Teams

Some of the Microsoft services have their own administration centers. In Chapter 10 we discussed Microsoft Teams. This service has its own administration center you use to configure Teams settings for your organization. In Chapter 11 we talked about SharePoint. SharePoint is a content management system, and it also has its own administration center.

You find these service specific administration centers using links in the main Microsoft 365 administration center. Expand the left navigation in the Microsoft 365 administration center using the Show All option. Then scroll down to the Admin Centers section to view links to the service specific admin centers, as shown in Figure 18-7.

In the Teams admin site, you can manage teams, users, devices, apps, and many other things. Think of the Teams admin center as the "backend" of Microsoft Teams for your organization. Likewise, in the SharePoint admin center you manage sites, policies, settings, content services, and many other settings. Again, you can think of the SharePoint admin center as the "backend" of the SharePoint product for your organization.

The Teams admin center is shown in Figure 18-8 and the SharePoint admin center is shown in Figure 18-9.

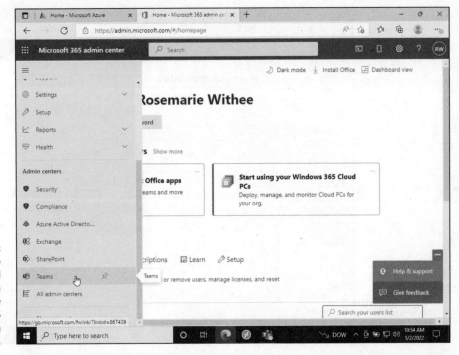

FIGURE 18-7:
Finding links to
the Teams and
SharePoint admin
centers from the
Microsoft 365
administration
center.

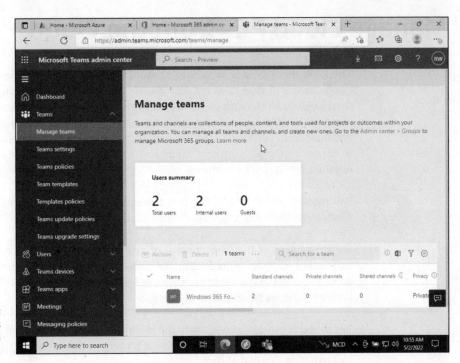

FIGURE 18-8:
The Teams
administration
center.

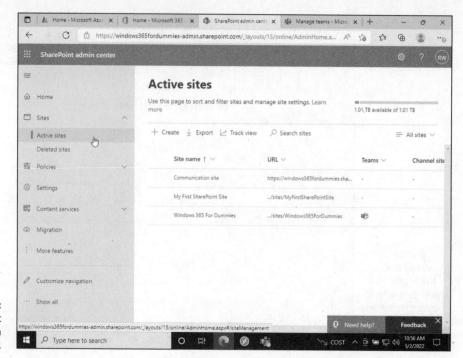

Manage Cloud PCs from the Cloud

The good news is that all administration happens through websites and all you really need is a web browser. We like to think that the operating system is the final holdout in moving to the cloud. When the operating system, which is your cloud PC, is in the cloud you don't have to worry about your physical computer anymore. Your physical computer is simply a means to connect and get work done. In other words, all administration and management for the cloud PCs in your organization happens in the cloud.

TIP

You manage cloud PCs in the cloud using the administrative websites for Windows 365, Microsoft 365, Azure, Teams, and SharePoint.

We are amazed at the development of new technologies and look forward to virtual reality and augmented reality devices that we can use to connect to our Windows 365 cloud PC. We also hope we live long enough to see direct brain interfaces such as the ones Neuralink is building.

The world is quickly moving into the realm of science fiction, and it can't get here soon enough for us. Though it can be a bit scary to think about, it is exciting and awe-inspiring nonetheless!

Getting Help from Microsoft

With any new product it is common to run into issues and unforeseen problems. When you get stuck with something, you can open a support ticket with Microsoft and someone will contact you to get you moving. You open a support ticket in the Microsoft 365 portal. To open a support ticket, expand the Support option in the left navigation and then click New Service Request, as shown in Figure 18-10.

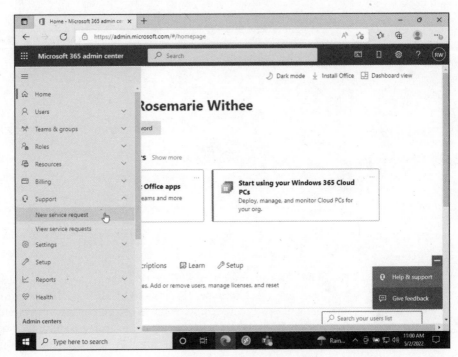

FIGURE 18-10:
Opening a new support ticket in the Microsoft 365 portal.

Keeping Windows 365 Business and Enterprise Plans in Mind

When your organization adopts Windows 365, one of the big choices is between signing up for the Business plan or the Enterprise plan. We discussed these plans in Chapter 17 and in Chapter 2. If your organization needs to scale up the management of cloud PCs, meaning you have a lot of people who need a cloud PC, then you will likely want to go with the Enterprise plan.

TIP

The Enterprise plan lets you take advantage of tools designed for managing a massive number of PCs. In particular, the tool you use is called Microsoft *Endpoint Manager*.

TIP

Managing cloud PCs using Microsoft Endpoint Manager is beyond the scope of this book, and for now you should just know that it is available when you need it.

6

The Part of Tens

IN THIS PART . . .

Discover how Windows 365 is the future of Windows

See where Windows is heading and what you need
to know

Convince your boss to adopt Windows 365 to make your
life easier and more productive

Chapter **19**

Ten Reasons Windows 365 Is the Future OS

As you learned throughout the book; Windows 365 is the future of Windows. Microsoft did the same thing with Office over a decade ago and now Office 365 (now called Microsoft 365) is one of Microsoft's most popular products.

In this chapter, we take a look at the top ten reasons that Windows 365 is the future operating system for Microsoft. You learn how to prepare for the Windows of the future and how to embrace the changes that are rapidly evolving the most popular operating system for PCs, ever.

Microsoft Is Committed to a Cloud-First World

Over the last decade, Microsoft has repositioned their products to a cloud-first strategy. The reason for this is fairly simple. The world has moved from an unconnected state to a connected state. The rapid advance of the Internet of Things (IoT) means that just about every device uses an Internet connection to provide value. We like to think of the paradigm shift as a wave of connectivity. We remember 20 years ago we were so amazed when we could use our laptop and not be plugged into a physical network connection. Then we were amazed again when our phones become "smart" and we started to use them for everything from communication to checking the weather to finding a ride and booking a hotel room.

We use our phones for just about everything now, and we just assume we have Internet connection. We often wonder what would be worse in the modern age — taking away our phone or taking away our power. We can always recharge our cell phones using off-the-shelf solar systems, but we would be hard-pressed to find much use in our modern smartphones should the Internet go down.

Microsoft has strategically positioned its products to excel (is there a pun there?) in a hyper-connected world. Windows has been slowly adding features for decades that leverage the Internet and Windows 365 is the final big leap to move the operating system to a cloud-first strategy.

The Same Thing Happened with Office

As we have described throughout the book, Microsoft started the cloud-first strategy over a decade ago with Office. It used to be that you would buy Office and install it on your local computer. Microsoft realized early on that cloud-connected software was the future, and they began transitioning their Office products to the cloud and dubbed them Office 365.

TIP

The 365 after a product name is a recurring theme in Microsoft cloud-first products. The 365 refers to the fact that your software can get updates any day of the year and because there are 365 days in a year . . . well, you get the point.

To peer into the future of what Microsoft is planning for Windows, we can just take a look back at what they did with Office when they transitioned it to Office 365. At first, the applications in Office, such as Word, Excel, and PowerPoint, were not really that much different from the same products that were bundled in the traditional old Office software package. Over time Microsoft started building Internet-connected features into the products and now, a decade later, these products hardly resemble the Office of old.

They might feel the same if you are not aware of what they are doing behind the scenes, but they are very different than previous products. A good example of this is how auto-save works with instant, real-time collaboration. When your Word document auto-saves to the cloud, you can start work on the document on one device and then switch to another device and continue working without having to move the file between devices.

Real-time collaboration means that you can work with someone on the other side of the world on a document and see what they are doing and they can see what you are doing, in real time, instantly. We can only speculate at the features that Microsoft is planning for Windows 365, and it will be exciting to see it unfold.

Windows Needs to Be Cloud-First to Provide the Value We Expect in the Future

An operating system that isn't built for the cloud is blind to the modern-day world. Windows needs the cloud in order to provide the value that we all expect from our devices. Windows 365 is designed to usher Windows into a cloud-first world. By developing a direct and tight integration with the cloud, the operating system can provide value to its users.

As an example, let's look at a smartphone. Our particular choice of smartphone is the iPhone. Our iPhones are always connected to the cloud and have become an extension of the way we think. In other words, our phone is our window (another pun) into the vast store of knowledge and connectivity known as the Internet. The operating system that runs on our phone is called iOS, and it is a cloud-first operating system. The same is true with Android.

Windows 365 provides a similar value moving into the future; however, instead of a physical device, like our phone, it will be a virtual PC. How we access our virtual PC will change over time. Many like to refer to this new virtual world as the *metaverse*. The way people access the metaverse can change as technology progresses. For example, if you play in online virtual worlds then you are accessing the metaverse through your physical PC. You might have an avatar in the virtual world or you might have a first-person view of a three-dimensional world using a virtual or augmented-reality headset.

We can envision a world where your metaverse PC is Windows 365 and you access it using whatever physical device you use to access the metaverse. For now though your access into your Windows 365 cloud PC is through a physical computer, phone, or laptop computer.

Security Is More Important Now Than Ever

The Internet has connected the world like never before. With all of the connectivity comes a risk though. It seems like hardly a day goes by without another major security incident.

We like to think about how things were when we were small children. Where we grew up, it was common for people not to lock their doors and everyone knew everyone else. If someone broke into a house, then chances are the community would figure out who did it rather quickly.

We now live in a major city, Seattle, and don't even leave valuable items in our car because break-ins are common practice. Imagine if the physical world was connected the same way the virtual world is connected. Everyone in Seattle, or any other major city around the world, could go knock on the doors and break into the houses of all the people that live in places where people don't even lock their doors.

We, as humans, are globally connected like never before and with that connection opens opportunity for criminals. Just like we take our physical security to a higher level now that we live in a city, everyone needs to take their virtual security to a higher level, too.

Windows 365 is hosted and managed by Microsoft. The nice thing with Microsoft is that they have a lot of smart people who are keeping tabs on global cybercriminals and keeping their data centers and virtual properties secure. When your PC is in the cloud with Windows 365, you can offload some of the security aspects to Microsoft and put more focus on being productive with your time.

Mundane IT Tasks Can Be Removed

Every few years hardware needs to be upgraded. It is often a fun thing to do but can also be a pain to get all of your software set up again just the way you need it in order to be productive. Using a cloud PC removes the upgrade cycle and enables you to focus on your work with your PC that never changes.

Microsoft takes care of updating and replacing the underlying hardware required to run your cloud PC and you just focus on your work. For very large enterprises your cloud PC can also be managed using Microsoft Endpoint Manager and Microsoft Intune.

TIP

Microsoft Intune and Microsoft Endpoint Manager are software packages designed for very large organizations. These tools enable an IT person to manage the specific PC in a way that conforms to the specifics of the organization's rules and procedures.

Improved Efficiency by Having a Single Computer Accessible from Anywhere

It takes time to boot up your computer and get all your windows set up just the way you want them in order to be productive. If you are like Ken, this boot up process can take seemingly half the day.

With your cloud PC, you never have to shut it down. You just stop working and when you decide to start working again, all of your windows and software and files are just how you left them. This might seem like a small thing but over time these little efficiency factors add up significantly. (See Figure 19-1.)

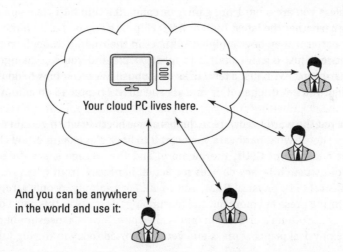

FIGURE 19-1:
Your PC lives in the cloud. You can access it from anywhere.

Your cloud PC lives here.

And you can be anywhere in the world and use it:

The State of the Computer and Your Work Are Always as You Left Them

Imagine that your computer is like a genie in a bottle. You say a magic word and the PC appears just as you previously left it. If you are working and get interrupted then the PC disappears in a puff of smoke and sits exactly as you left it until you say the word to make it appear again. Because the genie PC disappears and reappears wherever you are, then it doesn't matter if you forget your laptop and only have your tablet. Or if you are in a colleague's home office and the only computer available is theirs. The genie PC appears and is ready for you to work on it just the way you left it when it disappeared.

Your cloud PC is similar to just such a genie PC. You can be working on your cloud PC using your home laptop computer and spill coffee on it and the thing dies in a puff of gasping smoke. When you decide you want to work again and get into the office (or grab your tablet upstairs) and open up your cloud PC, it will be exactly as you left it. We like to think of our cloud PC as a genie though because it is such a nice thought experiment. We cover the concept of working on a single cloud PC from any device in Chapter 5.

Basic Computer Hardware Is Becoming a Commodity

Unless you are a hardcore gamer or computer chip buff then you probably aren't sure whether the latest Intel or AMD chips are any better than the last. They must be better if they have a higher number in their name, though, right? Well, in the future it just doesn't matter to most people and you can change your cloud PC "hardware" with just a few clicks of a mouse. We cover how to do this in Chapter 2 when you get things set up and also again in Chapter 18 on administration.

We put the word hardware in quotes above because when you set up your cloud PC you choose what hardware you want it to have. For example, you choose the number and type of CPUs, the memory, and the storage space. In reality, all these choices match legacy choices for actual hardware from when we used to have a physical CPU, physical RAM, and so on. For example, people rarely use a physical printing press anymore but the terminology persists to this day. For example, font sizes are often referred to in units called *pica*. Pica is a measurement developed for the physical printing press and yet is still used today in the digital age.

TIP

When you set up your cloud PC the choices could just as well be something like T-shirt sizes where you decide how "fast" and how much "storage" you want your cloud PC to have. The reason you can choose the hardware is because it makes the process familiar to setting up a physical PC.

Internet Connections Are Improving Globally

One critical requirement of the world becoming so connected is that devices require a high-speed and reliable Internet connection. In many places in the world, the Internet is iffy at best and completely disconnected and unavailable at worst. As the world moves into the metaverse, those without an Internet connection will be left behind.

The good news is that the Internet is improving globally. And even rural areas that don't make economic sense to implement wired network connections have the option of space Internet. Space Internet, think SpaceX Starlink, is finally here! Fast and reliable Internet will become standard around the world in the same way you can watch satellite TV in the most remote portions of the most desolate continent.

People Are Distributed and Will Interact and Interface Through the Metaverse

Say what? What does this have to do with anything? The metaverse is nothing new. It just means interacting with others over the Internet. Ken used to play online games in the "metaverse" back in the 1990s. Back then it was all text-based but it was a world unto itself. It was a universe unto itself. It was a world of dragons and wizards. It was a lot of fun. The modern-day equivalent is Elder Scrolls Online, or World of Warcraft.

Because people are distributed and interacting virtually, it only makes sense that all of their work, systems, and software are virtual, too. And Windows 365 is nothing more than a cloud-based personal computer (PC).

» **Learning how to become more productive with Windows 365**

» **Seeing how to get the most from your cloud PC**

» **Getting more work done when on the move**

Chapter **20**

Top Ten Reasons to Convince Your Boss to Move to Windows 365

indows 365 is squarely targeted at businesses (for now). Often only a handful of people get to actually make the decisions regarding the technology and systems that are used in the business. If you happen to be one of those decision makers, then congratulations (or perhaps our condolences) since you are responsible for technology in a world of blazing fast change. If you are not one of those decision makers, then we also say congratulations! Because you don't have to deal with a many of the headaches that come along with technology decisions.

In any case, there are many reasons that moving to a cloud PC model reduces stress and increases productivity. We made the exact same argument a decade ago when we started writing about Office moving to the cloud with Office 365. The same benefits apply, and in this chapter, we provide our top ten.

You Have Embraced the Post-Covid World and Your Physical Location Isn't Tied to the Office

In early 2020, the world changed, and nearly everyone that could began working remotely. As we continue in 2022, the world is still not back to normal and almost everyone we know is still working remotely. *Remotely* being the key word. Everyone is at a different stage in life, and remote might mean moving to a new location (which includes a beach) for younger workers, or it might mean turning an extra room or backyard shed into a home office.

Regardless of what *remote* means to you and your organization, things are different now. When everyone went remote a huge responsibility shift happened. Suddenly, individual workers were responsible for their own computers and equipment. This is a bit like asking everyone who drives a car to be a mechanic. It just isn't feasible, and yet people adapted.

When your organization moves to Windows 365, then everyone's main PC becomes virtual. The physical devices don't matter so much, and neither does where or how you connect to them. In this sense, using a cloud PC to maintain consistency in your work software and routine is an easy extension to a remote-first world.

You Want to Be Your Most Productive Self and If That Means Doing a Little Bit of Work on Your iPad While the Kids Are Doing Homework, Then So Be It

As writers, we often get something called writers' block. We can stare at a blank page with a blinking cursor for hours as our brain thinks about everything else except writing. Even getting to the point where we have our computer open and everything ready to go to work can be a challenge. We used to procrastinate by coming up with all sorts of excuses about how everything needed to be just perfect before we got started. Then, after we finally got all set up, we would just stare at the blank page for a while and then call it a wrap. We think everyone would agree: Procrastination can make it hard to get anything done.

What Windows 365 has done for us is create a persistent workspace that is always set up and ready to go. When we have an idea, we just connect to our cloud PC and start writing. In our case, our work is writing. In your case, it might be something else. Perhaps you use enterprise resource planning (ERP) software in accounting on a daily basis. Or perhaps you have a set of spreadsheets that define your work world, and you spend time toggling and interacting with them. Regardless of how you use your computer, when your computer is virtual and cloud-based it is always in the exact state that you left it the last time you disconnected. To start working again, you just have to connect to it from any device and you are instantly looking at your virtual desktop just the way you left it. What we have found is this creates a level of productivity that we didn't have before, and we like it.

TIP

Having a computer that doesn't change and that doesn't have to be set up again when you stop and start working from different devices can be a significant productivity booster.

You Want Your IT People to Help You with More Important Things, Like How to Use the Company ERP Software

If you are gifted, or cursed, with the ability to work with computers and solve incredibly difficult logic puzzles, then you might be known as an information technology (IT) person. If we could look back at our long careers and calculate how much time we have worked with IT solving some crazy computer problem, we would likely be shocked. Our time was wasted, and the person's time was also wasted.

IT people have a unique set of skills, and those skills are most impactful when used in supporting people with other impactful skills. By moving the burden of managing the PC to Microsoft, the IT people are free to focus their skills on other, more important, and more impactful areas of the business.

One of the most impactful pieces of software is called an enterprise resource planning (ERP) system. The ERP system handles things like accounting and inventory and all sorts of other critical business tasks. When an ERP system is used correctly, the business can take off like a drag car chugging nitrous oxide. Figure 20-1 illustrates how highly skilled people should be deployed to areas of the highest business impact whereas the lower business impact areas can be offloaded to companies such as Microsoft.

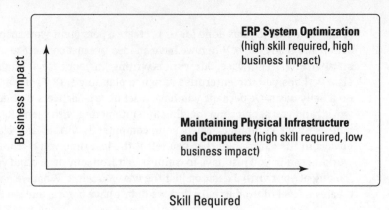

ERP System Optimization
(high skill required, high business impact)

Business Impact

Maintaining Physical Infrastructure and Computers (high skill required, low business impact)

Skill Required

FIGURE 20-1:
Move highly skilled IT people to areas of focus with the highest business impact.

TIP

IT people have a superpower that is best used on software that has the most business impact. Whenever an organization can focus their resources on the things that matter most, everyone wins.

You Don't Want to Lose Your Work Again by Spilling Coffee or Water on Your Keyboard

It takes days to get a new computer set up just how you want it. You must install software, and sign into everything, and configure certain things, and on and on. Just about the time you have everything set up some disaster inevitably seems to happen. It has happened to us more than once where we spilled coffee or water on a laptop and the thing fried. When you are working on your cloud PC it is no big deal. The physical computer might be fried but you can just pick up another computer and continue as if nothing happened, as illustrated in Figure 20-2.

TIP

Your cloud PC lives in the virtual world and is immune to coffee or water or other physical disasters.

We like to think of our physical device as a commodity. We might have a nice laptop we use for video editing, or we might have an old tablet sitting around that we use to check the news. Either one works to connect to, and use, our cloud PC. If you haven't been in the market for a computer recently you might be surprised to find out how affordable just a basic computer is. And that basic computer will work fine as your connection to your cloud PC where all the actual work happens. We cover requirements for connecting to your Windows 365 cloud PC in Chapter 16.

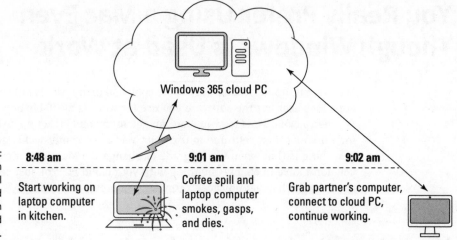

FIGURE 20-2:
Move between
physical
computers and
maintain
uninterrupted
work on cloud PC.

Windows 365 cloud PC

8:48 am

Start working on
laptop computer
in kitchen.

9:01 am

Coffee spill and
laptop computer
smokes, gasps,
and dies.

9:02 am

Grab partner's computer,
connect to cloud PC,
continue working.

TIP

Just about any physical computer will work as a dumb terminal to access your cloud PC. If your physical computer dies, you can run to Costco or Best Buy or any other retailer, grab a computer (after paying for it of course), and be up and running on your cloud PC in minutes.

Microsoft, Not Your Boss, Is Responsible for Your PC Now

The process of equipping everyone with a new PC every few years can be a grind. It takes time to keep track of who needs a new computer and when. Not to mention getting computers fixed when they break. Windows 365 provides a subscription price that is clear and predictable. After you have your cloud PC set up, it is yours for as long as you need.

Even a cloud PC has actual hardware running in a data center somewhere. The hardware is large and complicated and provides a virtual environment for computers, but it is still a significant factor. And the hardware has to be connected to the Internet and climate-controlled and maintained. Microsoft handles all of that. From your and your boss's point of view, your cloud PC is simply always on, always available, and always just how you left it. Shifting the burden of maintaining everything necessary to provide a computing environment might not seem like a huge deal, but the effort saved definitely adds up.

You Really Prefer Using a Mac Even Though Windows Is Used at Work

Let's face it, Apple products are super cool, and many people only use Macs. If you are a Mac user but the software you use for work is available only on a Windows PC, then a cloud PC is for you. You can get your cloud PC set up just how you need for work and then continue to use your Mac as your physical computer. And the best thing is that when you upgrade or change the Mac computer you are using, you don't have to change anything with your cloud PC. You just connect to it and use it from whatever physical computer you prefer at the time.

You Need to Use Your Laptop When on the Move and You Want to Still Be Productive by Accessing Your Work Computer

For many people work involves going into the office every day, sitting down at a work computer, and doing work. The problem is that your work is then tied to the computer in the office. The pandemic changed things, and IT teams all over the world had to scramble to figure out how to enable people to work remotely. All sorts of schemes have been put in place and many of those involve using special software called a Virtual Private Network (VPN). The VPN lets you connect to the network in your office remotely and your remote computer thinks it is in the office. This often works fine, although it provides complexity and a lot of moving parts to keep everything working.

When your work computer becomes a cloud PC it doesn't matter where you are when you connect to it. You can easily use your laptop when on the move and have the same experience whether you are sitting in your office, at home, or on a beach somewhere.

You Won't Have to Bug Your Boss with Ordering a New Computer Every Few Years

Your cloud PC experience is nearly identical whether you are using a $400 computer from Costco or a $4,000 high-end gaming computer. You might still want a new computer every few years. Who doesn't? But with a cloud PC you won't need to set up a new computer for work when you buy a new physical computer.

TIP

Your physical computer can adapt to your personal needs (that may change over time), and your cloud PC can stay the same and focused on work.

In our experience this allows leadership to provide expense budgets to people so that they can buy whatever computer they want or even just pocket the money. As far as work goes, the only computer that really matters is your cloud PC, and that is managed and maintained by Microsoft.

Your Boss Will Get the Benefits of a Cloud PC Too So They Might Want to Convince Their Boss

Being a boss is never what it is cracked up to be. And every boss has a boss of their own. Everyone in the organization likely enjoys the benefits of using a cloud PC. So, when convincing your boss might just mean introducing them to Windows 365 and then letting them convince their boss and on up the chain until everyone is migrated.

TIP

When we first heard about Windows 365 and cloud PCs, we were skeptical. We had a system in place to use our work desktop, laptops, tablets, and phones. It wasn't the most efficient system, but it worked. When people first learn about a virtual cloud PC, they are often skeptical, too. When you get used to the fact that your work computer is always on, always available, and always how you left it, and it doesn't matter what physical computer or device you use to access it, then it is easy to come around and become a fan.

Your Boss Can Offload the Risk of the Computer to Microsoft

We were once working with a friend in Boston. We spent a week working on code for a project and were set to fine-tune things on Friday before a Monday meeting. Walking home on Thursday evening, he was mugged, and his laptop was stolen. Devastation!

We had to spend the entire weekend working nearly 24 hours straight to complete the demo. It wasn't really something our boss could have controlled but if our computer had been a cloud PC, we wouldn't have lost any work. Or, we could have just backed it up, but we were tired and ready to get home, and nobody backed up the work from the laptop.

TIP

Computer hardware fails and data must be backed up and maintained. When you use Windows 365 you are offloading that risk of hardware failure to Microsoft.

Index

G

H

I

About the Authors

Rosemarie Withee is president of Portal Integrators (www.portalintegrators. com) and founder of Scrum Now in Seattle, Washington. Portal Integrators is a Scrum-based software and services firm. She is the author of *Microsoft Teams For Dummies* and lead author of *Microsoft SharePoint For Dummies*.

Rosemarie earned a Master of Science degree in economics at San Francisco State University and an Executive Master of Business Administration degree at Quantic School of Business and Technology. In addition, Rosemarie also studied marketing at UC Berkeley-Extension and holds a Bachelor of Arts degree in economics and a Bachelor of Science degree in marketing from De La Salle University, Philippines.

Ken Withee is the author and coauthor of several books on Microsoft technologies and currently writes articles on Azure for Microsoft. He earned a Master of Science degree in computer science at San Francisco State University and has recently completed his Master of Science degree in computer science at the University of Washington.

Dedication

We dedicate this book to our dad, Alfonso Supetran. He will be forever missed.

Author's Acknowledgments

We would like to acknowledge our families in both the United States and Philippines. An extraordinary amount of special thanks to Kelsey Baird and the rest of the *For Dummies* team for providing more support than we ever thought possible. It is truly amazing how much work goes into creating a single book.

Publisher's Acknowledgments

Acquisitions Editor: Kelsey Baird

Project Editor: Christopher Morris

Copy Editor: Christopher Morris

Technical Editor: Guy Hart-Davis

Production Editor: Tamilmani Varadharaj

Cover Image: © metamorworks/Shutterstock